Ninja Foodi
Recipe Book for Beginners

Nutrient-Rich & Mouth-Watering Ninja Recipes You Will Make on Repeat to Master Air Fryer, Pressure, Sauté, and Slow Cook

Yolanda Fincher

© Copyright 2024
– All Rights Reserved

This document is geared towards providing exact and reliable information with regards to the topic and issue covered. The publication is sold with the idea that the publisher is not required to render accounting, officially permitted, or otherwise, qualified services. If advice is necessary, legal, or professional, a practiced individual in the profession should be ordered. -From a Declaration of Principles which was accepted and approved equally by a Committee of the American Bar Association and a Committee of Publishers and Associations. In no way is it legal to reproduce, duplicate, or transmit any part of this document in either electronic means or in printed format. Recording of this publication is strictly prohibited and any storage of this document is not allowed unless with written permission from the publisher.

All rights reserved. The information provided herein is stated to be truthful and consistent, in that any liability, in terms of inattention or otherwise, by any usage or abuse of any policies, processes, or directions contained within is the solitary and utter responsibility of the recipient reader.

Under no circumstances will any legal responsibility or blame be held against the publisher for any reparation, damages, or monetary loss due to the information herein, either directly or indirectly. Respective authors own all copyrights not held by the publisher.

The information herein is offered for informational purposes solely, and is universal as so. The presentation of the information is without contract or any type of guarantee assurance. The trademarks that are used are without any consent, and the publication of the trademark is without permission or backing by the trademark owner.

All trademarks and brands within this book are for clarifying purposes only and are the owned by the owners themselves, not affiliated with this document.

CONTENTS

1 Introduction

2 Fundamentals of Ninja Foodi Deluxe Tendercrisp Pressure Cooker

9 4-Week Meal Plan

11 Chapter 1 Breakfast

22 Chapter 2 Vegetables and Sides

33 Chapter 3 Beans and Grains

41 Chapter 4 Soup and Salad

49 Chapter 5 Snacks and Starters

60 Chapter 6 Poultry Mains

70 Chapter 7 Beef, Pork, and Lamb

82 Chapter 8 Seafood Mains

90 Chapter 9 Desserts

100 Conclusion

101 Appendix 1 Measurement Conversion Chart

102 Appendix 2 Recipes Index

Introduction

Are you always eager for fried food but don't like the unhealthy outcome you experience? Do you need a kitchen appliance that will ease your cooking tasks and have healthy meals? Then, you need to try the Ninja Foodi Deluxe Tendercrisp Pressure Cooker. This is a revolutionary appliance that eases and quickens the process of cooking. You can do a lot with just this one appliance, ranging from one-pot dishes, soups, sides, appetizers, and desserts. And you are going to enjoy the bustling British kitchen.

This isn't just a mere cookbook. It goes beyond that to being a lovely invitation to British kitchens where you have the freedom to explore, experiment, and elevate. From the hills of Scotland to the bustling streets of London, this is your ticket to turning every meal into an ovation-worthy performance.

The Ninja Foodi Deluxe Tendercrisp Pressure Cooker will spare you time, especially for working individuals, and you won't need to go for pre-packaged junk foods. You will always enjoy your homemade dishes. The meal preparation is no longer tedious, and the time you spend in the kitchen is reduced. Even if you are a beginner, the appliance is great, and you will always come up with amazing dishes.

Whenever it comes to culinary gadgets, the Ninja Foodi Deluxe Tendercrisp Pressure Cooker is the best to consider, and it works as a hot air fryer for sizzling meals. Your meals are prepared quickly under pressure, and they have that crispy texture. Among the contemporary pressure cookers, the Ninja Foodi Deluxe Tendercrisp Pressure Cooker is redefining and elevating the very standards we thought we knew. It's not just a cooker; it's a culinary revolution! Give it a try!

Fundamentals of Ninja Foodi Deluxe Tendercrisp Pressure Cooker

Welcome to the British kitchen, where we meet a mix of sizzles, bubbles, and chopping sounds together with the new Ninja Foodi Deluxe Tendercrisp Pressure Cooker. An appliance that gives you amazing possibilities. This section is going to be a road map to the usage of the Ninja Foodi Deluxe Tendercrisp Pressure Cooker, guiding you to all the opportunities you will enjoy. These fundamentals will ensure that you and the Ninja Foodi Deluxe Tendercrisp Pressure Cooker waltz in perfect harmony.

What is Ninja Foodi Deluxe Tendercrisp Pressure Cooker

Picture this: An appliance that not only simmers your stews but can also, with the flick of a switch, transform them into golden, crispy treasures. It is a symphony of technology and culinary artistry, designed for the contemporary chef with a heart that beats for timeless classics.
We define the Ninja Foodi Deluxe Tendercrisp Pressure Cooker as an electric pressure cooker with an amazing exterior appearance. A beautiful appearance resonates well with the performance it offers. It is among the current multi-functional pressure cookers and stands out as the best that every chef yearns to possess. Ninja Foodi Deluxe Tendercrisp Pressure Cooker can act as a pressure cooker, including functions of an Air Fryer and Instant Pot. It uses the Tender Crisp technology to achieve the best of the functions.
Other functions you will enjoy include an air crisper, dehydrator, browning pan, broiler, slow cooker, roaster, and steamer. This gives you the opportunity and capability to prepare all types of your favorite dishes, from beef, poultry, seafood, stews, snacks, sides, and even desserts. The dehydrator is nice, especially when you want to preserve veggies and fruits.
The Ninja Foodi Deluxe Tendercrisp Pressure Cooker comes with a cooking pot, pressure lid, crisping lid, reversible rack, and cook & crisp™ basket. It is possible to sauté just as you would do on a stove, but here, you get the built-in timers and controls for advanced experience. Amid all those functions, do not perceive the Ninja Foodi Deluxe Tendercrisp Pressure Cooker to be too heavy to carry around. It is user-friendly and a handy cooker that everyone will love using.

Understanding the Tendercrisp Technology

The Tendercrisp Technology is a basic foundation that transforms the Ninja Foodi Deluxe Tendercrisp Pressure Cooker into an appealing and unique appliance. There is application of the Air Fryer technology in Ninja Foodi Deluxe Tendercrisp Pressure Cooker to crisp the external of your dishes. For uniformity of the inside and outside, there is a combination of air frying and pressure cooking, making all functions to be contained in one.
You achieve crispiness by the installation of a Crisping Lid and Crisping Basket set in the device. You then chose the Air Crisp

mode. So the whole process of first pressure cooking your meals and then crisping within the same appliance is what has the patent of Tendercrisp technology.

The Ninja Foodi Deluxe Tendercrisp Pressure Cooker is larger when you compare it to other pressure cookers since it performs several functions within a single unit.

It has an easy-to-use and amazing display at the front. The display has a touch panel where you can easily set the time and temperature. You can also adjust the pressure ranging from low to high and also select the type of cooking.

The back has several vents and drip cups. You can easily clean the drip tray by simply removing it. The Ninja Foodi Deluxe Tendercrisp Pressure Cooker has a 2-lid system attached to the appliance and acts as a lid for the air crisper or air fryer. The lid has a fan for air circulation to ensure the foods are crispy without the need for deep frying.

Benefits of Using It

Picture a kitchen appliance - stylish and compact, with promises of bringing revolutions in your kitchen experience. Yes, not just any other appliance, but this is Ninja Foodi Deluxe Tendercrisp Pressure Cooker. It comes with multiple hats to prepare your meals with amazing and delicious results. Here are some of the amazing benefits of catering to your taste and lifestyle.

1. Portable and space-efficient: You might have a cozy kitchen in your house in the city or a grand one located in your countryside, but you have nothing to worry about. The Ninja Foodi Deluxe Tendercrisp Pressure Cooker will comfortably fit in a rightful space within your kitchen counters and tables. The appliance is lightweight, making it easy to move around when on a journey.
2. It is a multi-tasker or has multiple functions: Here is a single solution offering lots of functions instead of having a cavalcade of gadgets in your kitchen. With the Ninja Foodi Deluxe Tendercrisp Pressure Cooker, you have an appliance that combines various functionalities, which saves you more space in your kitchen area, giving you value for your money. There is no need to buy other appliances.
3. You can easily operate and clean. With its intuitive design, even those who do not like the kitchen will find the Ninja Foodi Deluxe Tendercrisp Pressure Cooker a simple appliance to use. It is a plug-and-play gadget that can be used by both beginners and experts. And after the feast? You can easily remove the non-stick components and clean them in the dishwasher.
4. Pressure cooking and air frying combined. Many appliances are bringing together the functionalities of a slow cooker and pressure cooker. The Ninja Foodi Deluxe Tendercrisp Pressure Cooker stands out when you need something fried and crispy. Pressure cooking ensures succulence, while the air fryer bestows that golden, crispy perfection. The Ninja Foodi Deluxe Tendercrisp Pressure Cooker will brown the food and crisp it by using the hot air circulation to cook the food to perfection. It's a gastronomic duet, one that resonates with the Maillard reaction's delicious notes. The Ninja Foodi Deluxe Tendercrisp Pressure Cooker also makes food crunchy, tender on the inside, and a crispy exterior. Yes, pressure cooking and air frying benefits are combined within the same appliance.
5. It is fast and saves time (a time-maestro). Wouldn't you be happy enjoying delicious meals on a daily basis? I know you don't have the luxury of spending time in the kitchen. And here comes the Ninja Foodi Deluxe Tendercrisp Pressure Cooker, where scrumptious meals like chicken thighs coupled with aromatic Basmati rice and more come to reality, all under an hour.
6. No use of excessive oil. Remember the oil-splatter symphony? You must have cooked onion rings or French fries the traditional way. You understand how much oil is needed to make the food perfectly crispy. With the Ninja Foodi Deluxe Tendercrisp Pressure Cooker, your fried delicacies need just a spritz of oil or not at all – a healthier, cleaner, and crisper alternative. With the usage of less to no oil, you avoid dealing with splatters that normally happen when one is drying the food before the start of the cooking process.
7. Energy saving. Oven cooking often translates to sweaty brows and an escalating energy bill. But the Foodi performs its culinary magic efficiently without turning your house into a tropical rainforest. The Ninja Foodi Deluxe Tendercrisp Pressure Cooker transforms cooking into an amazing, comfortable experience and saves energy.
8. From ice to delight. Did you forget to thaw that steak before you start the cooking process? With the Ninja Foodi Deluxe Tendercrisp Pressure Cooker, the pressure cooking gently thaws (defrosts) and tenderizes, and then the air fryer adds the golden touch, ensuring last-minute plans are still gourmet. All this can happen in 30 minutes or less, meaning you don't need to order takeout food whenever you come home late.
9. Enjoy delicious and nutritious meals. Pressure-cooked or steamed, the Ninja Foodi Deluxe Tendercrisp Pressure Cooker retains the natural essence and nutrients, crafting dishes that delight both the palate and the body. Get into your kitchen and prepare delicious and nutritional meals with amazing flavors. Steamed or pressure-cooked veggies retain all the flavors.
10. Versatile heat. Whether it's a light simmer or a blazing sear, the Foodi's vast temperature range is ready to serve. Even frozen foods yield to its warmth, quickly transforming into gourmet delights.

For too long we have settled for convenience over flavor. Opting for takeout over a home-cooked meal or leaning on multi-cookers that don't deliver to answer the question, "What's for dinner?" With the Ninja Foodi Deluxe Tendercrisp Pressure Cooker Pressure Cooker, you no longer have to settle. Tendercrisp Technology unlocks unlimited possibilities for breakfast, lunch, dinner, dessert, and more.

Step-By-Step Using It

Ah, the Ninja Foodi Deluxe Tendercrisp Pressure Cooker! A culinary gem that promises a gastronomic journey unlike any other. But as

with all masterpieces, knowing its strokes is the key. The usage of circulating hot air cooks the food evenly and in a quick way. Using the appliance is as simple as placing the ingredients in the basket and setting the appropriate temperatures and time. The rest will be done with the appliance, making sure your food is cooked to perfection.

1. Gear Up for Cooking:

Before you start your culinary quest, ensure your Ninja Foodi Deluxe Tendercrisp Pressure Cooker is combat-ready:

- Give a quick check to ensure all its components are intact.
- Check the power cord for any wear and tear.
- Ensure all valves are in their good positions and the sealing ring sits well. If anything is not placed well, then your appliance will fail to function.
- If everything checks out, plug in the device and watch the LED screen of the control panel light up like a starry night.

2. The Recipe Canvas - Your Cooking Pot and Ingredients:

Whether you're about to sauté, steam, or stew:

- You can choose to pull out the cooking pot and add your ingredients before setting them inside.
- Or, if you're in for a sauté variety, leave the pot nestled inside and add the ingredients slowly.
- Remember, the inner pot markings aren't just for decoration! They guide the quantity and caution against overfilling or overcrowding. Respect the 2/3 full limit; your food will need room to breathe, boil, and bubble.

3. Lock and Load - Sealing the Lid:

- Opt for the pressure lid (with the integral valve) for those times when you need to pressure cook. Install it, seal it, and lock. Place it atop the appliance give it a little twist until it clicks into place. The arrow on the appliance should align with the lid's close marking as confirmation for being sealed.
- For that impeccable crispiness that makes you sigh in delight, the crisping lid is your friend.
- And always ensure the lid is locked and loaded. It's the Ninja Foodi Deluxe Tendercrisp Pressure Cooker's way of saying, "I've got your back!" If the lid isn't in position, it won't let you progress; the timer won't start – a safety feature we all appreciate.

4. Choose Your Culinary Tango - The Cooking Mode:

The beauty of the Ninja Foodi Deluxe Tendercrisp Pressure Cooker lies in its versatility:

- You enjoy the vast sea of cooking modes. Each button indicates a promise of a unique culinary experience with integrated settings where you can adjust the pressure and time accordingly.
- Whether you're in the mood for a quick steam, a long slow cook, or a crunchy air crisp, bake/roast, or keep warm, touch the button of your desire.
- Note: The Ninja Foodi Deluxe Tendercrisp Pressure Cooker is quite the perfectionist. It preheats for about 10 seconds, setting the stage, temperature, and pressure for the performance ahead.
- Once the food reaches its climax, the Foodi ensures it stays warm at low temperatures, letting flavors meld a little longer.

5. Personalize Your Experience:

Your relationship with the Ninja Foodi Deluxe Tendercrisp Pressure Cooker is personal:

- After selecting your preferred mode, tweak the time and temperature using the designated keys.
- Finally, like a conductor raising their baton, press the START/STOP button to commence or conclude your cooking concert.

Functions of Ninja Foodi Deluxe Tendercrisp Pressure Cooker

Now that we understand the benefits of the Ninja Foodi Deluxe Tendercrisp Pressure Cooker, it is time to learn about all of the different tasks you can accomplish with one pot.

Pressure

1. **Preparation:** Ensure your Ninja Foodi Deluxe Tendercrisp

Pressure Cooker is clean and all components are in place.
2. **Assemble:** Place your ingredients in the pot.
3. **Lid On:** Secure the pressure lid ensuring the valve is in the "Seal" position.
4. **Select:** Choose the "Pressure" function, adjusting the temperature and time as per the recipe.
5. **Release:** Once cooking completes, carefully release the pressure either naturally or manually.
6. **Dive in:** Open the lid, and let the aroma mesmerize you!

Steam
1. **Preparation:** Add water or broth to the pot.
2. **Rack in:** Place the reversible rack or Cook & Crisp™ Basket inside and top with your food.
3. **Lid Time:** Secure the pressure lid ensuring the valve is in the "Vent" position.
4. **Steam On:** Select the "Steam" function and set the time.
5. **Patience:** Allow a natural release, then unveil your gently-cooked meal.

When warming a leftover dish, simply place the dish in an aluminum pan and cover it with tin foil. Set it on top of the rack. Depending on the density of the leftover dish, place about 2 cups or more of water at the bottom of the rack. Set the steam function for 5 to 10 minutes. You will see that the heated dish will retain its moisture and not be overcooked.

The Ninja Foodi Deluxe Tendercrisp Pressure Cooker also allows you to reheat your leftovers whilst cooking rice at the same time.

Slow Cook
1. **Ingredients in:** Layer your ingredients inside.
2. **Seal:** Secure the pressure lid ensuring the valve is in the "Vent" position.
3. **The Long Game:** Select "Slow Cook" and set the temperature and duration. Let the Foodi work its magic over hours. Unlike pressure cooking that quickly cooks soups, stews and meats, this option builds flavor by braising food low and slow.
4. **Enjoy:** Open up to a pot of deep, melded flavors.

Sear/Sauté
1. **Preparation:** Select "Sear/Sauté" and let the pot preheat. You can alternate between Low, Medium Low, Medium, Medium High, and High as you continue the process
2. **Oil Splash:** Add a drizzle of oil.
3. **Sizzle:** Add your ingredients, stirring occasionally, until beautifully browned.
4. **Wind Down:** Press "Start/Stop" when done.

Air Crisp
1. **Preparation:** Place your food in the Cook & Crisp™ Basket or deluxe reversible rack.
2. **Basket in:** Insert the basket or rack into the pot.
3. **Crisp Mode:** Select "Air Crisp" adjusting temperature and time accordingly. Occasionally remove crisping lid, shake and return to ensure all the food is crisped well.
4. **Crunch Time:** Enjoy the crispy perfection without the guilt!

Bake/Roast
1. **Preparation:** Grease the pot or place an oven-proof dish inside.
2. **Mix & Pour:** Add your batter or roast.
3. **Bake/Roast:** Select "Bake/Roast" and set the temperature and time.
4. **Golden Perfection:** Extract your delicious creation.

Broil
1. **Place:** Keep the dish or ingredient you want to broil in the pot.
2. **Broil:** Select "Broil" and set the time.
3. **Watch:** Keep an eye for that golden-brown top!
4. **Serve:** Enjoy the intensified flavors and crispy top.

Dehydrate
1. **Thinly Slice:** Your fruits, veggies, or meat.
2. **Layer:** On the dehydrating rack and place it in the pot.
3. **Set:** Choose "Dehydrate" and adjust the time and temperature.
4. **Savor:** Enjoy your homemade dried treats!

Yogurt
1. **Preparation:** Add desired amount of milk to the pot.
2. **Lid On:** Secure the pressure lid ensuring the valve is in the "Vent" position.
3. **Slow Cook:** Choose the "Yogurt" function, adjusting the temperature and time as per the recipe.
4. **Enjoy:** When done, chill yogurt up to 12 hours and enjoy it.

Keep Warm
1. Done Cooking: But not ready to eat?
2. **Warm It:** Select the "Keep Warm" function.
3. **Just Right:** Your food stays warm without overcooking.
4. **Serve:** Enjoy a warm meal anytime.

Understanding the Basics of the Control Panel

Here are the core buttons:
FUNCTION: Press FUNCTION, then turn the START/STOP dial to choose a cooking function.
POWER: The Power button shuts the unit off and stops all cooking modes.
KEEP WARM: Button for keeping food at a food-safe temperature until when ready to serve.
START/STOP dial/button: Once you set the cooking function, cooking time, and cooking temperature, use the button to initiate or end cooking process.
TIME: Press TIME, then turn the START/STOP dial to adjust the cook time.
TEMP: Press TEMP, then turn the START/STOP dial to adjust cooking temperature.

Tips for Using Accessories

Let's face it, the Ninja Foodi Deluxe Tendercrisp Pressure Cooker is best gadget to be in your kitchen, but it has some other elements that make it work to its best. These accessories make your culinary experience amazing. In addition to the accessories that came with the Ninja Foodi Deluxe Tendercrisp Pressure Cooker, there are a few additional accessories you may buy to enjoy full benefits of the Ninja Foodi Deluxe Tendercrisp Pressure Cooker. Let's check some of the accessories:

Pressure Lid
Your pot may need to come to pressure. Seal it tight by setting it in the correct position for the selected function. Without this lid, and its locking technology, the pot can only cook like a regular pot on the stove.
When this lid is in place, pressure will build up within the Ninja Foodi Deluxe Tendercrisp Pressure Cooker, a good way to get your food safely and quickly. This method also kills germs. You can use this lid when you have chosen functions like Yoghurt, Steam, Pressure Cook, Slow Cooker, Steam, Sear and Saute.

You can quick clean by wiping it down after use to prevent the build-up of residue.

Crisping Lid
You can use this lid with air fryer feature. The design makes it easy for food to crisp up and maintain a moist interior. Use the lid when you select Bake, Air Crisp, Dehydrate, Grill or Roast functions. Make sure there is nothing obstructing its path when using this lid. It needs space to perform at its best.
The two lids give you freedom of seamlessly transitioning between all the cooking methods you like. Use the pressure lid to tenderize, then use the crisping lid to crisp up your food.
Safety should come first where you need to always use mitts whenever lifting since the lid can get very hot.

Cooking Pot
The pot is non-stick and ceramic-coated. It is PTFE PFOA free, and you can easily hand wash it. Insert in the Ninja Foodi Deluxe Tendercrisp Pressure Cooker to utilize as a crockpot and when you need to pressure cook. It has a capacity of 6L making it possible to serve a good number of people.
When using functions like Sear/Saute, stir it up occasionally for even results.

Cook & Crisp™ Basket
The crisp basket helps you in air frying and has a space of 3. 6L, ceramic-coated, non-stick, and PTFE PFOA-free. It is also dishwasher safe.
With the ceramic coating, the basket is PTFE PFOA-free, non-stick, and dishwasher safe.
No Overcrowding: Give your food space! This ensures the hot air circulates evenly.
Shake-a-Shake: For fries or veggies, give a gentle shake for that even golden crisp.

Reversible Rack
The rack has two layers necessary for stacking a whole meal within the Ninja Foodi Deluxe Tendercrisp Pressure Cooker. It is easy to clean and can allow food to steam and bake simultaneously. It is safe for cooking.
Dual Heights: Remember, the rack can be high for steaming or low for grilling. Position as per your recipe's needs.
Even Cooking: Rotate dishes midway for consistent results.

Dehydrate Rack
The rack is designed specifically to expand the amount of food one can dehydrate at once. Set ingredients in one layer and carefully place the rack in your cooking pot. Adhere to the Dehydrate Chart instructions to ensure you come up with your custom jerky, dried fruit snacks, vegetable chips, and more.

Detachable Diffuser
Keep it Clean: This controls the direction of steam. Ensure it's unclogged for smooth operation.
Attachment: Always attach it properly to prevent steam from escaping

in unintended directions.

8-Quart Removable Cooking Pot
Fill Wisely: Avoid filling past the 2/3 mark to allow space for food expansion and steam.
Easy Clean: Enjoy the convenience of tossing it in the dishwasher.

Heat Shield
Protection: This guards your countertops. Ensure it's positioned properly before setting your Ninja Foodi Deluxe Tendercrisp Pressure Cooker atop.

Control Panel
Gentle Touch: Use a soft, damp cloth to clean. No need for aggressive pressing; it's sensitive!

Cooker Base
Prime Position: Ensure it's on a flat, stable surface to prevent any toppling mishaps.

Pressure Release Valve & Float Valve
Safety Check: Before cooking, ensure they're clean and moving freely.
Hands Off: During cooking, never touch. Steam's hot!

Silicone Ring
Fitting: Ensure it's snug in the lid, without any twists or gaps.
Extra Packs: Handy to alternate between savory and sweet, preventing flavor crossover.

Anti-Clog Cap & Air Outlet Vent
Peak Performance: Regularly inspect for food particles and clear any blockages.
Clear Path: Ensure steam has a clear, unobstructed path to vent.

Condensation Collector
Routine Check: Empty after every use to avoid any overflow.
Cleanse: Clean occasionally to prevent residue build-up.

Glass Lid
See-Through Magic: Ideal for slow cooking and sautéing, where you can monitor your food without lifting the lid.

Loaf Tin/Pan
No Sticking: Grease lightly for easy loaf release.

Even Bake: Place in the center of the reversible rack for consistent baking.

Extra Pack of Silicone Rings
Alternate Use: Have dedicated rings for savory, sweet, and spicy, to keep flavors true.

Silicone Mitts
Safety Chic: Always use these stylish mitts to handle hot pots and lids. Safety, but make it fashion!

Crisper Pan
Layering: For best results, don't overlap food items. Give each piece its spotlight!

Other accessories may include the multi-purpose pan, multi-purpose sling and tube pan.

Straight from the Store

The excitement of unboxing a new gadget – always like a celebration. The box could be heavy with a promise of tools that will bring delicious meals on the table. Let's see what you will find in box that contains the Ninja Foodi Deluxe Tendercrisp Pressure Cooker.

- The Pressure Lid
- The Crisping Lid
- A 1,460 Watt Housing Unit
- A 8-Quart ceramic coated pot
- A reversible Steam/Broil rack (Stainless-Steel)
- 3. 6L Cook/Crisping Basket (Ceramic Coated)
- Cook and Crisp Layered Insert
- A recipe or cookbook
- Detachable diffuser
- Heat shield
- Valves, Silicone Rings, and Caps
- Condensation Collector

Cleaning and Caring for Ninja Foodi Deluxe Tendercrisp Pressure Cooker

It is advisable to clean the Ninja Foodi Deluxe Tendercrisp Pressure

Cooker after every use.
- Before you start the cleaning process, unplug from the wall socket. Electricity and water are a recipe for disaster.
- The cooker base and control panel are the brains and heart of the operation. Handle with care by gently cleaning them using a damp cloth.
- The other parts and accessories like reversible rack, pressure lid, Silicone Ring, Cook & Crisp™ Basket, cooking pot, and the detachable diffuser are all good to bath them in dishwasher.
- Use soap and warm water to manually clean the anti-clog cap and pressure release valve. Avoid the urge to disassemble pressure release or float valve assembly.
- Once the heat shield cools, take a damp cloth or a paper towel and wipe down the crisping lid.
- Ah, the stubborn morsels! If food residue clings onto the reversible rack, cooking pot, or Cook & Crisp™ Basket, add warm water to fill the pot and let it soak. Remember, the Ninja Foodi Deluxe Tendercrisp Pressure Cooker isn't fond of harsh scrubbers. So, avoid scouring pads. Instead, opt for a gentle nylon pad or brush paired with non-abrasive cleanser or liquid dish soap.
- Once you clean and dry everything, place them in the open air. All components should be air-dried.

Frequently Asked Questions & Notes

1. Why is the unit taking so long time to build up pressure?

It can be related to a number of factors like temperature settings, the chilliness of your cooking pot, and the warmth or amount of ingredients can influence this. Ensure the Silicone Ring is snugly placed, lock the pressure lid, and release valve shows 'SEAL'!

2. What are these PRE and rotating lights on my display when I use the Pressure or Steam function?

The lights indicate your Foodi is at work, building pressure or preheating. Once it's ready, your set cook time shall begin!

3. I can't get the pressure lid off! Is it locked forever?

The pressure lid loves safety. Ensure the unit is depressurized fully. Release the steam, wait for a while, and then try lifting the lid away from you.

4. My unit hisses like a disgruntled cat but isn't pressurizing. Why?

Ensure the release valve is on 'SEAL.' If hissing continues, recheck the position of your Silicone seal.

5. How long is this depressurizing process?

The duration depends on how stuffed your Foodi is. Wait till the float valve drops to remove the lid.

6. What is the difference between quick release and natural release?

Quick release is when you manually switch the pressure release valve to Vent position. Natural release occurs when you let the Ninja Foodi Deluxe Tendercrisp Pressure Cooker decrease in pressure naturally after cooking is complete.

4-Week Meal Plan

Week 1

Day 1:
Breakfast: Herbed Ham and Potatoes
Lunch: Delicious Potato and Cauliflower Curry
Snack: Broccoli, Potato, and Sausage Tots
Dinner: Lemony Garlic Chicken Breasts
Dessert: Simple Chocolate Molten Lava Cake

Day 2:
Breakfast: Soft Blueberry French Bread
Lunch: Freekeh Bowls with Chickpeas
Snack: Crispy Cheese Beef Meatballs
Dinner: Wonderful Pulled Beef Brisket
Dessert: Sweet Stewed Pears in Red Wine

Day 3:
Breakfast: Sweet Pecan Steel-Cut Oats
Lunch: Steamed Artichokes with Lemony Dijon Dipping Sauce
Snack: Classic Reuben Potato Skins
Dinner: Delicious Scallop Risotto with Spinach
Dessert: Tangy Dark Chocolate Fondue

Day 4:
Breakfast: Crustless Feta and Spinach Quiche
Lunch: Healthy Collard Greens with Bacon
Snack: Chicken Wings with Honey-Orange Sauce
Dinner: Creamy Mushroom and Chicken
Dessert: Chocolate Peanut Butter Popcorn

Day 5:
Breakfast: Cheesy Ham Strata
Lunch: Simple Sour Cream Cabbage
Snack: Pork Sausage-Stuffed Mushrooms
Dinner: Fried Cheese Prawns
Dessert: Easy Egg Custard

Day 6:
Breakfast: Easy Traditional Shakshuka
Lunch: Best Potatoes Au Gratin
Snack: Easy Boiled Peanuts
Dinner: Tangy Shredded Beef with Pineapple
Dessert: Almond Bundt Cake with Berries

Day 7:
Breakfast: Healthy Eggs in a Boat
Lunch: Herbed Carrots and Parsnips
Snack: Juicy Vinegary Beef Steak
Dinner: Homemade Chipotle Pulled Pork
Dessert: Creamy Cinnamon Raisin Brown Rice Pudding

Week 2

Day 1:
Breakfast: Sweet & Spicy Tomato Jam with Toast
Lunch: Smooth Celery Root and Cauliflower Mash
Snack: Chinese Vegetable Spring Rolls
Dinner: Cheesy Chicken Artichoke Casserole
Dessert: Basic Butter Vanilla Cake

Day 2:
Breakfast: Cheesy Baked Eggs
Lunch: Wholesome Cheese Corned Beef & Cabbage Slaw
Snack: Creamy Artichoke Crab Dip
Dinner: Classic Beef Burgundy
Dessert: Soft Vanilla Banana Bread

Day 3:
Breakfast: Creamy Blueberries Clafouti
Lunch: Lemony Garlic Smashed Red Potatoes
Snack: Delicious Hoisin Meatballs with Sesame Seeds
Dinner: Lemony-Buttered Lobster Tails
Dessert: Cinnamon Walnuts-Oats Stuffed Apples

Day 4:
Breakfast: Homemade Chocolate Banana Bread
Lunch: Tasty Herbed Veggie & Bread Casserole
Snack: Dill Pickle Dijon Deviled Eggs
Dinner: Mouthwatering Spiced Chicken Wings
Dessert: Yummy Creamy Rice Pudding

Day 5:
Breakfast: Fluffy Raspberry Breakfast Cake
Lunch: Crispy Fried Parmesan Polenta
Snack: Authentic Caribbean Chipotle Pork Sliders
Dinner: Authentic Pepperoncini Pot Roast
Dessert: Authentic Peach Cobbler

Day 6:
Breakfast: Classic Enchilada Casserole
Lunch: Red Wine Braised Mushroom with Carrot
Snack: Juicy Orange Pulled Pork Sliders
Dinner: Easy Crab Legs with Lemon Wedges
Dessert: Red Wine Braised Bartlett Pears

Day 7:
Breakfast: Egg White Bites with Ham
Lunch: Lemony Garlic Broccoli
Snack: Homemade Sour Cream Deviled Eggs with Olives
Dinner: Delicious Miso Pork Ramen
Dessert: Healthy Cinnamon Apples with Dates

Week 3

Day 1:
Breakfast: Veggie Bacon Frittatas
Lunch: Vegan Chickpeas Hummus
Snack: Crispy Avocado Fries
Dinner: Healthy Pesto Chicken Quinoa
Dessert: Quick Lemon Blueberry Compote

Day 2:
Breakfast: Crustless Mini Quiche Bites with Olives
Lunch: Coconut Rice and Red Beans
Snack: Flavourful Turkey Cabbage Dumplings
Dinner: Savoury Cheese Steak Mushroom Sloppy Joe
Dessert: Super-Simple Cheesecake

Day 3:
Breakfast: Cheesy Ham Polenta Muffins
Lunch: Super-Easy Cinnamon Applesauce
Snack: Crunchy Dill Pickles with Ranch Dip
Dinner: Quick Prawns Boil with Sausage
Dessert: Homemade Sweet Cranberry Applesauce

Day 4:
Breakfast: Yummy Mushroom Boat Eggs
Lunch: Lemony Roasted Cauliflower
Snack: Crispy Ranch Potato Chips
Dinner: Coconut Chicken and Mushroom Stroganoff
Dessert: Mouthwatering Chocolate Rice Pudding

Day 5:
Breakfast: Cheesy Ham Muffins
Lunch: Spicy Pinto Beans
Snack: Sesame Prawn Toasts
Dinner: Juicy Smoked Brisket Skewers
Dessert: Traditional Lava Cake

Day 6:
Breakfast: Crispy Toast Sticks
Lunch: Refreshing Lemony Broccoli Salad
Snack: Quick Avocado Fries with Salsa Fresca
Dinner: Garlicky Chili Fish Tacos
Dessert: Banana Pudding Cake with Pecans

Day 7:
Breakfast: Fried Banana PB&J Sandwich
Lunch: Artichoke and Spinach Stuffed Aubergine
Snack: Brie with Cherry Tomatoes
Dinner: Tender Pork Chops with Onion Gravy
Dessert: Sweet Cranberry Stuffed Apples

Week 4

Day 1:
Breakfast: Crustless Gruyère and Bacon Quiche
Lunch: Crispy Cheese Broccoli Pizza
Snack: Mozzarella Sandwich with Puttanesca Sauce
Dinner: Crispy Crusted Chicken Tenders
Dessert: Arroz con Leche

Day 2:
Breakfast: Nutty Carrot Muffins
Lunch: Cheesy White Beans with Lemon
Snack: Creamy Buffalo Cheese Chicken Dip
Dinner: Perfect Mexican Beef Casserole
Dessert: Classic Bread Pudding

Day 3:
Breakfast: Cheesy Egg in a Hole
Lunch: Easy Crispy Parmesan Artichokes
Snack: Coconut Chicken Bites
Dinner: Lemony Cocktail Prawns
Dessert: Flavourful Cinnamon Dried Fruit Compote

Day 4:
Breakfast: Oat Muffins with Dry Fruit
Lunch: Easy Chili Mac
Snack: Classic Reuben Potato Skins
Dinner: Flavourful Creamy Chicken and Brown Rice
Dessert: Delicious White Chocolate Pots De Crème

Day 5:
Breakfast: Honey Corn Muffins with Carrot and Pepper
Lunch: Authentic Bulgur Pilaf with Chickpeas
Snack: Broccoli, Potato, and Sausage Tots
Dinner: Hearty Lamb Ragù
Dessert: Perfect Lemony Tapioca Pudding

Day 6:
Breakfast: Herbed Ham and Potatoes
Lunch: Lemony Brussels Sprout
Snack: Crispy Cheese Beef Meatballs
Dinner: Thai Coconut Salmon Curry
Dessert: Fluffy Carrot Coconut Cake with Pecans

Day 7:
Breakfast: Sweet Pecan Steel-Cut Oats
Lunch: Sesame Carrots Sticks
Snack: Yummy Spicy Black Bean Dip
Dinner: Simple Beef Dinner Rolls
Dessert: Creamy Chocolate Cake

Chapter 1 Breakfast

Cheese Courgette Drop Biscuits 12	Sweet & Spicy Tomato Jam with Toast 16
Peach Oatmeal with Pecans 12	Crustless Mini Quiche Bites with Olives ... 17
Fluffy Garlic Cheese Bread..................... 12	Crustless Gruyère and Bacon Quiche 17
Jalapeño-Cheddar Bagel and Egg Casserole 12	Veggie Bacon Frittatas 17
Breakfast Kale Soufflé 13	Crispy Toast Sticks 17
Cinnamon Coconut Muesli Stuffed Apples... 13	Yummy Mushroom Boat Eggs 18
Chocolate-Strawberry Quinoa 13	Cheesy Ham Polenta Muffins 18
Spicy Sweet Potato Hash with Eggs 13	Cheesy Ham Muffins 18
Blueberry Muffins 14	Fried Banana PB&J Sandwich 18
Yogurt Egg Salad 14	Cheesy Egg in a Hole 19
Soft Blueberry French Bread 14	Nutty Carrot Muffins 19
Herbed Ham and Potatoes 14	Oat Muffins with Dry Fruit..................... 19
Sweet Pecan Steel-Cut Oats 15	Honey Corn Muffins with Carrot and Pepper 19
Savoury Sweet Potatoes and Bacon 15	Homemade Chocolate Banana Bread 20
Crustless Feta and Spinach Quiche............ 15	Classic Enchilada Casserole 20
Pepperoni Pizza Casserole 15	Egg White Bites with Ham 20
Easy Traditional Shakshuka 16	Healthy Eggs in a Boat 21
Cheesy Ham Strata 16	Creamy Blueberries Clafouti 21
Cheesy Baked Eggs............................. 16	Fluffy Raspberry Breakfast Cake 21

Cheese Courgette Drop Biscuits

Prep time: 25 minutes | Cook time: 25 minutes | Serves: 12

90 g shredded courgette
1¼ tsp. salt, divided
185 g plain flour
1 tbsp. baking powder
115 g cold butter, cubed
50 g shredded cheddar cheese

30 g shredded part-skim mozzarella cheese
25 g shredded Parmesan cheese
2 tbsp. finely chopped oil-packed sun-dried tomatoes, patted dry
2 tbsp. minced fresh basil or 2 tsp. dried basil
240 ml low fat milk

1. Put the courgette in a strainer on top of a plate, add ¼ tsp salt, and mix. 2. Leave it for 10 minutes, then rinse it and drain it well. Squeeze the courgette to get rid of any excess liquid, and dry it with a paper towel. 3. In a big bowl, mix together the flour, baking powder, and the rest of the salt. Cut in the butter until the mixture looks like coarse crumbs. Add the courgette, cheeses, tomatoes, and basil, and stir everything together. 4. Finally, pour in the milk and mix everything until it's just moistened. Drop by scant spoonfuls into a greased baking pan that can fit the pot. 5. Place the pan on the bottom layer of the Deluxe Reversible Rack in the lower position. 6. When the pot has preheated, place the rack with pan in the pot. Close the lid and make sure the slider is in the AIR FRY/STOVETOP. Select BAKE/ROAST, set temperature to 205°C, and set time to 25 minutes. Select START/STOP to begin cooking. Bake golden brown. 7. Serve warm.
Per Serving: Calories 196; Fat 9.85g; Sodium 371mg; Carbs 22g; Fibre 0.8g; Sugar 1.2g; Protein 4.84g

Peach Oatmeal with Pecans

Prep time: 10 minutes | Cook Time: 4 minutes | Serves: 4

960 ml water
160 g rolled oats
1 tablespoon light olive oil
1 large peach, peeled, pitted, and diced

¼ teaspoon salt
60 g toasted pecans
2 tablespoons maple syrup

1. Place water, oats, peach, oil, and salt in the pot. Stir well and close the lid. move slider to PRESSURE. Make sure the pressure release valve is in the SEAL position. The temperature will default to HIGH, which is the correct setting. Set time to 4 minutes. Select START/STOP to begin cooking. 2. When cooking is complete, turn the pressure relief valve to the VENT position for quick pressure relief. Move slider to the right to unlock the lid, then carefully open it. 3. Stir well. Serve oatmeal topped with pecans and maple syrup.
Per Serving: Calories 274; Fat 15.7g; Sodium 153mg; Carbs 43.72g; Fibre 9.1g; Sugar 10.89g; Protein 9.67g

Fluffy Garlic Cheese Bread

Prep time: 30 minutes | Cook time: 25 minutes | Serves:2

1 pkg. (5g) active dry yeast
300 ml warm water
2 tbsp. plus 2 tsp. olive oil
7 garlic cloves, minced
1 tbsp. sugar
Egg Wash:
1 large egg

½ tsp. salt
1½ tsp. white vinegar
170 g – 200 g bread flour
100 g cubed Asiago cheese

1 tbsp. Water

1. In a large bowl, dissolve yeast in warm water. Add the oil, garlic, sugar, salt, vinegar and 150 g flour. Beat until smooth. Stir in enough of the remaining flour to form a firm dough. Stir in cheese. 2. Turn onto a floured surface and knead until smooth and elastic, 6-8 minutes. Place in a greased bowl, turning once to grease the top. Cover and let rise in a warm place until doubled, about 1 hour. 3. Punch dough down; divide in half. Shape into 12cm -round loaves. Place on lightly greased baking sheets. Cover and let rise in a warm place until doubled, about 30 minutes. 4. For egg wash, in a small bowl, combine egg and water. Brush over loaves. 5. Place the baking sheets on the bottom layer of the Deluxe Reversible Rack in the lower position. 6. When the pot has preheated, place the rack with pan in the pot. Close the lid and make sure the slider is in the AIR FRY/STOVETOP. Select BAKE/ROAST, set temperature to 190°C, and set time to 25 minutes. Select START/STOP to begin cooking. 7. When cooking is complete, remove the rack with the baking sheets and let cool for 5 minutes, then serve warm.
Per Serving: Calories 822; Fat 52.83g; Sodium 823mg; Carbs 24.83g; Fibre 1.8g; Sugar 7.45g; Protein 61g

Jalapeño-Cheddar Bagel and Egg Casserole

Prep time: 10 minutes | Cook time: 20 minutes | Serves: 4

240 ml water
6 large eggs
60 g whipping cream
Salt
Freshly ground black pepper
1 jalapeño pepper, thinly sliced

1½ jalapeño-cheddar bagels, cut into 1 cm pieces
50 g shredded cheddar cheese
1 tbsp feta cheese crumbles
Unsalted butter, for baking dish
Chopped fresh coriander, for garnish

1. Pour the water into the pot of Ninja XL Pressure Cooker. 2. In a bowl, combine the cream, eggs, salt, black pepper, and the jalapeño and mix until the eggs are beaten. Stir in the bagel pieces and cheeses. Let sit for 3 minutes. 3. Butter a round baking dish that can fit the pot. Pour the egg mixture into the prepared baking dish. Place the pan on the bottom layer of the Deluxe Reversible Rack in the lower position. 4. Close the lid and move slider to PRESSURE. Ensuring the pressure release valve is in the SEAL position. The temperature will default to HIGH, which is the correct setting. Set time to 20 minutes. Select START/STOP to begin cooking. 5. When cooking is complete, release the pressure quickly by turning the pressure release valve to the VENT position. Move slider to the right to unlock the lid, then carefully open it. 6. Let the casserole cool for 5 minutes and then garnish with chopped fresh coriander.
Per Serving: Calories 336; Fat 21.32g; Sodium 1165mg; Carbs 22.44g; Fibre 1.8g; Sugar 4.96g; Protein 14g

Breakfast Kale Soufflé

Prep time: 15 minutes | Cook Time: 10 minutes | Serves: 4

1 tbsp (15 ml) extra-virgin olive oil
½ yellow onion, diced
135 g trimmed and chopped kale
Salt
Freshly ground black pepper
1 clove garlic, grated
240 ml water
Unsalted butter, for ramekins
4 large eggs
2 tsp (10 ml) heavy cream

1. Move slider to AIR FRY/STOVETOP. Select SEAR/SAUTÉ and set to 3. Select START/STOP to begin preheating. Allow unit to preheat for 5 minutes. After 5 minutes, add the olive oil. Heat the oil for 1 minute, then add the onion. Sauté for 2 minutes. 2. Mix in the kale and season with a little salt and pepper. Sauté for 3 to 4 minutes, or until tender and slightly wilted. Add the garlic, stir to combine and sauté for one more minute. Press START/STOP to turn off the SEAR/SAUTÉ function. 3. Remove the kale mixture and transfer to a small plate. 4. Clean the pot and return it to the device. Pour the water into the pot and place the bottom layer of the Deluxe Reversible Rack in the lower position in the pot. 5. Butter four small soufflé ramekins with unsalted butter. Place a little bit of the kale mixture in the bottom of each ramekin. 6. Crack an egg into each ramekin, then top each egg with ½ teaspoon of the heavy cream and sprinkle with salt and pepper. Place the ramekins on the rack. 7. Close the lid and move slider to PRESSURE. Make sure the pressure release valve is in the SEAL position. The temperature will default to HIGH, which is the correct setting. Set time to 3 minutes. Select START/STOP to begin cooking. 8. When the timer beeps, naturally release the pressure for 2 minutes. Then turn the pressure relief valve to the VENT position for quick pressure relief. Move slider to AIR FRY/ STOVETOP to unlock the lid, then carefully open it.
Per Serving: Calories 112; Fat 8.97g; Sodium 163mg; Carbs 4.83g; Fibre 0.7g; Sugar 2.43g; Protein 3.52g

Cinnamon Coconut Muesli Stuffed Apples

Prep time: 10 minutes | Cook Time: 3 minutes | Serves: 2

2 large unpeeled organic apples, cored
40 g coconut muesli
2 tablespoons butter, cubed
2 teaspoons packed brown sugar
½ teaspoon ground cinnamon
80 ml water

1. Remove the tops of the apples and slice the bottoms off just enough to help the apples sit flat in the cooker pot. 2. In a medium bowl, combine the muesli, brown sugar, butter, and cinnamon, mashing gently with a fork until combined. 3. Stuff each apple with the muesli mixture, then place them in the bottom of the cooker pot. Add the water to the pot. 4. Close the lid and move slider to PRESSURE. Make sure the pressure release valve is in the SEAL position. Set the heat to LOW and set time to 3 minutes. Select START/STOP to begin cooking. 5. When cooking is complete, naturally release the pressure for 10 minutes. Then turn the pressure relief valve to the VENT position for quick pressure relief. Move slider to AIR FRY/ STOVETOP to unlock the lid, then carefully open it. 6. Serve with Greek yogurt.
Per Serving: Calories 241; Fat 12.02g; Sodium 157mg; Carbs 36.05g; Fibre 6.4g; Sugar 27.2g; Protein 1.16g

Chocolate-Strawberry Quinoa

Prep time: 5 minutes | Cook Time: 12 minutes | Serves: 2

80 g uncooked quinoa
180 ml unsweetened coconut milk, plus more for serving
120 ml water
2 tablespoons maple syrup
1 tablespoon unsweetened cocoa powder
½ teaspoon vanilla extract (optional)
Pinch salt
30 g fresh strawberries
25 g chocolate shavings

1. Rinse the quinoa in a fine-mesh strainer for 2 minutes. Sort and pick out any discoloured pieces or pebbles by your hands. 2. Put the quinoa in the bowl and stir in the water, coconut milk, cocoa powder, maple syrup, vanilla (if using), and salt. 3. Close the lid and move slider to PRESSURE. Make sure the pressure release valve is in the SEAL position. Set the temperature to LOW and set time to 12 minutes. Select START/STOP to begin cooking. 4. When cooking is complete, naturally release the pressure for 10 minutes. Then turn the pressure relief valve to the VENT position for quick pressure relief. Move slider to AIR FRY/ STOVETOP to unlock the lid, then carefully open it. 5. Fluff the quinoa with a fork and spoon it into two cereal bowls. Add more coconut milk, and top with strawberries and chocolate shavings.
Per Serving: Calories 535; Fat 24.88g; Sodium 280mg; Carbs 73.16g; Fibre 7.1g; Sugar 34.78g; Protein 9.47g

Spicy Sweet Potato Hash with Eggs

Prep time: 10 minutes | Cook Time: 13 minutes | Serves: 4

1 tablespoon olive oil
675 g sweet potatoes, peeled and diced
1 yellow onion, chopped
1 red pepper, seeded and chopped
2 garlic cloves, minced
1 teaspoon dried oregano
½ teaspoon cayenne pepper
½ teaspoon salt
¼ teaspoon freshly ground black pepper
120 ml vegetable stock or store-bought low-sodium vegetable stock
4 large eggs

1. Move slider to AIR FRY/STOVETOP. Select SEAR/SAUTÉ and set to 3. Select START/STOP to begin preheating. Allow unit to preheat for 5 minutes. After 5 minutes, add the olive oil. When the oil is hot, add the sweet potatoes and sauté for 10 minutes, stirring occasionally, until the potatoes begin to brown and soften. 2. Stir in the onion, pepper, garlic, cayenne pepper, oregano, salt, and black pepper until well combined. Press START/STOP to turn off the SEAR/SAUTÉ function. 3. Stir in the stock, then crack the eggs on top of the potato mixture. Close the lid. 4. Move slider to PRESSURE. Make sure the pressure release valve is in the SEAL position. The temperature will default to HIGH, which is the correct setting. Set time to 3 minutes. Select START/STOP to begin cooking. 5. When the cook time is complete, quick release the pressure. 6. Carefully open the lid and serve.
Per Serving: Calories 199; Fat 11.32g; Sodium 331mg; Carbs 20.42g; Fibre 9.9g; Sugar 2.59g; Protein 7.8g

Blueberry Muffins

Prep time: 10 minutes | Cook Time: 10 minutes | Serves: 6

Nonstick cooking spray
125 g spelt flour
1 teaspoon baking powder
¼ teaspoon baking soda
⅛ teaspoon salt
1 egg, beaten

3 tablespoons nondairy milk
2 tablespoons coconut oil, melted
2 tablespoons honey
1 teaspoon vanilla extract
60 g fresh or frozen blueberries

1. Grease the outer 6 wells of a 7-well silicone egg bite mold with nonstick cooking spray. 2. In a medium bowl, mix together the flour, baking soda, baking powder, and salt. 3. In a small bowl, whisk the egg, coconut oil, milk, honey, and vanilla. Add the egg mixture to the flour mixture and stir until combined into a thick batter. 4. Divide the batter between the prepared egg bite wells, filling each well about halfway. Gently press the blueberries into the top of each muffin. Place the lid on the mold. 5. Pour 240 ml of water into the pot and place the bottom layer of the Deluxe Reversible Rack in the lower position in the pot. Place the egg bite mold on the rack. 6. Close the lid and move slider to PRESSURE. Make sure the pressure release valve is in the SEAL position. The temperature will default to HIGH, which is the correct setting. Set time to 10 minutes. Select START/STOP to begin cooking. 7. When the cook time is complete, let the pressure release naturally for 10 minutes, then quick release any remaining pressure. 8. Open the lid carefully and lift out the mold. Uncover the muffins and let them rest for 3 to 5 minutes, until the mold is cool to the touch, then pop the muffins out. 9. Serve warm or store at room temperature in an airtight container for up to 3 days.
Per Serving: Calories 194; Fat 7.22g; Sodium 130mg; Carbs 28.71g; Fibre 3.5g; Sugar 9.39g; Protein 6.03g

Yogurt Egg Salad

Prep time: 10 minutes | Cook Time: 10 minutes | Serves: 6

6 large eggs
240 ml water
1 tablespoon olive oil
1 medium red pepper, seeded and chopped

¼ teaspoon salt
¼ teaspoon ground black pepper
120 g low-fat plain Greek yogurt
2 tablespoons chopped fresh dill

1. Fill a large bowl with ice water. Place the bottom layer of the Deluxe Reversible Rack in the lower position in the pot. 2. Arrange eggs on rack and add water to the pot. Close the lid. Close the lid and move slider to PRESSURE. Make sure the pressure release valve is in the SEAL position. The temperature will default to HIGH, which is the correct setting. Set time to 5 minutes. Select START/STOP to begin cooking. 3. When cooking is complete, naturally release the pressure for 5 minutes. Then turn the pressure relief valve to the VENT position for quick pressure relief. Move slider to AIR FRY/ STOVETOP to unlock the lid, then carefully open it. 4. Carefully transfer eggs to the bowl of ice water. Let stand in ice water for 10 minutes, then peel, chop, and add eggs to a medium bowl. 5. Clean out pot, dry well, and return to machine. Move slider to AIR FRY/STOVETOP. Select SEAR/SAUTE and set to 3. Select START/STOP to begin cooking. Heat oil in the pot. Add pepper, salt, and black pepper. Cook, stirring frequently, until pepper is tender, about 5 minutes. Transfer to bowl with eggs. 6. Add yogurt and dill to bowl, and fold to combine. Cover and chill for 1 hour before serving.
Per Serving: Calories 101; Fat 7.46g; Sodium 122mg; Carbs 4.64g; Fibre 0.9g; Sugar 2.46g; Protein 4.35g

Soft Blueberry French Bread

Prep time: 15 minutes | Cook Time: 15 minutes | Serves: 4

2 large eggs
240 ml whole milk
2 tbsp light brown sugar
1 tsp. pure vanilla extract
½ tsp. ground cinnamon

1 small loaf French bread, cut into 1.3-cm cubes
Nonstick cooking spray, for pan
75 g blueberries, plus more for serving (optional)
240 ml water
Pure maple syrup, for serving

1. Beat the eggs in a medium bowl, then add the milk, brown sugar, vanilla and cinnamon, and whisk well until thoroughly combined. 2. Add the bread cubes and press into the liquid until completely submerged. Cover the bowl and refrigerate for 30 minutes (or overnight if you want to make it ahead). 3. Spray a cake pan with nonstick cooking spray. Take the bread mixture out of the refrigerator and fold in the blueberries. Pour the mixture into the prepared pan. 4. Pour the water into the pot and insert the rack. Tent the cake pan with foil and place on the rack. 5. Close the lid, turn the pressure release valve to SEAL position, and then move the slider to PRESSURE. Select HI and set the cooking time to 15 minutes. Press START/STOP to begin cooking. When finished, release the pressure quickly. 6. Cut the French toast and serve with maple syrup and more fresh blueberries, if desired.
Per Serving: Calories 296; Fat: 5.66g; Sodium: 372mg; Carbs: 52.06g; Fibre: 1.9g; Sugar: 24.43g; Protein: 9.41g

Herbed Ham and Potatoes

Prep time: 15 minutes | Cook Time: 15 minutes | Serves: 4-6

1 tbsp extra-virgin olive oil
2 tbsp unsalted butter
2 yellow onions, diced
115 g diced thick-cut ham
½ tsp. chopped fresh rosemary

3 sprigs thyme
3 large russet potatoes cut into 2.5-cm cubes
Salt
Freshly ground black pepper
60 ml chicken stock

1. Select SEAR/SAUTÉ. Select Lo3, and then press START/STOP to begin cooking. 2. When the pot is hot, add olive oil and butter; once the butter melts, add the onions and cook them for 9 minutes until the onions start to caramelize; add ham, rosemary and thyme, and sauté them for another 3 minutes. 3. Stop the process, and stir in the potatoes, salt, pepper, and the stock, scraping up any bits from the bottom of the pan. 4. Close the lid, turn the pressure release valve to SEAL position, and then move the slider to PRESSURE. Select HI and set the cooking time to 3 minutes. Press START/STOP to begin cooking. When finished, release the pressure naturally. 5. Remove the lid, stir and add more salt or pepper if needed. Serve and enjoy.
Per Serving: Calories 216; Fat: 4.53g; Sodium: 313mg; Carbs: 37.42g; Fibre: 3.1g; Sugar: 2.86g; Protein: 7.98g

Sweet Pecan Steel-Cut Oats

Prep time: 15 minutes | Cook Time: 5 minutes | Serves: 4

320 g steel-cut oats
710 ml water
1 (400-ml) can full-fat coconut milk, divided
80 ml pure maple syrup, plus more to taste
½ tsp. sea salt
55 g toasted pecan pieces
2 tsp. ground cinnamon (optional)

1. Combine the oats, maple syrup, water, 240 ml of the coconut milk, and salt in the pot, and then give the mixture a quick stir. 2. Close the lid, turn the pressure release valve to SEAL position, and then move the slider to PRESSURE. Select HI and set the cooking time to 4 minutes. Press START/STOP to begin cooking. When finished, release the pressure naturally. 3. Remove the lid and stir in the remaining coconut milk and additional maple syrup to taste. 4. Serve with the toasted pecans and sprinkle with the cinnamon (if using).
Per Serving: Calories 581; Fat: 38.52g; Sodium: 3228mg; Carbs: 77.65g; Fibre: 15.8g; Sugar: 20.63g; Protein: 17.33g

Savoury Sweet Potatoes and Bacon

Prep time: 15 minutes | Cook Time: 5 minutes | Serves: 4-6

1 tbsp. extra-virgin olive oil
7 slices thick-cut bacon, diced
1 yellow onion, diced
1 tsp. Worcestershire sauce
60 ml bourbon or beef stock
3 sweet potatoes (about 540 g total), peeled and cut into large cubes
80 ml water
Salt
Freshly ground black pepper
40 g loosely packed light brown sugar
¼ tsp. cayenne pepper

1. Select SEAR/SAUTÉ. Select Lo3, and then press START/STOP to begin cooking. 2. When the pot is hot, add olive oil and bacon, and sauté them for 10 minutes until crispy; add the onion and sauté for 5 to 7 minutes until the onion is starting to caramelize. 3. Deglaze the pot with the Worcestershire and bourbon, and scrape up all the browned bacon bits from the bottom of the pot. Sauté them for 2 more minutes. 4. Stop the process and stir in the sweet potatoes along with the water, salt and black pepper. 5. Close the lid, turn the pressure release valve to SEAL position, and then move the slider to PRESSURE. Select HI and set the cooking time to 3 minutes. Press START/STOP to begin cooking. When finished, release the pressure quickly. 6. Stir in the brown sugar and cayenne pepper. Let the potato mixture cool slightly before tasting and adjusting the salt and pepper, if needed. Enjoy.
Per Serving: Calories 291; Fat: 13.49g; Sodium: 253mg; Carbs: 35.43g; Fibre: 4.4g; Sugar: 2.76g; Protein: 7.99g

Crustless Feta and Spinach Quiche

Prep time: 10 minutes | Cook Time: 30 minutes | Serves: 4

Nonstick cooking spray
6 large eggs, beaten
60 ml skim milk
30 g crumbled feta
1 shallot, finely chopped
¼ teaspoon salt
¼ teaspoon freshly ground black pepper
75 g frozen chopped spinach

1. Grease a cake pan with nonstick cooking spray. 2. Mix up the eggs and milk in a large bowl until frothy; stir in the feta, shallot, salt, and pepper. 3. Spread the spinach over the bottom of the prepared cake pan, and then pour the egg mixture over the spinach. Cover the pan with aluminum foil. 4. Pour 240 ml of water into the pot and insert the rack. Place the cake pan on top of the rack. 5. Close the lid, turn the pressure release valve to SEAL position, and then move the slider to PRESSURE. Select HI and set the cooking time to 30 minutes. Press START/STOP to begin cooking. When finished, release the pressure naturally. 6. Carefully remove the lid and lift out the cake pan. 7. Cut the quiche into four slices and serve.
Per Serving: Calories 167; Fat: 9.59g; Sodium: 402mg; Carbs: 6.71g; Fibre: 2.4g; Sugar: 3.33g; Protein: 14.15g

Pepperoni Pizza Casserole

Prep time: 15 minutes | Cook Time: 25 minutes | Serves: 6

Grass-fed butter, ghee or avocado oil, for casserole dish
85 g pepperoni, divided
5 large eggs
120 ml milk or heavy cream
1 tsp sea salt
1½ tsp (4.5 g) garlic granules
½ tsp onion powder
½ tsp dried oregano
½ tsp dried thyme
3 small tomatoes, seeded and chopped
15 g chopped fresh flat-leaf parsley
70 g sliced mushrooms
50 g pitted and sliced black olives
115 g shredded mozzarella cheese
40 g shredded Parmesan cheese
240 ml water

1. Grease a casserole dish that fits inside the pot with oil. Set it aside. 2. Chop 28g of the pepperoni, reserving the remaining pepperoni (left whole). 3. In a large bowl, whisk together the eggs and milk. Add the salt, onion powder, garlic granules, thyme, oregano, parsley, mushrooms, tomatoes, olives, the chopped pepperoni and the cheeses, gently stirring to combine. 4. Pour the mixture into the prepared casserole dish. In a uniform layer, place the remaining whole pieces of pepperoni on top of the filling. 5. Cover the casserole dish with its glass lid or you can cover the top of the dish with unbleached parchment paper, then put foil on top and secure it around the edges. 6. Pour water into the pot and place the bottom layer of the Deluxe Reversible Rack in the lower position in the pot. Carefully place the covered casserole dish on top of the rack. 7. Close the lid and move slider to PRESSURE. Make sure the pressure release valve is in the SEAL position. The temperature will default to HIGH, which is the correct setting. Set time to 25 minutes. Select START/STOP to begin cooking. 8. When cooking is complete, naturally release the pressure for 10 minutes. Then turn the pressure relief valve to the VENT position for quick pressure relief. Move slider to AIR FRY/ STOVETOP to unlock the lid, then carefully open it. 9. Carefully remove the casserole dish from the pot and remove the lid from the dish. 10. Lest it rest for 15 minutes, serve.
Per Serving: Calories 241; Fat 18.02g; Sodium 947mg; Carbs 5.15g; Fibre 1.2g; Sugar 1.93g; Protein 14.8g

Easy Traditional Shakshuka

Prep time: 15 minutes | Cook Time: 11 minutes | Serves: 2

2 tbsp (30 ml) avocado oil or olive oil
1 small yellow onion, diced
1 green pepper, seeded and diced
1 clove garlic, minced
60 ml water
1 (800-g) can whole tomatoes, with juices

1½ tsp (3.5 g) smoked paprika
½ tsp ground cumin
½ tsp sea salt
4 large eggs
15 g chopped fresh parsley or (10 g) coriander, for serving
3 tbsp (28 g) crumbled feta cheese, for serving (optional)

1. Move slider to AIR FRY/STOVETOP. Select SEAR/SAUTÉ and set to 3. Select START/STOP to begin preheating. Allow unit to preheat for 5 minutes. After 5 minutes, add oil to the bottom of the pot and add the onion and pepper. Sauté for 2 to 3 minutes, then add the garlic. Cook for 1 more minute, or until the vegetables are softened and fragrant. Press START/STOP to turn off the SEAR/SAUTÉ function. 2. Add water to the pot. Then, add the tomatoes with their juices, cumin, paprika and salt. 3. Close the lid and move the slider to PRESSURE. Ensure the pressure release valve is in the SEAL position. The temperature will default to HIGH, which is the correct setting. Set time to 6 minutes. Select START/STOP to begin cooking. 4. When cooking is complete, turn the pressure release valve to the vent position for a quick pressure release. Move slider to the right to unlock the lid, then carefully open it. 5. Gently crack each egg into a ladle or large wooden spoon and slowly lower into the tomato sauce. 6. Close the lid once again, and select PRESSURE and 0 minutes (yes, zero). 7. Use a quick release and remove the lid. You can leave the lid on longer for a more cooked egg. 8. Serve hot with the fresh parsley or coriander, and feta cheese.
Per Serving: Calories 396; Fat 28.98g; Sodium 1460mg; Carbs 24.95g; Fibre 9.7g; Sugar 15.43g; Protein 13.79g

Cheesy Ham Strata

Prep time: 15 minutes | Cook Time: 20 minutes | Serves: 4

1 tbsp unsalted butter
250 ml water
6 large eggs
¼ tsp ground cumin
¼ tsp mustard powder
80 ml heavy cream
Salt

Freshly ground black pepper
95 g leftover mole carnitas or store-bought cooked pulled pork
75 g cubed ham
85 g shredded Swiss cheese
100 g cubed French bread
1 small to medium kosher dill pickle, thinly sliced

1. Butter a round baking dish that can fit the pot. Pour water into the pot and place the Deluxe Reversible Rack in the lower position in the pot. 2. Combine together the eggs, cumin, cream, salt, mustard powder, and pepper in a bowl. 3. Stir in the mole carnitas, bread, Swiss, ham, and pickle. Let the mixture sit for 2 minutes and then transfer to the prepared baking dish. 4. Carefully place the baking dish on the rack. 5. Close the lid and move the slider to PRESSURE. Ensure the pressure release valve is in the SEAL position. The temperature will default to HIGH, which is the correct setting. Set time to 20 minutes. Select START/STOP to begin cooking. 6. When cooking is complete, turn the pressure release valve to the vent position for a quick pressure release. Move slider to the right to unlock the lid, then carefully open it. 7. Lift the rack and baking dish out of the pot. Let the strata cool slightly before slicing.
Per Serving: Calories 362; Fat 23.18g; Sodium 716mg; Carbs 18.02g; Fibre 0.9g; Sugar 6.49g; Protein 19.84g

Cheesy Baked Eggs

Prep time: 15 minutes | Cook Time: 10 minutes | Serves: 3

6 large eggs
115 g full-fat cottage cheese
60 g Mexican-blend shredded cheese

1 jalapeño pepper, minced
1 green onion, minced
240 ml water

1. In a high-powered blender, pulse all the ingredients except the water. 2. Pour the water into the pot and place the bottom layer of the Deluxe Reversible Rack in the lower position in the pot. Evenly divide the egg mixture among the wells of a six-bite egg mold. 3. Carefully lower the mold onto the rack. 4. Close the lid and move the slider to PRESSURE. Ensure the pressure release valve is in the SEAL position. The temperature will default to HIGH, which is the correct setting. Set time to 10 minutes. Select START/STOP to begin cooking. 5. When cooking is complete, naturally release the pressure for 10 minutes. Then quick release pressure by turning the pressure release valve to the VENT position. Move slider to AIR FRY/ STOVETOP to unlock the lid, then carefully open it. 6. Carefully remove the eggs from the molds and serve immediately.
Per Serving: Calories 247; Fat 17.32g; Sodium 86mg; Carbs 8.57g; Fibre 1.8g; Sugar 2.7g; Protein 15.04g

Sweet & Spicy Tomato Jam with Toast

Prep time: 10 minutes | Cook Time: 10 minutes | Serves: 6

455 g tomatoes, cut into eighths
100 g sugar
60 ml white wine vinegar
¼ to ½ tsp crushed red pepper flakes

¼ tsp salt
15 ml water
Toast or crackers, for serving

1. In the pot, mix together all the ingredients except the toast. 2. Close the lid and move the slider to PRESSURE. Ensure the pressure release valve is in the SEAL position. The temperature will default to HIGH, which is the correct setting. Set time to 10 minutes. Select START/STOP to begin cooking. 3. When the timer beeps, quick release the pressure. 4. Open the lid and mash the tomatoes into small pieces with a potato masher. As the jam cools, it will thicken. 5. When the jam is completely cool, transfer to a pint-size Mason jar with a lid. Store in the refrigerator for up to 3 weeks. 6. Spread the jam on toast or crackers.
Per Serving: Calories 51; Fat 0.17g; Sodium 130mg; Carbs 11.63g; Fibre 0.8g; Sugar 8.29g; Protein 1.02g

Crustless Mini Quiche Bites with Olives

Prep time: 20 minutes | Cook Time: 10 minutes | Serves: 4

1 tsp. extra-virgin olive oil
5 large eggs
½ tsp. onion salt
½ tsp. dried basil
½ tsp. chopped fresh dill
½ tsp. chopped fresh parsley
75 g sliced cherry tomatoes
25 g chopped pitted green olives
75 g crumbled goat cheese
240 ml water

1. Place the olive oil on a paper towel and then use the paper towel to oil each well of the egg bite mold. 2. Whisk the eggs, onion salt, basil, dill and parsley in a medium bowl. 3. Add ¼ to ½ teaspoon each of the tomatoes, olives and goat cheese to the bottom of each well in the mold. Pour the egg mixture over the toppings to fill each well about three-quarters of the way up. Add the remaining tomatoes, olives and cheese on top of the egg mixture. 4. Pour the water in the pot and place in the rack, and then place the egg mold on the rack. 5. Close the lid, turn the pressure release valve to SEAL position, and then move the slider to PRESSURE. Select HI and set the cooking time to 8 minutes. Press START/STOP to begin cooking. When finished, release the pressure naturally. 6. Remove the egg bite mold. Flip the mini quiches out onto a serving dish. Enjoy.
Per Serving: Calories 191; Fat: 13.89g; Sodium: 192mg; Carbs: 1.35g; Fibre: 0.1g; Sugar: 0.83g; Protein: 14.61g

Crustless Gruyère and Bacon Quiche

Prep time: 20 minutes | Cook Time: 35 minutes | Serves: 4

6 slices bacon
355 ml water
Nonstick cooking spray, for pan
6 large eggs
175 ml heavy cream
55 g shredded Gruyère cheese
1 tbsp chopped fresh parsley
½ tsp. coarse salt
Freshly ground black pepper

1. Select SEAR/SAUTÉ. Select Lo3, and then press START/STOP to begin cooking. 2. When the pot is hot, put the bacon and cook for about 5 minutes or until browned and crispy, and then transfer the bacon to paper towels to drain any excess fat. Discard the drippings without wiping clean. 3. Stop the process and scrape up any browned bits from the bottom of the pot. 4. Pour the water into the pot and place the rack in it. 5. Spray a suitable cake pan with nonstick cooking spray. 6. In a medium bowl, whisk together the eggs and cream until frothy. Crumble the bacon and stir it in along with the shredded cheese, parsley, salt and pepper. Arrange the mixture onto the prepared cake pan and place the pan on the rack. 7. Close the lid, turn the pressure release valve to SEAL position, and then move the slider to PRESSURE. Select HI and set the cooking time to 30 minutes. Press START/STOP to begin cooking. When finished, release the pressure quickly. 8. Carefully remove the cake pan from the pot. Slice the quiche and serve immediately.
Per Serving: Calories 390; Fat: 34.47g; Sodium: 706mg; Carbs: 2.04g; Fibre: 0g; Sugar: 1.59g; Protein: 17.56g

Veggie Bacon Frittatas

Prep time: 20 minutes | Cook Time: 15 minutes | Serves: 4

2 tbsp. grass-fed butter or ghee, plus more for jars
35 g cleaned and thinly sliced white button or cremini mushrooms
1 large celery rib, thinly sliced
15 g prewashed finely chopped fresh spinach
6 large eggs
60 ml milk of choice
½ tsp. sea salt
½ tsp. garlic granules or garlic powder
¼ tsp. onion powder
¼ tsp. dried thyme
2 tbsp chopped fresh flat-leaf parsley, plus more for garnish
60 g shredded sharp or mild cheddar cheese
20 g shredded Parmesan, provolone or Gruyère cheese
4 slices cooked crispy bacon, crumbled
355 ml water

1. Select SEAR/SAUTÉ. Select Lo3, and then press START/STOP to begin cooking. 2. When the pot is hot, melt the healthy fat you chose; add the mushrooms and celery, and sauté them for 7 minutes until lightly caramelized; add the spinach and sauté for 2 minutes or just until wilted. Stop the process. 3. Butter 4 wide-mouth ramekins. Set them aside. 4. In a large bowl, whisk together the eggs and your milk of choice until the eggs are fully incorporated. Add the sautéed veggies, salt, garlic granules, onion powder, thyme, parsley, shredded cheeses and crumbled bacon. 5. Evenly pour the mixture into the prepared ramekins, and cover the tops of the ramekins with unbleached parchment paper, then top them with foil and secure it around the edges. 6. Pour the water into the pot and place the rack in it, and then place the ramekins on the rack. 7. Close the lid, turn the pressure release valve to SEAL position, and then move the slider to PRESSURE. Select HI and set the cooking time to 5 minutes. Press START/STOP to begin cooking. When finished, release the pressure naturally. 8. Allow the frittatas to rest for 5 minutes before serving.
Per Serving: Calories 362; Fat: 28.68g; Sodium: 712mg; Carbs: 6.01g; Fibre: 1.1g; Sugar: 1.95g; Protein: 20.11g

Crispy Toast Sticks

Prep time: 5 minutes | Cook Time: 5–7 minutes | Serves: 4

2 eggs
120ml milk
⅛ teaspoon salt
½ teaspoon pure vanilla extract
30g crushed cornflakes
6 slices sandwich bread, each slice cut into 4 strips
Oil for misting or cooking spray
Maple syrup or honey

1. Place the Cook & Crisp Basket in your Pressure Cooker Steam Fryer. 2. In a suitable bowl, beat eggs, milk, salt, and vanilla. 3. Place crushed cornflakes on a plate or in a shallow dish. 4. Dip bread strips in egg mixture, shake off excess, and roll in cornflake crumbs. 5. Spray both sides of bread strips with oil. 6. Place bread strips in Cook & Crisp Basket in single layer. 7. Put on the Smart Lid on top of the Ninja Foodi Steam Fryer. 8. Move the Lid Slider to the "Air Fry/Stovetop". Select the "Air Fry" mode for cooking. 9. Air Fry the strips at 200°C for 5 to 7 minutes or until they're dark golden brown. 10. Repeat to cook remaining toast sticks. 11. Serve with maple syrup or honey for dipping.
Per Serving: Calories: 282; Fat: 19g; Sodium: 354mg; Carbs: 15g; Fibre: 5.1g; Sugar 8.2g; Protein 12g

Yummy Mushroom Boat Eggs

Prep time: 10 minutes | Cook Time: 10 minutes | Serves: 4

4 postulate rolls
1 teaspoon butter
25g diced fresh mushrooms
½ teaspoon dried onion flakes
4 eggs

½ teaspoon salt
¼ teaspoon dried dill weed
¼ teaspoon dried parsley
1 tablespoon milk

1. Place the Cook & Crisp Basket in your Pressure Cooker Steam Fryer. 2. Cut a small rectangle in the top of each roll and scoop out centre, leaving 1 cm shell on the sides and bottom. 3. Place butter, mushrooms, and dried onion in the Cook & Crisp Basket. 4. Put on the Smart Lid on top of the Ninja Foodi Steam Fryer. Move the Lid Slider to the "Air Fry/Stovetop". Select the "Air Fry" mode for cooking. Cook at 200°C for around 1 minute. Stir and cook for 3 more minutes. 5. In a suitable bowl, beat the eggs, salt, dill, parsley, and milk. Pour mixture into basket with mushrooms. 6. Air Fry the eggs at 200°C for 2 minutes. Stir. Continue cooking for around 3 or 4 minutes, stirring every minute, until eggs are scrambled to your liking. 7. Remove basket from Pressure Cooker Steam Fryer and fill rolls with scrambled egg mixture. 8. Place filled rolls in Cook & Crisp Basket. Select the "Air Fry" mode for cooking. Air Fry at 200°C for 2 to 3 minutes or until rolls are browned.
Per Serving: Calories: 334; Fat: 12.9g; Sodium: 414mg; Carbs: 11g; Fibre: 5g; Sugar 9g; Protein 11g

Cheesy Ham Polenta Muffins

Prep time: 10 minutes | Cook Time: 8 minutes | Serves: 8

120g yellow polenta
30g flour
1½ teaspoons baking powder
¼ teaspoon salt
1 egg, beaten

2 tablespoons rapeseed oil
120ml milk
50g shredded sharp Cheddar cheese
70g diced ham

1. Place the Cook & Crisp Basket in your Pressure Cooker Steam Fryer. 2. In a suitable bowl, stir the polenta, flour, baking powder, and salt. 3. Add egg, oil, and milk to dry recipe ingredients and mix well. 4. Stir in shredded cheese and diced ham. 5. Divide batter among the muffin cups. 6. Place 4 filled muffin cups in Cook & Crisp Basket. Put on the Smart Lid on top of the Ninja Foodi Steam Fryer. Move the Lid Slider to the "Air Fry/Stovetop". Select the "Air Fry" mode for cooking. Air-fry 200°C for around 5 minutes. 7. Reduce temperature to 165°C and cook for around 1 to 2 minutes or until toothpick inserted in centre of muffin comes out clean. 8. Repeat to cook remaining muffins.
Per Serving: Calories: 284; Fat: 9g; Sodium: 441mg; Carbs: 7g; Fibre: 4.6g; Sugar 5g; Protein 19g

Cheesy Ham Muffins

Prep time: 10 minutes | Cook Time: 9 minutes | Serves: 4

4 eggs
Black pepper and salt
Olive oil

4 English muffins, split
100g shredded cheddar cheese
4 slices ham or bacon

1. Place the Cook & Crisp Basket in your Pressure Cooker Steam Fryer. 2. Beat eggs and add black pepper and salt to taste. Spray the Cook & Crisp Basket with oil and add eggs. Put on the Smart Lid on top of the Ninja Foodi Steam Fryer. 3. Move the Lid Slider to the "Air Fry/Stovetop". Select the "Air Fry" mode for cooking. Cook at 200°C for around 2 minutes, stir, and continue cooking for around 3 or 4 minutes, stirring every minute, until eggs are scrambled to your preference. Remove the Cook & Crisp Basket. 4. Place bottom halves of English muffins in Cook & Crisp Basket. Take half of the shredded cheese and divide it among the muffins. Top each with a slice of ham and one-quarter of the eggs. Sprinkle the remaining cheese on top of the eggs. Use a fork to press the cheese into the egg a little so it doesn't slip off before it melts. Transfer the basket to Pressure Cooker Steam Fryer. 5. Put on the Smart Lid on top of the Ninja Foodi Steam Fryer. 6. Move the Lid Slider to the "Air Fry/Stovetop". Select the "Air Fry" mode for cooking. 7. Air Fry at 180°C for around 1 minute. Add English muffin tops. Cook for around 2 to 4 minutes to heat through and toast the muffins.
Per Serving: Calories: 221; Fat: 7.9g; Sodium: 704mg; Carbs: 6g; Fibre: 3.6g; Sugar 6g; Protein 18g

Fried Banana PB&J Sandwich

Prep time: 10 minutes | Cook Time: 6–8 minutes | Serves: 4

20g cornflakes, crushed
25g shredded coconut
8 slices oat nut bread or any whole-grain, oversize bread
6 tablespoons peanut butter

2 medium bananas, cut into 1 cm-thick slices
6 tablespoons pineapple preserves
1 egg, beaten
Oil for misting or cooking spray

1. Place the Cook & Crisp Basket in your Pressure Cooker Steam Fryer. 2. In a shallow dish, mix the coconut and cornflake crumbs. 3. For each sandwich, brush one bread slice with 1½ tablespoons of peanut butter. Top with the banana slices. Brush another bread slice with 1½ tablespoons of preserves. 4. Use a pastry brush to brush top of sandwich with the beaten egg. Sprinkle with about 1½ tablespoons of crumb coating and press it in to make it stick. Coat with the oil. 5. Turn the sandwich over and repeat to coat and grease the other side. 6. Put on the Smart Lid on top of the Ninja Foodi Steam Fryer. 7. Move the Lid Slider to the "Air Fry/Stovetop". Select the "Air Fry" mode for cooking. 8. Cook at 180°C for around 6 to 7 minutes or until coating is golden brown and crispy. If the sandwich isn't brown enough, brush with a little more oil and cook for another minutes. 9. Cut cooked sandwiches in half and serve warm.
Per Serving: Calories: 372; Fat: 20g; Sodium: 891mg; Carbs: 29g; Fibre: 3g; Sugar 8g; Protein 7g

Cheesy Egg in a Hole

Prep time: 5 minutes | Cook Time: 6–7 minutes | Serves: 1

1 slice bread
1 teaspoon soft butter
1 egg

Black pepper and salt
1 tablespoon shredded Cheddar cheese
2 teaspoons diced ham

1. Place the Cook & Crisp Basket in your Pressure Cooker Steam Fryer. 2. Using a 6 cm biscuit cutter, cut a hole in centre of bread slice. 3. Brush the softened butter on both sides of bread. 4. Lay the bread slice in the Cook & Crisp Basket and crack egg into the hole. Top egg with black pepper and salt to taste. 5. Put on the Smart Lid on top of the Ninja Foodi Steam Fryer. 6. Move the Lid Slider to the "Air Fry/Stovetop". Select the "Air Fry" mode for cooking. 7. Cook at 165°C for 5 minutes. 8. Turn the toast over and top it with the shredded cheese and diced ham. 9. Cook for around 1 to 2 more minutes or until the yolk is done to your liking.
Per Serving: Calories: 372; Fat: 20g; Sodium: 891mg; Carbs: 29g; Fibre: 3g; Sugar 8g; Protein 7g

Nutty Carrot Muffins

Prep time: 15 minutes | Cook Time: 11 minutes | Serves: 8

60g 2 tablespoons whole-wheat flour
25g oat bran
2 tablespoons flaxseed meal
55g brown sugar
½ teaspoon baking soda
½ teaspoon baking powder
¼ teaspoon salt
½ teaspoon cinnamon
120ml buttermilk
2 tablespoons melted butter

1 egg
½ teaspoon pure vanilla extract
50g grated carrots
30g chopped pecans
30g chopped walnuts
1 tablespoon pumpkin seeds
1 tablespoon sunflower seeds
16 foil muffin cups, paper liners removed
Cooking spray

1. Place the Cook & Crisp Basket in your Pressure Cooker Steam Fryer. 2. In a suitable bowl, stir the flour, bran, flaxseed meal, sugar, baking soda, baking powder, salt, and cinnamon. 3. In a suitable bowl, beat the buttermilk, butter, egg, and vanilla. Pour into the prepared flour mixture and stir just until dry recipe ingredients moisten. Do not beat. 4. Gently stir in carrots, pecans, nuts, and seeds. 5. Double up the foil cups so you have 8 total and spray with cooking spray. 6. Place 4 foil cups in Cook & Crisp Basket and divide half the prepared batter among them. 7. Put on the Smart Lid on top of the Ninja Foodi Steam Fryer. 8. Move the Lid Slider to the "Air Fry/Stovetop". Select the "Air Fry" mode for cooking. 9. Air-fry at 165°C for around 9 to 11 minutes or until toothpick inserted in centre comes out clean. 10. Repeat to cook remaining 4 muffins.
Per Serving: Calories: 349; Fat: 2.9g; Sodium: 511mg; Carbs: 12g; Fibre: 3g; Sugar 8g; Protein 7g

Oat Muffins with Dry Fruit

Prep time: 10 minutes | Cook Time: 12 minutes | Serves: 8

60g oat bran
60g flour
55g brown sugar
1 teaspoon baking powder
½ teaspoon baking soda
⅛ teaspoon salt

120ml buttermilk
1 egg
2 tablespoons rapeseed oil
75g chopped dates, raisins, or dried cranberries
24 paper muffin cups
Cooking spray

1. Place the Cook & Crisp Basket in your Pressure Cooker Steam Fryer. 2. In a suitable bowl, mix the flour, oat bran, brown sugar, baking soda, baking powder, and salt. 3. In a suitable bowl, beat the buttermilk, egg, and oil. 4. Pour the prepared buttermilk mixture into bowl with dry recipe ingredients and stir just until moistened. Do not beat. 5. Gently stir in dried fruit. 6. Use baking cups to help muffins hold shape during baking. Grease them with cooking spray, place 4 sets of cups in Cook & Crisp Basket at a time, and fill each one ¾ full of batter. 7. Put on the Smart Lid on top of the Ninja Foodi Steam Fryer. 8. Move the Lid Slider to the "Air Fry/Stovetop". Select the "Air Fry" mode for cooking. 9. Cook at 165°C for around 12 minutes, until top springs back when touched and toothpick inserted in centre comes out clean. 10. Repeat for remaining muffins.
Per Serving: Calories: 334; Fat: 10.9g; Sodium: 454mg; Carbs: 10g; Fibre: 3.1g; Sugar 5.2g; Protein 10g

Honey Corn Muffins with Carrot and Pepper

Prep time: 10 minutes | Cook time: 15 minutes | Serves: 12

145 g yellow polenta
65 g flour
65 g whole wheat flour
1 tsp. baking powder
¾ tsp. salt
1 large egg

240 ml unsweetened almond milk
60 ml rapeseed oil
70 g honey
60 g finely shredded carrot
75 g finely chopped green pepper

1. Coat 12 muffin cups with cooking spray. 2. Combine the polenta, flours, baking powder and salt in a bowl. In a separate bowl, mix together the milk, egg, oil and honey. Add to polenta mixture; stir just until moistened. Fold in the vegetables. Fill prepared cups two-thirds full. 3. Place the muffin cups on the bottom layer of the Deluxe Reversible Rack in the lower position, then place the rack in the pot. 4. Close the lid and make sure the slider is in the AIR FRY/STOVETOP. Select BAKE/ROAST, set temperature to 205°C, and set time to 15 minutes. Select START/STOP to begin cooking. 5. Bake until a toothpick inserted in centre comes out clean. Let Cool for 5 minutes before removing from the rack. Serve warm.
Per Serving: Calories 172; Fat 6.05g; Sodium 193mg; Carbs 27.17g; Fibre 1.7g; Sugar 7.3g; Protein 3.28g

Homemade Chocolate Banana Bread

Prep time: 10 minutes | Cook Time: 40 minutes | Serves: 2

3 tablespoons unsalted butter, at room temperature, plus more for greasing
60 g applesauce
2 tablespoons packed brown sugar
1 egg, at room temperature
2 very ripe bananas, mashed
60 ml milk
½ teaspoon vanilla extract
125 g flour
1 teaspoon baking soda
¼ teaspoon Salt
45 g chocolate chips

1. Add 240 ml to the pot and place the Deluxe Reversible Rack in the lower position in the pot. 2. Coat a 16-cm loaf pan with butter, set aside. 3. Combine together 3 tablespoons of butter, the applesauce, and the brown sugar in a medium bowl. Add the egg and stir in the mashed bananas, milk, and vanilla. 4. Stir in the flour, salt and baking soda. Fold in the chocolate chips. Pour the batter into the prepared loaf pan and cover with foil, then place on the rack inside the pot. 5. Close the lid and move the slider to PRESSURE. Ensure the pressure release valve is in the SEAL position. The temperature will default to HIGH, which is the correct setting. Set time to 40 minutes. Select START/STOP to begin cooking. 6. When cooking is complete, naturally release the pressure for 10 minutes. Then quick release pressure by turning the pressure release valve to the VENT position. Move slider to AIR FRY/ STOVETOP to unlock the lid, then carefully open it. 7. Carefully remove the pan and place on a cooling rack. Remove the foil, being sure to avoid dripping any condensation onto the bread. 8. Make sure the bread centre is fully cooked with a toothpick and no more than a few moist crumbs should be on the toothpick. End with a quick release. Let cool at room temperature for at least 45 minutes. 9. When the banana bread has thoroughly cooled, cut into thick slices.
Per Serving: Calories 751; Fat 32.35g; Sodium 1100mg; Carbs 101.85g; Fibre 5.4g; Sugar 33.58g; Protein 15.33g

Classic Enchilada Casserole

Prep time: 35 minutes | Cook Time: 25 minutes | Serves: 4-6

240 ml water
1 tbsp. extra-virgin olive oil
20 small flour tortillas
170 g cooked breakfast sausage links, diced
1 red pepper, seeded and stemmed and thinly sliced
½ yellow onion, thinly sliced
85 g drained and rinsed canned black beans
175 ml canned red enchilada sauce
4 large eggs
1 tsp. heavy cream
¼ tsp. dried oregano
¼ tsp. crushed red pepper flakes
Salt
Freshly ground black pepper
175 g shredded Mexican-blend cheese

1. Coat a suitable baking pan with olive oil. Arrange 2 or 3 tortillas on the bottom of the pan, enough to cover the bottom. 2. Place ⅓ of the sausage, ⅓ of the sliced red pepper, ⅓ of the sliced onion and ⅓ of the black beans on top of the tortillas; top them with 2 to 3 tablespoons of the enchilada sauce. 3. Mix the eggs, cream, oregano, salt, red pepper flakes, and black pepper in a small bowl. Pour ⅓ of the egg mixture over the veggie- and bean-topped tortilla. Sprinkle a big pinch of cheese over the eggs and then top with 2 or 3 more tortillas. 4. Do the same with the next two layers, ending with tortillas. 5. When the layers of tortillas and fillings have just about reached the edge of the dish, pour the remaining enchilada sauce and the remaining cheese to the top of the tortillas. 6. Cover the pan with foil. 7. Pour the water into the pot and place in the rack, and the place the pan on the rack. 8. Close the lid, turn the pressure release valve to SEAL position, and then move the slider to PRESSURE. Select HI and set the cooking time to 25 minutes. Press START/STOP to begin cooking. When finished, release the pressure quickly. 9. Take out the pan, remove the foil and let the dish sir for at least for 10 minutes before slicing. 10. Serve and enjoy.
Per Serving: Calories 743; Fat: 28.46g; Sodium: 1532mg; Carbs: 91.8g; Fibre: 6.3g; Sugar: 8.23g; Protein: 28.72g

Egg White Bites with Ham

Prep time: 20 minutes | Cook Time: 25 minutes | Serves: 7 egg bites

15 g unsalted butter
½ yellow onion, sliced
Salt
Freshly ground black pepper
85 g thick-cut ham, diced
240 ml water
55 g shredded Swiss and Gruyère cheese blend
6 large egg whites
15 ml heavy cream
½ tsp. prepared ground horseradish
¼ tsp. dried thyme

1. Select SEAR/SAUTÉ. Select Lo3, and then press START/STOP to begin cooking. 2. Once the pot is hot, melt the butter. When the butter melts, place in the onion, and sauté for about 10 minutes or until caramelized, then season them with salt and pepper. Stir in the diced ham and sauté for 5 more minutes. 3. Transfer the ham and caramelized onion to a plate to cool. Clean out the inside of the pot and return it to the device. Pour the water into the pot and insert the rack. 4. Place some caramelized onion and ham along with cheese in the bottom of each well of a silicone egg bite mold. 5. In a small bowl, whisk together the egg whites, cream, horseradish, salt, pepper and thyme. Pour the egg mixture over the ham mixture, filling each mold about three-quarters of the way full. 6. Carefully place the silicone egg bite mold on the rack. Close the lid, turn the pressure release valve to SEAL position, and then move the slider to PRESSURE. Select HI and set the cooking time to 8 minutes. Press START/STOP to begin cooking. When finished, release the pressure naturally. 7. Cut around the edges and release the egg bites from the mold. Flip the egg bites out onto a plate. Season them with more salt and pepper, if needed.
Per Serving: Calories 83; Fat: 4.53g; Sodium: 211mg; Carbs: 3.13g; Fibre: 0.2g; Sugar: 1.57g; Protein: 7.45g

Healthy Eggs in a Boat

Prep time: 15 minutes | Cook Time: 5 minutes | Serves: 6

120 ml water
3 to 4 demi-baguettes
15 g mixed fresh baby spinach and rocket
6 grape tomatoes, halved

6 to 8 large eggs
Salt
Freshly ground black pepper
Crushed red pepper flakes

1. Pour the water into the pot and place the Deluxe Reversible Rack in the lower position in the pot. 2. Cut each demi-baguette to create a lid and well in the bread. Slice length-wise from end to end at a 45-degree angle about three-quarters of the way through the bread. Use your fingers to pull the "lid" off the baguette. Remove any stray pieces of bread from inside the well. Ensuring there is enough room for the eggs. 3. To each demi-baguette, add a few leaves of spinach and rocket along with a few tomato halves. Crack 2 eggs into each bread boat. Top with salt, black pepper and a tiny pinch of red pepper flakes. 4. Arrange up to three bread boats on top of the rack. 5. Close the lid and move the slider to PRESSURE. Ensure the pressure release valve is in the SEAL position. The temperature will default to HIGH, which is the correct setting. Set time to 4 minutes. Select START/STOP to begin cooking. 6. When cooking is complete, naturally release the pressure for 3 minutes. Then quick release pressure by turning the pressure release valve to the VENT position. Move slider to AIR FRY/ STOVETOP to unlock the lid, then carefully open it. 7. Remove the boats with tongs and transfer to a plate. Allow the boats to cool for a minute or two so the bread will harden up a bit again, before slicing and serving.
Per Serving: Calories 151; Fat 8.9g; Sodium 392mg; Carbs 9.47g; Fibre 1g; Sugar 3.9g; Protein 8.27g

Creamy Blueberries Clafouti

Prep time: 5 minutes | Cook Time: 15 minutes | Serves: 2

Butter, at room temperature, for greasing
3 tablespoons granulated sugar, plus more for sprinkling
80 g fresh blueberries
1 egg
1 tablespoon plain flour
1 teaspoon rum

60 g heavy cream
60 ml whole milk
¼ teaspoon grated lemon zest
¼ teaspoon vanilla extract
Pinch salt
Icing sugar, for garnish

1. Pour 240 ml of water into the pot and place the bottom layer of the Deluxe Reversible Rack in the lower position in the pot. 2. Butter two ramekins, then sprinkle a bit of granulated sugar in each of them and tip to coat. Divide the blueberries between the ramekins, set aside. 3. In a medium bowl, whisk together the egg and 3 tablespoons of granulated sugar until well combined. Stir in the flour, rum, cream, milk, vanilla, lemon zest, and salt for about 1 minute until smooth. Pour the batter over the berries, filling the ramekins about three-quarters full. 4. Put the ramekins on the rack and place a square of aluminum foil loosely on top. 5. Close the lid and move the slider to PRESSURE. Ensure the pressure release valve is in the SEAL position. The temperature will default to HIGH, which is the correct setting. Set time to 11 minutes. Select START/STOP to begin cooking. 6. When cooking is complete, quick release the pressure in the pot. 7. Move slider to AIR FRY/STOVETOP position. Select BROIL and set time to 4 minutes, Select START/STOP to begin cooking. 8. The top should be browned, then transfer to a cooling rack and allow to cool for 10 to 15 minutes. Garnish with icing sugar and serve.
Per Serving: Calories 290; Fat 13.7g; Sodium 228mg; Carbs 34.69g; Fibre 1.1g; Sugar 27.22g; Protein 6.52g

Fluffy Raspberry Breakfast Cake

Prep time: 10 minutes | Cook Time: 30 minutes | Serves: 2

120 g plain flour, plus more for dusting and coating
55 g unsalted butter, at room temperature, plus more for greasing
1 teaspoon baking powder
¼ teaspoon salt
65 g granulated sugar
1 egg, at room temperature

½ teaspoon vanilla extract
½ teaspoon almond extract
60 ml buttermilk
160 g fresh raspberries
Icing sugar, for garnish (optional)

1. Add 240 ml of water to the pot and place the bottom layer of the Deluxe Reversible Rack in the lower position in the pot. 2. Coat a 16 cm cake pan with butter and then with flour. Set aside. 3. Mix flour, the baking powder, and the salt in a bowl. Reserve 2 tablespoons of the flour mixture in another small bowl. 4. In a big bowl, mix the granulated sugar and 55 g of butter with an electric hand mixer until well combined, scraping down the sides of the bowl as necessary. 5. Add in the egg, vanilla, and almond extract, mix to combine well. 6. Put the flour mixture and the buttermilk in alternating batches to the batter, mixing well after each addition. 7. In a medium bowl, lightly toss the raspberries with some flour to coat. Gently fold the berries into the cake batter. Arrange the batter onto the prepared pan and put the pan on the rack in the pressure cooker. 8. Close the lid and move the slider to PRESSURE. Ensure the pressure release valve is in the SEAL position. The temperature will default to HIGH, which is the correct setting. Set time to 30 minutes. Select START/STOP to begin cooking. 9. When cooking is complete, quick release the pressure in the pot, then remove the lid and immediately transfer the cake to a cooling rack. 10. Let cool for 10 to 15 minutes, then dust with powdered sugar (if desired). Serve warm.
Per Serving: Calories 632; Fat 21.44g; Sodium 418mg; Carbs 97.4g; Fibre 6g; Sugar 43.92g; Protein 14.01g

Chapter 2 Vegetables and Sides

Freekeh Bowls with Chickpeas	23	Szechuan Beans with Sesame Seeds	28
Delicious Potato and Cauliflower Curry	23	Sesame Carrots Sticks	28
Healthy Collard Greens with Bacon	23	Lemony Brussels Sprout	28
Steamed Artichokes with Lemony Dijon Dipping Sauce	23	Super-Easy Cinnamon Applesauce	28
Best Potatoes Au Gratin	24	Easy Crispy Parmesan Artichokes	29
Simple Sour Cream Cabbage	24	Crispy Cheese Broccoli Pizza	29
Herbed Carrots and Parsnips	24	Artichoke and Spinach Stuffed Aubergine	29
Lemony Garlic Smashed Red Potatoes	24	Refreshing Lemony Broccoli Salad	29
Smooth Celery Root and Cauliflower Mash	25	Lemony Roasted Cauliflower	29
Tasty Herbed Veggie & Bread Casserole	25	Vegan Chickpeas Hummus	30
Red Wine Braised Mushroom with Carrot	25	Spicy Pinto Beans	30
Crispy Fried Parmesan Polenta	26	Mashed Potatoes and Cauliflower	30
Lemony Garlic Broccoli	26	Herbed Mashed Sweet Potatoes	30
Wholesome Cheese Corned Beef & Cabbage Slaw	26	Garlicky Potatoes and Kale	31
Garlic Cannellini Beans with Tomatoes	26	Quinoa Endive Boats	31
Classic Indian Spiced Kidney Bean Stew	27	Tasty Butternut Squash Mash	31
Minty Red Lentil and Bulgur Soup	27	Butter-Maple Glazed Carrots	31
Garlic Chickpea Curry	27	Sweet & Spicy Red Cabbage	32
Classic Lentils & Bulgur	28	Flavourful Aubergine, Courgette & Tomatoes	32
		Easy Cauliflower "Rice"	32

Freekeh Bowls with Chickpeas

Prep Time: 20 minutes | Cook Time: 10 minutes | Serves: 4

1 medium aubergine, cut into 5 cm cubes
Salt
300 ml store-bought vegetable or chicken stock, or homemade
95 g cracked freekeh
1 tablespoon za'atar
2 tablespoons extra-virgin olive oil
1 can chickpeas, drained and rinsed
150 g cherry tomatoes, halved
1 tablespoon red wine vinegar
1 medium garlic clove, finely chopped and smashed with the side of a knife
Freshly ground black pepper

1. Toss the aubergine with 1 teaspoon salt and set aside for 10 minutes to draw out the bitter juices. Pat the aubergine dry with paper towels. Rinse briefly and dry with paper towels again. 2. Combine the stock, freekeh, za'atar, ½ teaspoon salt, and 1 tablespoon of the oil in the pot; add the chickpeas and then layer the aubergine on top, but don't stir it into the stock mixture. 3. Close the lid, turn the pressure release valve to SEAL position, and then move the slider to PRESSURE. Select HI and set the cooking time to 5 minutes. Press START/STOP to begin cooking. When finished, release the pressure naturally. 4. Transfer the grain mixture to a large serving bowl. 5. In a small bowl, mix up the remaining 1 tablespoon oil with the tomatoes, vinegar, garlic, and several grinds of pepper. 6. Gently toss the dressing with the grain mixture and serve warm or at room temperature.
Per Serving: Calories 197; Fat: 5.09g; Sodium: 530mg; Carbs: 33.77g; Fibre: 9.1g; Sugar: 16.74g; Protein: 7.06g

Delicious Potato and Cauliflower Curry

Prep Time: 20 minutes | Cook Time: 10 minutes | Serves: 4

2 tablespoons safflower oil
1 tablespoon brown mustard seeds
1 medium yellow onion, chopped
1 tablespoon hot curry powder
225 g chopped ripe tomatoes
3 medium Yukon Gold potatoes, unpeeled, cut into 2.5 cm cubes
Salt and freshly ground black pepper
1 medium cauliflower, cut into large (8 cm) florets, stalk and core discarded

1. Select SEAR/SAUTÉ. Select Lo3, and then press START/STOP to begin cooking. 2. When the pot is hot, heat the oil, then add the mustard seeds and cook them for 1 minute until they have popped and turned gray; add onion and curry powder, and cook them for 4 minutes until the onion is tender; add tomatoes and cook for 2 minutes until they break down a bit. 3. Stop the process, and stir in the potatoes, 120 ml water, 1 teaspoon salt, and several grinds of pepper. Arrange the cauliflower florets over the potato mixture, but don't stir. 4. Close the lid, turn the pressure release valve to SEAL position, and then move the slider to PRESSURE. Select LO and set the cooking time to 2 minutes. Press START/STOP to begin cooking. When finished, release the pressure quickly. 5. Add the mixture into a large serving bowl, breaking up the cauliflower a bit with a spoon. Serve immediately.
Per Serving: Calories 344; Fat: 8.39g; Sodium: 66mg; Carbs: 61.73g; Fibre: 11.2g; Sugar: 7.75g; Protein: 9.85g

Healthy Collard Greens with Bacon

Prep Time: 15 minutes | Cook Time: 15 minutes | Serves: 4

3 slices thick-cut pepper bacon, chopped
1 small yellow onion, chopped
3 medium garlic cloves, chopped
180 ml store-bought chicken or vegetable stock, or homemade
2 large bunches collard greens or kale, tough centre stems discarded,
leaves torn
2 tablespoons cider vinegar or red wine vinegar
1 teaspoon smoked paprika
Salt and freshly ground black pepper

1. Select SEAR/SAUTÉ. Select Lo3, and then press START/STOP to begin cooking. 2. When the pot is hot, add bacon and onion, and cook them for 8 minutes until the bacon is browned; add garlic and sauté them for 45 seconds until fragrant. 3. Stop the process, add stock and scrape up the browned bits on the bottom of the pot, then add greens, vinegar, paprika, several grinds of pepper, and ½ teaspoon salt, and toss them to coat the greens with the liquid. 4. Close the lid, turn the pressure release valve to SEAL position, and then move the slider to PRESSURE. Select HI and set the cooking time to 5 minutes. Press START/STOP to begin cooking. When finished, release the pressure naturally. 5. Season the dish with salt and pepper. Serve the greens immediately.
Per Serving: Calories 88; Fat: 2.81g; Sodium: 220mg; Carbs: 13.89g; Fibre: 3.5g; Sugar: 4.28g; Protein: 4.36g

Steamed Artichokes with Lemony Dijon Dipping Sauce

Prep Time: 15 minutes | Cook Time: 15 minutes | Serves: 4

4 (250 g) whole artichokes, rinsed and drained
110 g unsalted butter, at room temperature
2 garlic cloves, chopped
2½ tablespoons fresh lemon juice
1 tablespoon Dijon mustard
Salt and freshly ground black pepper

1. Trim the artichoke stems to within 2.5 cm of the base. Place the rack in the pot and add 360 ml warm water. Place the artichokes stem-side down on the rack. 2. Close the lid, turn the pressure release valve to SEAL position, and then move the slider to PRESSURE. Select HI and set the cooking time to 10 minutes. Press START/STOP to begin cooking. When finished, release the pressure quickly. 3. To check the doneness, pull a leaf from near the centre of an artichoke and scrape the tender bottom of the leaf off with your teeth; the flesh should come away easily. If they're not done, lock on the lid and cook under HIGH pressure for a minute or so more. 4. Transfer the artichokes to serving plates with tongs, cover loosely, and set them aside. Take the rack out of the pot and discard the cooking water. Return the pot to the appliance. 5. Select SEAR/SAUTÉ. Select Hi5, and then press START/STOP to begin cooking. 6. When the pot is hot, add butter and garlic, and cook them for 1 minute until the garlic is sizzling and fragrant. 7. Stop the process and whisk in the lemon juice and mustard; season them with salt and pepper. 8. Pour the butter mixture into dipping bowls and serve with the artichokes.
Per Serving: Calories 223; Fat: 15.83g; Sodium: 206mg; Carbs: 18.42g; Fibre: 9g; Sugar: 1.89g; Protein: 6.5g

Best Potatoes Au Gratin

Prep Time: 25 minutes | Cook Time: 10 minutes | Serves: 4

2 tablespoons butter
2 medium garlic cloves, sliced
900 g Yukon Gold potatoes, peeled and cut into ½ cm-thick slices
Salt and freshly ground black pepper
160 ml store-bought vegetable or chicken stock, or homemade
150 g grated cheese of your choice (cheddar, Gruyère, or Swiss)
60 g heavy cream, warmed

1. Select SEAR/SAUTÉ. Select Lo3, and then press START/STOP to begin cooking. 2. When the pot is hot, melt the butter, add the garlic and cook them for 45 seconds until fragrant; add potatoes, several grinds of pepper, and 1 teaspoon salt, and stir them to coat the potatoes with the garlic butter. 3. Stop the process, and add the stock. 4. Close the lid, turn the pressure release valve to SEAL position, and then move the slider to PRESSURE. Select HI and set the cooking time to 2 minutes. Press START/STOP to begin cooking. When finished, release the pressure naturally. 5. Pour the potato mixture into a baking dish and gently fold in 100 g of the cheese and the cream with a rubber spatula. Sprinkle the remaining 50 g cheese on the top. 6. Place the rack in the pot in the higher broil position and then place the baking pan on it. Close the lid and move slider to AIR FRY/STOVETOP, then use the dial to select BROIL. Set the cooking time to 5 minutes and then press START/STOP to begin cooking. 7. When cooked, serve and enjoy.
Per Serving: Calories 457; Fat 25.57g; Sodium: 536mg; Carbs: 41.19g; Fibre: 5g; Sugar: 2.32g; Protein: 17.06g

Simple Sour Cream Cabbage

Prep Time: 15 minutes | Cook Time: 5 minutes | Serves: 6

240 ml water
1 medium-large green or savoy cabbage, sliced
55 g grass-fed butter
115 g sour cream
¾ tsp sea salt
114 g precooked crispy bacon or turkey bacon, crumbled, for garnish (optional)

1. Pour the water into the pot and put the bottom layer of the Deluxe Reversible Rack in the lower position in the pot. Layer the sliced cabbage on the rack. 2. Close the lid and move the slider to PRESSURE. Ensure the pressure release valve is in the SEAL position. The temperature will default to HIGH, which is the correct setting. Set time to 2 minutes. Select START/STOP to begin cooking. 3. Once the timer beeps, press START/STOP. Quick release pressure by turning the pressure release valve to the VENT position. Move slider to the right to unlock the lid, then carefully open it. 4. Carefully remove the cabbage and the rack, setting the cabbage aside. Pour out and discard the water that remains in the pot. 5. Place the butter in the pot and select SEAR/SAUTÉ and set to 3. Press START/STOP to begin cooking. Once the butter has melted, return the cabbage to the pot and sauté for 1 minute, stirring occasionally. Add the sour cream and salt and sauté for 2 minutes, stirring occasionally. Press START/STOP to turn off the SEAR/SAUTÉ function. 6. Serve immediately, garnished with the crumbled crispy bacon (if using).
Per Serving: Calories 196; Fat 15.51g; Sodium 623mg; Carbs 12.87g; Fibre 3.4g; Sugar 5.4g; Protein 4.77g

Herbed Carrots and Parsnips

Prep Time: 15 minutes | Cook Time: 8 minutes | Serves: 6

240 ml water
4 large carrots, peeled and thickly sliced on the diagonal
3 medium parsnips, peeled and sliced on the diagonal
45 g grass-fed butter or ghee
2 cloves garlic, minced
1 tsp sea salt
1 tsp dried thyme
1 tsp dried dill

1. Pour the water into the pot and put the bottom layer of the Deluxe Reversible Rack in the lower position in the pot. Layer the carrots and parsnips in the on the rack. 2. Close the lid and move the slider to PRESSURE. Ensure the pressure release valve is in the SEAL position. The temperature will default to HIGH, which is the correct setting. Set time to 3 minutes. Select START/STOP to begin cooking. 3. When cooking is complete, turn the pressure release valve to the vent position for a quick pressure release. Move slider to the right to unlock the lid, then carefully open it. 4. Carefully remove the carrots and parsnips and the rack, setting the carrots and parsnips aside. Pour out and discard the water that remains in the pot. 5. Place your healthy fat of choice in the pot and press SEAR/SAUTÉ and set to 3. Press START/STOP to begin cooking. Once the fat has melted, add the garlic and sauté for 1 minute, stirring occasionally. 6. Add the carrots and parsnips back to the pot along with the salt, thyme and dill. Give everything a stir, then sauté for 3 minutes, stirring occasionally. Press START/STOP. Serve immediately.
Per Serving: Calories 104; Fat 6.02g; Sodium 397mg; Carbs 12.72g; Fibre 3.4g; Sugar 3.3g; Protein 1g

Lemony Garlic Smashed Red Potatoes

Prep Time: 15 minutes | Cook Time: 11 minutes | Serves: 4

680 g baby red potatoes
240 ml water
2 tbsp (30 ml) avocado oil or extra-virgin olive oil
3 cloves garlic, minced
½ tsp sea salt, plus more to taste
½ tsp freshly ground black pepper
2 tbsp (30 ml) fresh lemon juice

1. Wash and dry the potatoes. Pour the water into the pot and put the bottom layer of the Deluxe Reversible Rack in the lower position in the pot. Place the potatoes on the rack. 2. Close the lid and move the slider to PRESSURE. Ensure the pressure release valve is in the SEAL position. The temperature will default to HIGH, which is the correct setting. Set time to 6 minutes. Select START/STOP to begin cooking. 3. When cooking is complete, turn the pressure release valve to the vent position for a quick pressure release. Move slider to the right to unlock the lid, then carefully open it. 4. Remove the potatoes and place on a large baking sheet. Using a glass or the back of a spoon, gently press down on the potatoes, or smash them. 5. Combine the oil and garlic in a small bowl. Brush over each of the potatoes, then sprinkle with salt and pepper. 6. Place the potatoes on the rack in the pot. Move slider to AIR FRY/STOVETOP. Select BROIL. Broil for 4 to 5 minutes, or until crispy. 7. Remove and drizzle with the lemon juice. Sprinkle with additional salt to taste. Serve hot.
Per Serving: Calories 185; Fat 7.08g; Sodium 323mg; Carbs 28.56g; Fibre 3.1g; Sugar 2.41g; Protein 3.42g

Smooth Celery Root and Cauliflower Mash
Prep Time: 15 minutes | Cook Time: 13 minutes | Serves: 8

6 tbsp (85 g) grass-fed butter or ghee, divided
1 yellow onion, sliced
¾ tsp sea salt, divided
240 ml water
4 small celery roots, peeled and cut into large cubes
1 small head cauliflower, cut into florets
2 small parsnips, peeled and cut into large cubes
2 tbsp (30 ml) chicken or vegetable stock, or bone stock
Leaves from 2 sprigs thyme
½ tsp garlic granules or powder

1. Place 2 tablespoons (28 g) of your healthy fat of choice in the pot. Move slider to AIR FRY/STOVETOP. Select SEAR/SAUTÉ and set to 3. Select START/STOP to begin cooking. 2. Once the fat has melted, add the onion and ¼ teaspoon of the salt and sauté for about 7 minutes, stirring occasionally, or until the onion is light golden brown and caramelized. Press START/STOP, transfer the caramelized onion to a bowl or plate, set aside. 3. Pour the water into the pot and put the bottom layer of the Deluxe Reversible Rack in the lower position in the pot. Layer the celery roots, cauliflower and parsnips on the rack. 4. Close the lid and move the slider to PRESSURE. Ensure the pressure release valve is in the SEAL position. The temperature will default to HIGH, which is the correct setting. Set time to 5 minutes. Select START/STOP to begin cooking. 5. When cooking is complete, naturally release the pressure for 10 minutes. Then quick release pressure by turning the pressure release valve to the VENT position. Move slider to AIR FRY/ STOVETOP to unlock the lid, then carefully open it. 6. Carefully remove the vegetables with a large slotted spoon and place them in a blender or food processor. Add the remaining 4 tablespoons (57 g) of your healthy fat of choice plus the stock, thyme, remaining ½ teaspoon of salt and the garlic granules. Pulse or blend for 30 seconds to 1 minute, or until completely smooth. 7. Serve the mash immediately, topped with the reserved caramelised onions.
Per Serving: Calories 108; Fat 9.43g; Sodium 244mg; Carbs 5.6g; Fibre 1.7g; Sugar 1.85g; Protein 1.16g

Tasty Herbed Veggie & Bread Casserole
Prep Time: 15 minutes | Cook Time: 35 minutes | Serves: 8

1 (455-g) loaf gluten-free sourdough bread, cubed
6 tbsp (85 g) grass-fed butter, ghee or avocado oil, plus more for casserole dish
1 small yellow onion, diced
2 celery ribs, diced
1 small fennel bulb, diced
50 g cauliflower rice
2 cloves garlic, finely chopped
1 small sweet apple, cored, peeled and diced (I like Fuji, Gala or Honey crisp apples)
30 g dried cranberries or raisins (optional)
1 tbsp (3 g) chopped fresh sage
1 tbsp (2 g) chopped fresh thyme
1 tbsp (4 g) chopped fresh flat-leaf parsley
1¼ tsp (8 g) sea salt
240 ml chicken or vegetable stock, or bone stock
240 ml water

1. Toast the bread cubes: You can do this on a dry baking sheet in a 180°C oven for 25 minutes. Transfer the toasted bread cubes to a large bowl and set aside. 2. Use your healthy fat of choice to grease a 1.5-L casserole dish that fits inside the pot. Set it aside. 3. Place your healthy fat of choice in the pot. Move slider to AIR FRY/STOVETOP. Select SEAR/SAUTÉ and set to 3. Select START/STOP to begin cooking. Once the fat has melted, add the onion and sauté, stirring occasionally, for 7 minutes, or until light golden brown. Add the celery and fennel and sauté, stirring occasionally, for 3 minutes. Add the cauliflower and garlic and sauté, stirring often, for 2 minutes. Add the apple, dried fruit (if using), parsley, sage, thyme, and salt, stirring to combine. Press START/STOP. 4. Carefully transfer the vegetable mixture and stock into the bowl that contains the toasted bread cubes and gently stir to combine for about 30 seconds, allowing some of the stock to absorb into the bread. 5. Pour the stuffing mixture into the prepared casserole dish, patting down as needed. Cover the casserole dish with its glass lid. 6. Pour the water into the pot and place the Deluxe Reversible Rack in the lower position in the pot. 7. Carefully set the covered casserole dish on top of the rack. 8. Close the lid and move the slider to PRESSURE. Ensure the pressure release valve is in the SEAL position. The temperature will default to HIGH, which is the correct setting. Set time to 23 minutes. Select START/STOP to begin cooking. 9. When cooking is complete, turn the pressure release valve to the vent position for a quick pressure release. Move slider to the right to unlock the lid, then carefully open it. 10. Using an oven mitt, carefully remove the casserole dish and place on a wire rack. Carefully remove the hot lid without dripping any condensation onto the stuffing. 11. Allow the stuffing to cool on a wire rack at room temperature for 20 minutes before serving.
Per Serving: Calories 153; Fat 10.75g; Sodium 571mg; Carbs 13.86g; Fibre 3.6g; Sugar 5.4g; Protein 3.68g

Red Wine Braised Mushroom with Carrot
Prep Time: 15 minutes | Cook Time: 35 minutes | Serves: 6

2 tbsp (30 ml) extra-virgin olive oil
2 tbsp (28 g) unsalted butter
455 g whole white mushrooms, cut in half
1 yellow onion, diced
2 carrots, peeled and sliced
1 celery rib, diced
Salt
Freshly ground black pepper
½ tsp dried thyme
1 clove garlic, grated
1 tbsp (15 ml) balsamic vinegar
240 ml dry red wine
240 ml water
175 ml beef or vegetable stock, divided
30 g dried shiitake mushrooms
1 tbsp (8 g) cornflour
2 tbsp (32 g) tomato paste

1. Move slider to AIR FRY/STOVETOP. Select SEAR/SAUTÉ and set to 3. Select START/STOP to begin preheating. Allow unit to preheat for 5 minutes. After 5 minutes, add the oil and butter. When the butter melts, add the white mushrooms and cook for 15 minutes, or until the mushrooms are golden. 2. Add the onion, carrots, celery, thyme, salt and pepper, and garlic. Sauté for 3 minutes. Press START/STOP, then mix in the red wine, vinegar, water, 115 ml of the stock and the dried mushrooms. 3. Close the lid and move the slider to PRESSURE. Ensure the pressure release valve is in the SEAL position. The temperature will default to HIGH, which is the correct setting. Set time to 9 minutes. Select START/STOP to begin cooking. 4. When cooking is complete, turn the pressure release valve to the vent position for a quick pressure release. Move slider to the right to unlock the lid, then carefully open it. 5. In a bowl, whisk together the cornflour and remaining 60 ml of stock. 6. Stir the cornflour slurry into the pot along with the tomato paste. Adjust the salt and pepper to taste.
Per Serving: Calories 116; Fat 5.67g; Sodium 395mg; Carbs 11.24g; Fibre 2.9g; Sugar 4.48g; Protein 4.83g

Crispy Fried Parmesan Polenta

Prep Time: 10 minutes | Cook Time: 25 minutes | Serves: 4

2 tablespoons olive oil
2 medium garlic cloves, thinly sliced
960 ml store-bought chicken or vegetable stock, warmed
1 bay leaf
Salt and freshly ground black pepper
125 g polenta (not quick-cooking)
50 g grated Parmesan cheese

1. Add the oil to the pot. Select SEAR/SAUTÉ. Select Lo3, and then press START/STOP to begin cooking. 2. When the oil is hot, add the garlic and cook for 30 seconds. Pour in the stock, bay leaf, and ½ teaspoon salt, and when the liquid comes to simmer, gradually whisk in the polenta. 3. Stop the process. 4. Close the lid, turn the pressure release valve to SEAL position, and then move the slider to PRESSURE. Select LO and set the cooking time to 9 minutes. Press START/STOP to begin cooking. When finished, release the pressure naturally. 5. Unlock the lid. It will look watery at first, but will come together and thicken as it stands. Whisk in the cheese and season with salt and pepper. Discard the bay leaf before serving. 6. For solid polenta to pan-fry, transfer the polenta to a storage container without lid and refrigerate them for at least 2 hours until solid. 7. Cut into squares and pan-fry in a nonstick sauté pan over medium heat with a few tablespoons of olive oil for 5 minutes on each side or until golden brown. 8. Serve warm.
Per Serving: Calories 296; Fat: 17.32g; Sodium: 814mg; Carbs: 25.78g; Fibre: 3.8g; Sugar: 7.01g; Protein: 10.62g

Lemony Garlic Broccoli

Prep Time: 15 minutes | Cook Time: 5 minutes | Serves: 4

4 medium garlic cloves, unpeeled, left whole
455 g broccoli, cut into 2.5 – 3 cm florets, stems thinly sliced
2 tablespoons fresh lemon juice
1 teaspoon Dijon mustard
60 ml olive oil
Salt and freshly ground black pepper

1. Place 240 ml warm water and the garlic in the pot. Set the Cook & Crisp Basket in the pot and place the broccoli in the basket. 2. Close the lid, turn the pressure release valve to SEAL position, and then move the slider to PRESSURE. Select HI and set the cooking time to 1 minute. Press START/STOP to begin cooking. When finished, release the pressure quickly. 3. Transfer the broccoli to a large serving bowl. Remove the basket from the pot. 4. Transfer the garlic to a cutting board, discard the peels, and chop the cloves. In a medium bowl, combine the lemon juice, garlic, and mustard. Gradually whisk in the oil. 5. Toss the broccoli with the dressing and season with salt and pepper.
Per Serving: Calories 151; Fat: 14.13g; Sodium: 52mg; Carbs: 4.84g; Fibre: 3.2g; Sugar: 0.66g; Protein: 3.86g

Wholesome Cheese Corned Beef & Cabbage Slaw

Prep Time: 15 minutes | Cook Time: 85 minutes | Serves: 6

237 ml beef stock
1.4 kg corned beef
295 g mayonnaise
10 ml cider vinegar
¼ tsp celery seeds
1 small head green cabbage, sliced thinly, core removed
110 g diced Swiss cheese

1. Combine the beef stock and the corned beef along with the contents of its seasoning packet in the pot. 2. Close the lid and move the slider to PRESSURE. Ensure the pressure release valve is in the SEAL position. The temperature will default to HIGH, which is the correct setting. Set time to 85 minutes. Select START/STOP to begin cooking. 3. When cooking is complete, turn the pressure release valve to the vent position for a quick pressure release. Move slider to the right to unlock the lid, then carefully open it. Arrange the corned beef onto a cutting board to cool. 4. In the meantime, mix together the mayonnaise, vinegar and celery seeds in a small bowl. Chop the corned beef into bite-size pieces. In a big bowl, combine the beef, mayonnaise mixture, cabbage and cheese and stir well. 5. Refrigerate for at least 1 hour before serving.
Per Serving: Calories 553; Fat 35.06g; Sodium 683mg; Carbs 3.37g; Fibre 0.6g; Sugar 1g; Protein 56.27g

Garlic Cannellini Beans with Tomatoes

Prep Time: 20 minutes | Cook Time: 30 minutes | Serves: 4-6

455 g dried cannellini beans (see note), rinsed and drained
Salt and ground black pepper
½ teaspoon baking soda
3 tablespoons extra-virgin olive oil, plus more to serve
1 medium yellow onion, chopped
4 medium garlic cloves, thinly sliced
1 tablespoon fennel seeds
½ teaspoon red pepper flakes
360g can diced tomatoes
1 piece Parmesan cheese rind (optional), plus shaved Parmesan to serve
20 g lightly packed fresh basil, torn

1. Stir the beans, 2 teaspoons salt, the baking soda and 1.4 L water in the pot, then distribute in an even layer. 2. Close the lid, turn the pressure release valve to SEAL position, and then move the slider to PRESSURE. Select HI and set the cooking time to 5 minutes. Press START/STOP to begin cooking. When finished, release the pressure quickly. 3. Carefully remove the pot from the unit and drain the beans in a colander; return the pot to the unit. Rinse the beans under cool water, set aside. 4. Add the oil to the pot. Select SEAR/SAUTÉ. Select Lo3, and then press START/STOP to begin cooking. 5. When the oil is shimmering, add garlic, onion, pepper flakes, fennel seeds, and 1 teaspoon salt, and cook them for 3 minutes until the onion begins to soften; add the tomatoes with the juices and cook them for 6 to 7 minutes until the liquid has almost evaporated; add the beans and Parmesan rind (optional), then stir in 720 ml water; distribute in an even layer. 6. Close the lid, turn the pressure release valve to SEAL position, and then move the slider to PRESSURE. Select HI and set the cooking time to 16 minutes. Press START/STOP to begin cooking. When finished, release the pressure naturally. 7. Let the dish stand for about 15 minutes, then remove and discard the Parmesan rind (if used). Taste and season the dish with salt and pepper, then stir in half of the basil. 8. Serve topped with the remaining basil, shaved Parmesan, black pepper and additional oil.
Per Serving: Calories 49; Fat: 0.74g; Sodium: 424mg; Carbs: 10.24g; Fibre: 3.8g; Sugar: 4.07g; Protein: 2.3g

Classic Indian Spiced Kidney Bean Stew

Prep Time: 25 minutes | Cook Time: 30 minutes | Serves: 4-6

455 g dried red kidney beans, rinsed and drained
Salt and ground black pepper
½ teaspoon baking soda
3 tablespoons extra-virgin olive oil
1 large yellow onion, halved and thinly sliced
6 medium garlic cloves, finely chopped
3 tablespoons finely grated fresh ginger
2 tablespoons garam masala
1 tablespoon ground cumin
2 teaspoons curry powder
700 g can whole peeled tomatoes, drained, 240 ml juices reserved, tomatoes crushed by hand
20 g finely chopped fresh coriander

1. Stir the beans, 2 teaspoons salt, the baking soda and 1.4 L water in the pot. 2. Close the lid, turn the pressure release valve to SEAL position, and then move the slider to PRESSURE. Select HI and set the cooking time to 5 minutes. Press START/STOP to begin cooking. When finished, release the pressure naturally. 3. Carefully remove the pot from the unit and drain the beans in a colander; return the pot to the unit. Rinse the beans under cool water; set aside. 4. Add the oil to the pot. Select SEAR/SAUTÉ. Select Lo3, and then press START/STOP to begin cooking. 5. When the oil is hot, add the garlic, ginger, garam masala, cumin and curry powder, and cook them for 30 seconds until fragrant. Stir in the tomatoes and reserved juices, scraping up any browned bits. Stir in 720 ml water, beans, and 1½ teaspoons salt, then distribute in an even layer. 6. Close the lid, turn the pressure release valve to SEAL position, and then move the slider to PRESSURE. Select HI and set the cooking time to 15 minutes. Press START/STOP to begin cooking. When finished, release the pressure naturally. 7. Stir the beans, and cook the food at Hi5 on SEAR/SAUTÉ mode for 5 to 8 minutes. 8. Let the dish stand for 10 minutes, then stir in the coriander. Taste and season the dish with salt and pepper.
Per Serving: Calories 161; Fat: 4.12g; Sodium: 447mg; Carbs: 25.84g; Fibre: 9.3g; Sugar: 6.92g; Protein: 7.61g

Minty Red Lentil and Bulgur Soup

Prep Time: 15 minutes | Cook Time: 20 minutes | Serves: 4

180 g plain whole-milk yogurt
2 teaspoons grated lemon zest, plus lemon wedges to serve
30 g lightly packed fresh mint leaves, finely chopped, divided
Salt and ground black pepper
6 tablespoons salted butter, cut into 1 tablespoon-pieces, divided
285 g red lentils, rinsed and drained
50 g coarse bulgur
1 large yellow onion, finely chopped
2 medium garlic cloves, finely chopped
3 tablespoons tomato paste
2 tablespoons harissa, plus more to serve
2 tablespoons sweet paprika

1. In a small bowl, stir together the lemon zest, yogurt, half the mint, and ¼ teaspoon each salt and pepper. Cover the bowl and refrigerate the mixture until ready to serve. 2. Select SEAR/SAUTÉ. Select Lo3, and then press START/STOP to begin cooking. 3. Add 3 tablespoons of butter and cook for 1 to 2 minutes until it begins to smell nutty and the milk solids at the bottom begin to brown. 4. Stop the process, and carefully remove the pot from the unit and pour the browned butter into a small microwave-safe bowl, scraping out the butter with a silicone spatula. 5. Return the pot to the unit, then add the remaining 2 tablespoons butter, bulgur, onion, garlic, tomato paste, lentils, harissa, paprika and 2 teaspoons salt. Stir them, then pour in 1.7 L water and distribute the mixture in an even layer. 6. Close the lid, turn the pressure release valve to SEAL position, and then move the slider to PRESSURE. Select HI and set the cooking time to 15 minutes. Press START/STOP to begin cooking. When finished, release the pressure naturally. 7. Stir the soup, scraping the bottom of the pot, then stir in the remaining mint. Taste and season the dish with salt. If the browned butter has solidified, microwave on high for 10 to 15 seconds until melted. 8. Ladle the soup into bowls, drizzle with browned butter and dollop with the yogurt mixture, then sprinkle with additional pepper. Offer lemon wedges and additional harissa on the side.
Per Serving: Calories 471; Fat: 17.86g; Sodium: 202mg; Carbs: 61.13g; Fibre: 10.8g; Sugar: 7.97g; Protein: 21.31g

Garlic Chickpea Curry

Prep Time: 35 minutes | Cook Time: 40 minutes | Serves: 4-6

455 g dried chickpeas, rinsed and drained
Salt and ground black pepper
½ teaspoon baking soda
10 cm piece fresh ginger, peeled and cut into 4 pieces
1 serrano chili, stemmed, halved and seeded
6 medium garlic cloves, smashed and peeled
1 tablespoon ground coriander
1 tablespoon ground cumin
1 bunch coriander, stems and leaves roughly chopped
4 spring onions, roughly chopped
3 tablespoons coconut oil
3 tablespoons lime juice, plus lime wedges to serve
Whole-milk yogurt, to serve

1. Mix together the chickpeas, 2 teaspoons salt, the baking soda and 1.4 L water in the pot, then distribute in an even layer. 2. Close the lid, turn the pressure release valve to SEAL position, and then move the slider to PRESSURE. Select HI and set the cooking time to 5 minutes. Press START/STOP to begin cooking. When finished, release the pressure naturally. 3. Drain the chickpeas in a colander; return the pot to the unit. Rinse the chickpeas under cool water; set aside. 4. In a food processor, combine the chili, garlic, coriander, ginger, and cumin. Process them for 1 minute until finely chopped, scraping the bowl as needed. Transfer the mixture to a small bowl. 5. Add the coriander, spring onions and 120 ml water to the now-empty food processor, and then process them for 30 seconds until smooth. Transfer the mixture to another small bowl, press plastic wrap directly against the surface and refrigerate until ready to use. 6. Select SEAR/SAUTÉ. Select Lo3, and then press START/STOP to begin cooking. 7. Add the coconut oil and let melt, then add the chili mixture and cook for 1 minute until fragrant. Add the chickpeas, 1½ teaspoons salt and 960 ml water; stir them to combine, and then distribute them in an even layer. 8. Close the lid, turn the pressure release valve to SEAL position, and then move the slider to PRESSURE. Select HI and set the cooking time to 20 minutes. Press START/STOP to begin cooking. When finished, release the pressure naturally. 9. Stir the chickpeas and cook them at Hi5 for 8 to 10 minutes until the liquid is slightly thickened. 10. Carefully remove the pot from the unit and let the dish stand for about 10 minutes. Stir in the coriander puree and the lime juice. Taste and season the dish with salt and pepper. Serve with lime wedges and yogurt.
Per Serving: Calories 335; Fat: 11.27g; Sodium: 140mg; Carbs: 47.3g; Fibre: 9g; Sugar: 8.35g; Protein: 14.63g

Classic Lentils & Bulgur

Prep Time: 30 minutes | Cook Time: 35 minutes | Serves: 4-6

60 ml extra-virgin olive oil
2 medium yellow onions, halved and thinly sliced
3 bay leaves
2½ teaspoons ground cumin
½ teaspoon ground allspice
Salt and ground black pepper

180 g coarse bulgur
210 g brown lentils, rinsed and drained
4 spring onions, thinly sliced
10 g chopped fresh flat-leaf parsley
Plain yogurt, to serve

1. Add oil to the pot. Select SEAR/SAUTÉ. Select Lo3, and then press START/STOP to begin cooking. 2. When the oil is shimmering, add the onions and cook them for 20 minutes until deeply browned. 3. Transfer about half the onions to a paper towel–lined plate; set aside. Add the bay, cumin, allspice and 2 teaspoons salt to the pot, and then cook them for 30 seconds until fragrant. Pour in 720 ml water, scraping up any browned bits. 4. Stop the process, and stir in the bulgur and lentils, then distribute in an even layer. 5. Close the lid, turn the pressure release valve to SEAL position, and then move the slider to PRESSURE. Select HI and set the cooking time to 10 minutes. Press START/STOP to begin cooking. When finished, release the pressure quickly. 6. Drape a kitchen towel across the pot and re-cover without locking the lid in place. Let stand for 10 minutes. 7. Open the pot, and then fluff the mixture with a fork, removing and discarding the bay. Taste and season the dish with salt and pepper. Transfer to a serving dish and sprinkle with the reserved onions, the spring onions and parsley. 8. Serve the food with yogurt.
Per Serving: Calories 87; Fat: 4.3g; Sodium: 89mg; Carbs: 10.99g; Fibre: 2.3g; Sugar: 0.84g; Protein: 2.89g

Szechuan Beans with Sesame Seeds

Prep Time: 10 minutes | Cook Time: 9 minutes | Serves: 4

455g fresh green beans, trimmed
1 tablespoon sesame oil
½ teaspoon garlic powder

1 tablespoon soy sauce
Sea salt and Szechuan pepper, to taste
2 tablespoons sesame seeds, toasted

1. Place the Cook & Crisp Basket in your Pressure Cooker Steam Fryer. 2. Mix the green beans with the sesame oil and garlic powder; then, arrange them in the Ninja Foodi Pressure Steam Fryer basket. 3. Put on the Smart Lid on top of the Ninja Foodi Steam Fryer. 4. Move the Lid Slider to the "Air Fry/Stovetop". Select the "Air Fry" mode for cooking. 5. Cook the green beans at 195°C for around 7 minutes; make sure to check the green beans halfway through the cooking time. 6. Toss the green beans with the remaining recipe ingredients and stir to mix well. Enjoy!
Per Serving: Calories: 334; Fat: 7.9g; Sodium: 704mg; Carbs: 6g; Fibre: 3.6g; Sugar 6g; Protein 18g

Sesame Carrots Sticks

Prep Time: 10 minutes | Cook Time: 20 minutes | Serves: 3

340g carrots, trimmed and cut into sticks
2 tablespoons butter, melted

Salt and white pepper, to taste
1 tablespoon sesame seeds, toasted

1. Place the Cook & Crisp Basket in your Pressure Cooker Steam Fryer. 2. Toss the carrots with the butter, salt, and white pepper; then, arrange them in the Ninja Foodi Pressure Steam Fryer basket. 3. Put on the Smart Lid on top of the Ninja Foodi Steam Fryer. 4. Move the Lid Slider to the "Air Fry/Stovetop". Select the "Air Fry" mode for cooking. 5. Cook the carrots at 195°C for around 15 minutes; make sure to check the carrots halfway through the cooking time. 6. Top the carrots with the sesame seeds. Serve.
Per Serving: Calories: 382; Fat: 7.9g; Sodium: 704mg; Carbs: 6g; Fibre: 3.6g; Sugar 6g; Protein 18g

Lemony Brussels Sprout

Prep Time: 10 minutes | Cook Time: 12 minutes | Serves: 3

340g Brussels sprouts, trimmed
2 tablespoons olive oil
Sea salt and black pepper, to taste

½ teaspoon dried dill weed
1 tablespoon fresh lemon juice
1 tablespoon rice vinegar

1. Place the Cook & Crisp Basket in your Pressure Cooker Steam Fryer. 2. Mix the Brussels sprouts with the oil and spices until they are well coated on all sides; then, arrange the Brussels sprouts in the Ninja Foodi Pressure Steam Fryer basket. 3. Put on the Smart Lid on top of the Ninja Foodi Steam Fryer. 4. Move the Lid Slider to the "Air Fry/Stovetop". Select the "Air Fry" mode for cooking. 5. Cook the Brussels sprouts at 195°C for around 10 minutes, shaking the basket halfway through the cooking time. 6. Mix the Brussels sprouts with lemon juice and vinegar. Enjoy!
Per Serving: Calories: 184; Fat: 5g; Sodium: 441mg; Carbs: 17g; Fibre: 4.6g; Sugar 5g; Protein 9g

Super-Easy Cinnamon Applesauce

Prep Time: 10 minutes | Cook time: 10 minutes | Serves: 6

1.2kg apples (such as Fuji or McIntosh), peeled and sliced
½ teaspoon ground cinnamon

120ml water

1. Add the apples, cinnamon, and water to the cooking pot. 2. Install the pressure lid and turn the pressure release valve to the SEAL position. 3. Select PRESSURE COOK, set the cooking temperature to HI and adjust the cooking time to 10 minutes. 4. When cooked, let the unit naturally release pressure. 5. Use a potato masher or blender to puree the apples to the consistency of your choice. 6. Serve the applesauce warm, or transfer it to an airtight container and chill in the fridge until ready to serve. 7. Store the applesauce in the fridge for 1 week or in the freezer for 3 months.
Per Serving: Calories 118; Fat 0.39g; Sodium 3mg; Carbs 31.5g; Fibre 5.6g; Sugar 23.57g; Protein 0.6g

Easy Crispy Parmesan Artichokes

Prep Time: 10 minutes | Cook Time: 10 minutes | Serves: 4

2 medium artichokes, with the centres removed
2 tablespoon coconut oil, melted
1 egg, beaten

50g parmesan cheese, grated
30g blanched, finely flour

1. Place the Cook & Crisp Basket in your Pressure Cooker Steam Fryer. 2. Place the artichokes in a suitable bowl with the coconut oil and stir well, then dip the artichokes into a suitable bowl of beaten egg. 3. In another bowl, mix up the parmesan cheese and the flour. 4. Mix with artichoke, making sure to coat each piece well. Transfer the artichoke to the basket. 5. Put on the Smart Lid on top of the Ninja Foodi Steam Fryer. 6. Move the Lid Slider to the "Air Fry/Stovetop". Select the "Air Fry" mode for cooking. 7. Air Fry artichoke at 200°C. Cook for 10 minutes, shaking occasionally throughout the cooking time. Serve hot.
Per Serving: Calories: 372; Fat: 20g; Sodium: 891mg; Carbs: 29g; Fibre: 3g; Sugar 8g; Protein 7g

Crispy Cheese Broccoli Pizza

Prep Time: 10 minutes | Cook Time: 30 minutes | Serves: 1

265g broccoli rice, steamed
50g parmesan cheese, grated
1 egg

3 tablespoon low-carb Alfredo sauce
55g mozzarella cheese, grated

1. Place the Cook & Crisp Basket in your Pressure Cooker Steam Fryer. 2. Drain the broccoli rice and mix with the parmesan cheese and egg in a suitable bowl, mixing well. 3. Cut a piece of parchment paper the size of the base of the basket. Using a spoon, place four equal-sized amounts of the broccoli mixture on the paper. And press each part into the shape of a pizza crust. You may have to complete this part in two batches. Transfer the parchment to the Cook & Crisp Basket. 4. Put on the Smart Lid on top of the Ninja Foodi Steam Fryer. 5. Move the Lid Slider to the "Air Fry/Stovetop". Select the "Air Fry" mode for cooking. 6. Air Fry broccoli at 185°C. Cook for 5 minutes. When the crust is firm, flip over. Cook for an additional 2 minutes. 7. Pour the sauce and mozzarella cheese on top of the crusts. Cook for an additional 7 minutes until the sauce and cheese melt. 8. Serve hot.
Per Serving: Calories: 295; Fat: 12.9g; Sodium: 414mg; Carbs: 11g; Fibre: 5g; Sugar 9g; Protein 11g

Artichoke and Spinach Stuffed Aubergine

Prep Time: 10 minutes | Cook Time: 35 minutes | Serves: 2

1 large aubergine
¼ medium yellow onion, diced
2 tablespoons red pepper, diced

30g spinach
45g artichoke hearts, chopped
Cooking spray

1. Place the Cook & Crisp Basket in your Pressure Cooker Steam Fryer. 2. Slice the aubergine lengthwise and scoop out the flesh with a spoon, leaving a shell about 1 cm thick. Chop it up and set aside. 3. Set a suitable frying pan over a suitable heat and spritz with cooking spray. Cook the onions for about 3 to 5 minutes to soften. Then add the pepper, spinach, artichokes, and the flesh of aubergine. Fry for a further 5 minutes, then remove from the heat. 4. Scoop this mixture in equal parts into the aubergine shells and place each one in the basket. 5. Put on the Smart Lid on top of the Ninja Foodi Steam Fryer. 6. Move the Lid Slider to the "Air Fry/Stovetop". Select the "Air Fry" mode for cooking. 7. Cook for 20 minutes at 160°C until the aubergine shells are soft. Serve warm.
Per Serving: Calories: 122; Fat: 7.9g; Sodium: 704mg; Carbs: 6g; Fibre: 3.6g; Sugar 6g; Protein 18g

Refreshing Lemony Broccoli Salad

Prep Time: 10 minutes | Cook Time: 15 minutes | Serves: 2

265g fresh broccoli florets
2 tablespoon coconut oil, melted

40g sliced spring onion
½ medium lemon, juiced

1. Place the Cook & Crisp Basket in your Pressure Cooker Steam Fryer. 2. Fill the broccoli florets on the Cook & Crisp Basket. Pour the melted coconut oil over the broccoli and add in the sliced spring onion. Toss together. Put the basket in the Ninja Foodi Pressure Steam Fryer. 3. Put on the Smart Lid on top of the Ninja Foodi Steam Fryer. 4. Move the Lid Slider to the "Air Fry/Stovetop". Select the "Air Fry" mode for cooking. 5. Air Fry at 195°C for 7 minutes, stirring at the halfway point. 6. Place the broccoli in a suitable bowl and drizzle the lemon juice over it.
Per Serving: Calories: 221; Fat: 19g; Sodium: 354mg; Carbs: 15g; Fibre: 5.1g; Sugar 8.2g; Protein 12g

Lemony Roasted Cauliflower

Prep Time: 10 minutes | Cook Time: 20 minutes | Serves: 2

1 medium head cauliflower
2 tablespoon salted butter, melted
1 medium lemon

1 teaspoon dried parsley
½ teaspoon garlic powder

1. Place the Cook & Crisp Basket in your Pressure Cooker Steam Fryer. 2. Having removed the leaves from the cauliflower head, brush it with the melted butter. Grate the rind of the lemon over it and then drizzle some juice. Finally add the parsley and garlic powder on top. 3. Transfer the cauliflower to the basket of the Pressure Cooker Steam Fryer. 4. Put on the Smart Lid on top of the Ninja Foodi Steam Fryer. 5. Move the Lid Slider to the "Air Fry/Stovetop". Select the "Air Fry" mode for cooking. 6. Cook for 15 minutes at 175°C, checking regularly to ensure it doesn't overcook. The cauliflower is ready when it is hot and fork tender. 7. Take care when removing it from the fryer, cut up and serve.
Per Serving: Calories: 219; Fat: 10g; Sodium: 891mg; Carbs: 22.9g; Fibre: 4g; Sugar 4g; Protein 13g

Vegan Chickpeas Hummus

Prep Time: 5 minutes | Cook time: 50 minutes | Serves: 4-5

175g dried chickpeas (not soaked)
840ml water
65g tahini
2 tablespoons freshly squeezed lemon juice
2 cloves garlic, minced
1 teaspoon fine sea salt
1 teaspoon ground cumin
Freshly ground black pepper

1. Place the dried chickpeas in the cooking pot and add 720ml of the water. 2. Install the pressure lid and turn the pressure release valve to the SEAL position. 3. Select PRESSURE COOK, set the cooking temperature to HI and adjust the cooking time to 50 minutes. 4. When cooked, let the unit naturally release pressure. 5. Drain the cooked chickpeas in a colander. 6. To blend the hummus, you can either return the cooked chickpeas to the cooking pot and use an immersion blender, or add the chickpeas to a food processor or blender. 7. Add the tahini, the remaining water, the lemon juice, garlic, salt, cumin, and several grinds of black pepper and blend until smooth. Adjust the seasonings to your taste. 8. Serve the hummus right away or store it in an airtight container in the fridge for 7 days.
Per Serving: Calories 228; Fat 9g; Sodium 493mg; Carbs 29.02g; Fibre 6.2g; Sugar 4.52g; Protein 10.45g

Spicy Pinto Beans

Prep Time: 10 minutes | Cook time: 20 minutes | Serves: 4

180g dried pinto beans, soaked for 8 hours and drained
720ml water
½ yellow onion, chopped
2 cloves garlic, minced
1 teaspoon ground cumin
1 teaspoon chili powder
¼ teaspoon freshly ground black pepper
Pinch of cayenne pepper (optional)
½ to ¾ teaspoon fine sea salt
Chopped fresh coriander, for garnish
Lime wedges, for garnish

1. Combine the drained beans, water, onion, and garlic in the cooking pot. Stir them well, making sure the beans are submerged. 2. Install the pressure lid and turn the pressure release valve to the SEAL position. 3. Select PRESSURE COOK, set the cooking temperature to HI and adjust the cooking time to 20 minutes. 4. When cooked, let the unit naturally release pressure. 5. Drain the beans, reserving the liquid. Return the cooked beans to the cooking pot, and stir in 120ml of the reserved cooking liquid, cumin, black pepper, cayenne, chili powder, and ½ teaspoon salt. 6. Mash the cooked beans with a potato masher until smooth, leaving some texture if you like. 7. Taste and adjust the seasoning, adding more salt as needed, and serve warm with a garnish of coriander and a squeeze of lime juice. 8. Store the leftover beans in an airtight container in the fridge for 7 days.
Per Serving: Calories 191; Fat 2g; Sodium 322mg; Carbs 33.12g; Fibre 8.1g; Sugar 1.76g; Protein 10.78g

Mashed Potatoes and Cauliflower

Prep Time: 10 minutes | Cook time: 10 minutes | Serves: 6

900g Yukon gold potatoes
1 yellow onion, chopped
100g cremini mushrooms, chopped
2 cloves garlic, minced
2 tablespoons soy sauce or tamari
Fine sea salt and freshly ground black pepper
240ml water
455g cauliflower, cut into florets
2 tablespoons chopped fresh chives
Cut the potatoes into 2.5cm chunks, reserving one cut-up potato for the gravy

1. Add the water to the cooking pot, place the Cook & Crisp Basket on top of diffuser and press down firmly, and then combine the onion, mushrooms, the reserved cut-up potato, the garlic, soy sauce, ¼ teaspoon salt, several grinds of black pepper, and the water in the basket; place the cauliflower florets and the remaining potatoes into the basket. 2. Install the pressure lid and turn the pressure release valve to the SEAL position. 3. Select PRESSURE COOK, set the cooking temperature to HI and adjust the cooking time to 10 minutes. 4. When cooked, let the unit naturally release pressure. 5. Transfer the cauliflower and potatoes to a large bowl. Use a potato masher to mash them and then season generously with salt and pepper to taste. Stir in the chives. 6. Use a blender to blend the gravy directly in the bottom of the cooking pot. Alternatively, you can pour the mixture into a blender and blend until smooth. Taste and adjust the seasonings. 7. Serve the mash immediately with the gravy on top. Store the leftovers in an airtight container in the fridge for 5 days.
Per Serving: Calories 276; Fat 3.14g; Sodium 121mg; Carbs 58.24g; Fibre 8.9g; Sugar 5.21g; Protein 8.21g

Herbed Mashed Sweet Potatoes

Prep Time: 10 minutes | Cook time: 8 minutes | Serves: 4

900g sweet potatoes, peeled and cut into 2.5cm chunks
1 teaspoon minced fresh thyme
½ teaspoon minced fresh rosemary
1 tablespoon extra-virgin olive oil (optional)
½ teaspoon fine sea salt
Freshly ground black pepper

1. Add the water to the cooking pot, place the reversible rack in the pot in the lower position and drop the lower rack through the reversible rack handles. 2. Arrange the sweet potatoes onto the rack. 3. Install the pressure lid and turn the pressure release valve to the SEAL position. 4. Select PRESSURE COOK, set the cooking temperature to HI and adjust the cooking time to 8 minutes. 5. When cooked, let the unit naturally release pressure. 6. Pour the water out of the pot. 7. Pour the drained sweet potatoes back into the pot and use a potato masher to mash the potatoes. Add the thyme, rosemary, olive oil, salt, and several grinds of pepper and stir well to combine. 8. Taste and adjust the seasonings, then serve warm. 9. Store the leftovers in an airtight container in the fridge for 5 days.
Per Serving: Calories 189; Fat 1.71g; Sodium 334mg; Carbs 39.71g; Fibre 5g; Sugar 1.77g; Protein 4.61g

Garlicky Potatoes and Kale
Prep Time: 10 minutes | Cook Time: 10 minutes | Serves: 4

1 tablespoon olive oil
1 small onion, peeled and diced
1 stalk celery, diced
2 cloves garlic, minced
4 medium potatoes, peeled and diced
2 bunches kale, washed, deveined, and chopped
360 ml vegetable stock
2 teaspoons salt
½ teaspoon ground black pepper
¼ teaspoon caraway seeds
1 tablespoon apple cider vinegar
4 tablespoons sour cream

1. Move slider to AIR FRY/STOVETOP. Select SEAR/SAUTÉ and set to Lo1. Select START/STOP to begin preheating. Allow unit to preheat for 5 minutes. After 5 minutes, heat oil. Add onion and celery and stir-fry 3 to 5 minutes until onions are translucent. Add garlic and cook for an additional minute. 2. Add potatoes in an even layer. Add chopped kale in an even layer. Add stock. 3. Close the lid and move slider to PRESSURE. Make sure the pressure release valve is in the SEAL position. The temperature will default to HIGH, which is the correct setting. Set time to 5 minutes. Select START/STOP to begin cooking. 4. When cooking is complete, naturally release the pressure for 10 minutes. Then turn the pressure relief valve to the VENT position for quick pressure relief. Move slider to AIR FRY/ STOVETOP to unlock the lid, then carefully open it. Then drain stock. 5. Stir in salt, pepper, caraway seeds, and vinegar; slightly mash the potatoes in the pot. Garnish each serving with 1 tablespoon sour cream.
Per Serving: Calories 364; Fat 5.35g; Sodium 1419mg; Carbs 72.26g; Fibre 9.9g; Sugar 5.53g; Protein 9.76g

Quinoa Endive Boats
Prep Time: 10 minutes | Cook Time: 3 minutes | Serves: 4

1 tablespoon walnut oil
160 g quinoa
600 ml water
205 g chopped jarred artichoke hearts
300 g diced tomatoes, seeded
½ small red onion, peeled and thinly sliced
2 tablespoons olive oil
1 tablespoon balsamic vinegar
2 heads chicory
120 g roasted pecans

1. Move slider to AIR FRY/STOVETOP. Select SEAR/SAUTÉ and set to Lo1. Select START/STOP to begin cooking. Heat walnut oil. Add quinoa and toss for 1 minute until slightly browned. Add water. 2. Close the lid and move slider to PRESSURE. Make sure the pressure release valve is in the SEAL position. The temperature will default to HIGH, which is the correct setting. Set time to 2 minutes. Select START/STOP to begin cooking. 3. When timer beeps, let pressure release naturally for 10 minutes. Then turn the pressure relief valve to the VENT position for quick pressure relief. Move slider to AIR FRY/ STOVETOP to unlock the lid, then carefully open it. 4. Drain the liquid and transfer quinoa to a serving bowl. 5. Toss the remaining ingredients except chicory leaves and pecans into quinoa. Refrigerate mixture covered until cooled for 1 hour up to overnight. 6. To prepare boats, separate the chicory leaves. Rinse, drain, and divide them among four plates. Top each with ¼ of the quinoa mixture. 7. Distribute 30 g toasted pecans over the top of each endive boat and serve.
Per Serving: Calories 519; Fat 31.33g; Sodium 143mg; Carbs 52.2g; Fibre 18.7g; Sugar 5.35g; Protein 14.9g

Tasty Butternut Squash Mash
Prep Time: 15 minutes | Cook Time: minutes | Serves: 6

360 ml water
900 g butternut squash, peeled, halved, seeded, and cut into 10 cm pieces
55 g butter
2 tablespoons heavy cream, or whole milk
1 tablespoon packed fresh sage leaves, minced
½ teaspoon table salt
½ teaspoon ground black pepper

1. Pour the water into the pot. Then place the bottom layer of the Deluxe Reversible Rack in the lower position in the pot. Pile the butternut squash pieces onto the rack. 2. Close the lid and move slider to PRESSURE. Make sure the pressure release valve is in the SEAL position. The temperature will default to HIGH, which is the correct setting. Set time to 8 minutes. Select START/STOP to begin cooking. 3. When cooking is complete, turn the pressure relief valve to the VENT position for quick pressure relief. Move slider to the right to unlock the lid, then carefully open it. 4. Pick up the rack with food and take it out of the pot. Drain the liquid in the pot. Return all the butternut squash pieces to the pot. 5. Move slider to AIR FRY/STOVETOP. Select SEAR/SAUTÉ and set to Lo1. Select START/STOP to begin cooking. 6. Use a potato masher to begin mashing the squash. Add the butter, sage, salt, cream, and pepper. Continue to mash the ingredients together until as smooth as you like, about 1 minute. Turn off the SEAR/SAUTÉ function. Serve warm.
Per Serving: Calories 148; Fat9.73 g; Sodium 263mg; Carbs 16.46g; Fibre 2.5g; Sugar 0.34g; Protein 1.5g

Butter-Maple Glazed Carrots
Prep Time: 15 minutes | Cook Time: 7 minutes | Serves: 8

900 g medium carrots, peeled and cut into 2.5 cm pieces
480 ml water
3 tablespoons butter
2 tablespoons maple syrup
½ teaspoon table salt

1. Put the carrots and water in the pot. 2. Close the lid and move slider to PRESSURE. Make sure the pressure release valve is in the SEAL position. The temperature will default to HIGH, which is the correct setting. Set time to 3 minutes. Select START/STOP to begin cooking. 3. When cooking is complete, turn the pressure relief valve to the VENT position for quick pressure relief. Move slider to the right to unlock the lid, then carefully open it. Drain the carrots into a colander set in the sink. 4. Move slider to AIR FRY/STOVETOP. Select SEAR/SAUTÉ and set to 3. Select START/STOP to begin cooking. 5. Melt the butter in the cooker. Stir in the syrup and salt until bubbling. Add the carrots and continue cooking, stirring constantly, until the carrots are glazed, 2 to 3 minutes. 6. Turn off the SEAR/SAUTÉ function and remove the pot from the cooker to stop the cooking. Pour the carrots and any remaining glaze into a serving bowl and cool for a couple of minutes before serving.
Per Serving: Calories 98; Fat 4.59g; Sodium 260mg; Carbs 14.22g; Fibre 3.2g; Sugar 8.4g; Protein 1.1g

Sweet & Spicy Red Cabbage

Prep Time: 15 minutes | Cook Time: 14 minutes | Serves: 8

240 ml pomegranate juice
120 ml plus 1 tablespoon water
55 g packed light brown sugar
1 canned chipotle chile in adobo sauce, stemmed, seeded (if desired), and minced
1 tablespoon adobo sauce from the can of chipotle chiles
¼ teaspoon table salt
900 g cored and shredded red cabbage
3 large thyme sprigs
2 teaspoons corn flour

1. Stir the juice, 120 ml water, brown sugar, adobo sauce, chipotle chile, and salt in pot until the brown sugar dissolves. Add the cabbage and thyme sprigs. Toss well until evenly and thoroughly coated. 2. Close the lid and move slider to PRESSURE. Make sure the pressure release valve is in the SEAL position. The temperature will default to HIGH, which is the correct setting. Set time to 12 minutes. Select START/STOP to begin cooking. 3. When cooking is complete, turn the pressure relief valve to the VENT position for quick pressure relief. Move slider to the right to unlock the lid, then carefully open it. 4. Move slider to AIR FRY/STOVETOP. Select SEAR/SAUTÉ and set to 3. Select START/STOP to begin cooking. 5. Whisk the remaining 1 tablespoon water and the corn flour in a small bowl until smooth. Stir this slurry into the bubbling cabbage mixture. 6. Continue cooking, stirring constantly, until the liquid in the pot thickens to a sauce, 1 to 2 minutes. Press START/STOP to turn off the SEAR/SAUTÉ function. 7. Pour the cabbage and any sauce into a large serving bowl and cool for a couple of minutes before serving.
Per Serving: Calories 107; Fat 4.11g; Sodium 192mg; Carbs 15.26g; Fibre 2.8g; Sugar 8.97g; Protein 4.21g

Flavourful Aubergine, Courgette & Tomatoes

Prep Time: 15 minutes | Cook Time: 7 minutes | Serves: 6

One can diced tomatoes with or without chiles
2 medium courgette, diced
1 medium aubergine, stemmed and diced (no need to peel)
1 small yellow onion, chopped
Up to 4 medium garlic cloves, peeled and minced (4 teaspoons)
2 tablespoons olive oil
1 tablespoon fresh lemon juice
1 teaspoon dried oregano
1 teaspoon dried thyme
½ teaspoon table salt
½ teaspoon ground black pepper
1 bay leaf

1. Combine all the ingredients in the pot. 2. Close the lid and move slider to PRESSURE. Make sure the pressure release valve is in the SEAL position. The temperature will default to HIGH, which is the correct setting. Set time to 7 minutes. Select START/STOP to begin cooking. 3. When cooking is complete, turn the pressure relief valve to the VENT position for quick pressure relief. Move slider to the right to unlock the lid, then carefully open it. 4. Stir well; fish out and discard the bay leaf. Set the lid askew over the pot and set aside for 5 minutes to blend the flavours before serving in small bowls.
Per Serving: Calories 202; Fat 10.05g; Sodium 354mg; Carbs 12g; Fibre 4.1g; Sugar 6.3g; Protein 16.91g

Easy Cauliflower "Rice"

Prep Time: 5 minutes | Cook time: 1 minutes | Serves: 4

1 head cauliflower, cut into florets
Fine sea salt

1. Add 240ml of water to the cooking pot, place the reversible rack in the pot in the lower position and drop the lower rack through the reversible rack handles. 2. Arrange the cauliflower florets onto the rack. 3. Install the pressure lid and turn the pressure release valve to the SEAL position. 4. Select PRESSURE COOK, set the cooking temperature to HI and adjust the cooking time to 20 minutes. 5. When cooked, let the unit naturally release pressure. 6. Lift the steam basket out of the pot with oven mitts and pour out any water from the pot. 7. Add the cooked cauliflower back to the pot. Season generously with salt and use a potato masher to break up the cauliflower into a rice-like consistency. Serve warm. 8. Store the leftovers in an airtight container in the fridge for 5 days.
Per Serving: Calories 53; Fat 0.59g; Sodium 102mg; Carbs 10.44g; Fibre 4.2g; Sugar 4.01g; Protein 4.03g

Chapter 3 Beans and Grains

Farro with Cremini Mushrooms and Parmesan   34

Authentic Bulgur Pilaf with Chickpeas ……   34

Coconut Rice and Red Beans ………………   34

Lemony Mashed Chickpeas with Spring Onions……………………………………   34

Flavourful Brown Basmati Rice Pilaf with Spiced Beef……………………………   35

Herbed White Beans ………………………   35

Cheesy White Beans with Lemon …………   35

Turmeric Basmati Rice with Yellow Onion   35

Greek Fried Rice with Eggs and Cucumber   36

Simple Asian Quinoa and Carrot Salad ……   36

Savoury Cheese Mushroom Risotto ………   36

Basil Green Beans with Tomatoes and Pine Nuts……………………………………   36

Homemade Parmesan-Lemon Chicken Risotto   37

Spicy Red Kidney Beans & Sausage Stew with Rice ……………………………………   37

Stir-Fried Vegetables and Brown Rice ……   37

Herbed Black-Eyed Peas and Swiss Chard…   38

Fresh Barley & Beans Taco Salad with Zesty Lime Vinaigrette ………………………   38

Traditional Hummus ………………………   38

Quick Spicy Lentil & Walnut Tacos ………   39

Fantastic Braised Chickpeas with Swiss Chard 39

Hearty Cranberry Beans with Spanish Chorizo & Red Cabbage …………………………   39

Chinese Vegetable Fried Rice ………………   40

Spanish Rice with Salsa ……………………   40

Cheesy Black Bean and Corn Quesadillas …   40

Yummy Chipotle Black Beans with Bacon…   40

Farro with Cremini Mushrooms and Parmesan

Prep Time: 35 minutes | Cook Time: 35 minutes | Serves: 4

4 tablespoons extra-virgin olive oil, divided
455 g cremini mushrooms, trimmed and quartered
Salt and ground black pepper
1 large yellow onion, finely chopped
4 medium garlic cloves, finely chopped
195 g farro
120 ml dry white wine
3 tablespoons salted butter, cut into 3 pieces
125 g container baby rocket, roughly chopped
½ teaspoon minced fresh rosemary
40 g Parmesan cheese, finely grated

1. Select SEAR/SAUTÉ. Select Hi5, and then press START/STOP to begin cooking. 2. When the pot is hot, heat 2 tablespoons of oil until shimmering; add mushrooms and ½ teaspoon salt, and cook them for 6 to 8 minutes until well browned and most of the liquid released by the mushrooms has evaporated; transfer them to a small bowl. 3. Heat 2 tablespoons of oil in the pot under the same setting; add onion and sauté them for 5 to 7 minutes until lightly browned. Add the garlic and cook them for 30 seconds until fragrant. Add the farro, 2 teaspoons salt and ¾ teaspoon pepper, stirring to coat the grains with oil; add the wine and cook for 1 to 2 minutes until most of the liquid evaporates, scraping up any browned bits. 4. Pour in 720 ml water, stir them to combine, and then distribute the mixture in an even layer. Stop the process. 5. Close the lid, turn the pressure release valve to SEAL position, and then move the slider to PRESSURE. Select HI and set the cooking time to 12 minutes. Press START/STOP to begin cooking. When finished, release the pressure naturally. 6. Serve the dish with the remaining Parmesan on the side.
Per Serving: Calories 571; Fat: 21.38g; Sodium: 606mg; Carbs: 92.28g; Fibre: 14.2g; Sugar: 4.87g; Protein: 18.51g

Authentic Bulgur Pilaf with Chickpeas

Prep Time: 20 minutes | Cook Time: 10 minutes | Serves: 4

4 tablespoons salted butter
2½ teaspoons garam masala
1 bunch spring onions, thinly sliced, whites and greens reserved separately
130 g coarse bulgur, rinsed and drained
Salt and ground black pepper
2 cans chickpeas, rinsed and drained
35 g lightly packed fresh dill, roughly chopped
35 g lightly packed fresh flat-leaf parsley, roughly chopped
90 g toasted pistachios, chopped

1. Select SEAR/SAUTÉ. Select Hi5, and then press START/STOP to begin cooking. 2. When the pot is hot, melt the butter; add garam masala and spring onion whites, and cook for 1 minute until fragrant; add bulgur and stir them to coat the grains with butter. 3. Stop the process, stir in 360 ml water, 2 teaspoons salt and ½ teaspoon pepper, and then distribute the mixture in an even layer. 4. Close the lid, turn the pressure release valve to SEAL position, and then move the slider to PRESSURE. Select HI and set the cooking time to 5 minutes. Press START/STOP to begin cooking. When finished, release the pressure quickly. 5. Stir in the chickpeas and about half of the spring onion greens, half of the dill and half of the parsley. Taste and season the dish with the pepper and salt. 6. Transfer the dish to a serving dish, sprinkle with the remaining spring onion greens, the remaining dill and the remaining parsley, then top with the pistachios. Enjoy.
Per Serving: Calories 332; Fat: 14.89g; Sodium: 386mg; Carbs: 40.54g; Fibre: 11.6g; Sugar: 5.94g; Protein: 12.57g

Coconut Rice and Red Beans

Prep Time: 15 minutes | Cook Time: 50 minutes | Serves: 4

3 tablespoons coconut oil (preferably unrefined), melted
300 g long-grain white rice, rinsed and drained
1 bunch spring onions, thinly sliced
4 medium garlic cloves, finely chopped
1 small red pepper, stemmed, seeded and chopped
2 tablespoons minced fresh corinader stems, plus 20 g chopped fresh
corinader leaves, reserved separately
600 ml coconut water
1 teaspoon ground cumin
1 teaspoon white sugar
Salt and ground black pepper
390 g small red beans or kidney beans, rinsed and drained

1. Stir together the oil, rice, spring onions, garlic, pepper and corinader stems in the pot; stir in the coconut water, cumin, sugar, 2 teaspoons salt and 1 teaspoon pepper. Distribute the mixture in an even layer. 2. Close the lid, turn the pressure release valve to SEAL position, and then move the slider to PRESSURE. Select LO and set the cooking time to 10 minutes. Press START/STOP to begin cooking. When finished, release the pressure naturally. 3. Carefully remove the insert from the housing. Without fluffing the rice, scatter the beans over the surface, then drape a kitchen towel across the top and re-cover without locking the lid in place. 4. Let the dish stand for 10 minutes. Uncover and add the corinader leaves, and then fluff the rice, stirring in the beans and corinader. 5. Taste and season the dish with the pepper and salt.
Per Serving: Calories 762; Fat: 12.38g; Sodium: 181mg; Carbs: 132.95g; Fibre: 20.2g; Sugar: 8.47g; Protein: 31.71g

Lemony Mashed Chickpeas with Spring Onions

Prep Time: 25 minutes | Cook Time: 25 minutes | Serves: 6

985 g cooked chickpeas, plus 120 ml reserved cooking liquid
1 tablespoon garam masala
2 teaspoons ground turmeric
¼ teaspoon cayenne pepper
1 bunch spring onions, thinly sliced, white and green parts reserved
separately
4 tablespoons extra-virgin olive oil, divided, plus more to serve
2 teaspoons grated lemon zest, plus 60 ml lemon juice, plus lemon wedges to serve
Salt and ground black pepper

1. Mash 165 g of the chickpeas in a large bowl; stir in the remaining whole chickpeas, the garam masala, turmeric, cayenne and spring onion whites. 2. Select SEAR/SAUTÉ. Select Lo3, and then press START/STOP to begin cooking. 3. When the pot is hot, heat 2 tablespoons of oil until barely smoking; add about half of the chickpea mixture and cook for 2 to 3 minutes until heated through. 4. Transfer the mixture to a large bowl and cover with foil to keep warm. Repeat with remaining oil and the remaining chickpea mixture. 5. Add the reserved chickpea cooking liquid and lemon juice and zest, and then stir to combine. 6. Taste and season them with salt and pepper. Sprinkle the dish with the spring onion greens and drizzle with additional oil. 7. Serve and enjoy.
Per Serving: Calories 767; Fat: 12.19g; Sodium: 123mg; Carbs: 128.72g; Fibre: 25g; Sugar: 22.38g; Protein: 41.34g

Flavourful Brown Basmati Rice Pilaf with Spiced Beef

Prep Time: 25 minutes | Cook Time: 70 minutes | Serves: 4

200 g 85 percent lean beef mince
2 tablespoons tomato paste
1¾ teaspoons ground cinnamon
1¾ teaspoons ground turmeric
Salt and ground black pepper

2 tablespoons extra-virgin olive oil, divided
200 g green beans, trimmed and cut into 2.5 cm pieces
300 g brown basmati rice, rinsed and drained
30 g golden raisins
30 g chopped fresh corinader

1. Mix together the beef, tomato paste, cinnamon, turmeric, 1¾ teaspoons salt and 1 teaspoon pepper in a medium bowl; set aside. 2. Select SEAR/SAUTÉ. Select Lo3, and then press START/STOP to begin cooking. 3. When the pot is hot, heat 1 tablespoon of the oil, add the green beans and cook them for 8 to 9 minutes until browned in spots; transfer the green beans to a bowl and set aside. 4. Add the remaining 1 tablespoon oil and the beef mixture to the pot, and cook them for 2 to 4 minutes until the beef is no longer pink, breaking up the meat into small pieces. 5. Stop the process, and then stir in the rice and half the raisins. Pour in 360 g water; stir them to combine, and then distribute the mixture in an even layer. 6. Close the lid, turn the pressure release valve to SEAL position, and then move the slider to PRESSURE. Select HI and set the cooking time to 22 minutes. Press START/STOP to begin cooking. When finished, release the pressure quickly. 7. Scatter the green beans and remaining raisins over the surface of the rice mixture. Drape a kitchen towel across the pot and re-cover without locking the lid in place. 8. Let stand for 10 minutes. 9. Fluff the pilaf, stirring in the beans and raisins, then stir in the corinader. 10. Taste and season the dish with the pepper and salt.
Per Serving: Calories 376; Fat: 21.99g; Sodium: 298mg; Carbs: 37.19g; Fibre: 12.3g; Sugar: 8.6g; Protein: 22.25g

Herbed White Beans

Prep Time: 20 minutes | Cook Time: 1 hour 30 minutes | Serves: 6

455 g dried cannellini beans, rinsed and drained
Salt and ground black pepper
½ teaspoon baking soda
2 tablespoons extra-virgin olive oil

1 medium yellow onion, chopped
4 medium garlic cloves, smashed and peeled
3 bay leaves
2 tablespoons chopped fresh sage

1. Stir together the beans, 2 teaspoons salt, the baking soda and 1.4 L water in the pot, then distribute in an even layer. 2. Close the lid, turn the pressure release valve to SEAL position, and then move the slider to PRESSURE. Select HI and set the cooking time to 5 minutes. Press START/STOP to begin cooking. When finished, release the pressure quickly. 3. Carefully remove the insert from the housing and drain the beans in a colander. Return the insert to the housing. Rinse the beans under the cool water and set aside. 4. Select SEAR/SAUTÉ. Select Hi5, and then press START/STOP to begin cooking. 5. When the pot is hot, heat the oil until shimmering; add onion, garlic, bay, sage, and 1 teaspoon, and then cook them for 5 minutes until the onion is softened. 6. Return the beans to the pot and add 1.4 L water, stir them and then distribute in an even layer. Stop the process. 7. Close the lid, turn the pressure release valve to SEAL position, and then move the slider to PRESSURE. Select HI and set the cooking time to 16 minutes. Press START/STOP to begin cooking. When finished, release the pressure naturally. 8. Carefully remove the insert from the housing and drain the beans in a colander. Remove and discard the garlic and bay. 9. Taste and season the dish with salt and pepper. Serve and enjoy.
Per Serving: Calories 131; Fat: 8.58g; Sodium: 268mg; Carbs: 14.18g; Fibre: 3.4g; Sugar: 1.19g; Protein: 2.89g 4.06g; Protein: 1.77g

Cheesy White Beans with Lemon

Prep Time: 15 minutes | Cook Time: 15 minutes | Serves: 4-6

3 tablespoons extra-virgin olive oil, plus more to serve
1 medium yellow onion, chopped
2 carrots, peeled, halved and thinly sliced
160 g cherry or grape tomatoes
Salt and ground black pepper
4 medium garlic cloves, finely chopped

½ teaspoon red pepper flakes
320 g "White Beans with Chopped Onion"
10 g finely chopped fresh dill
55 g feta cheese, crumbled
Lemon wedges, to serve

1. Select SEAR/SAUTÉ. Select Lo4, and then press START/STOP to begin cooking. 2. When the pot is hot, heat the oil until shimmering; stir in the onion, carrots, tomatoes and 1 teaspoon salt, then cover the lid and cook the vegetables for 10 minutes until the tomatoes begin to burst and the vegetables are tender. 3. Remove the lid, and add garlic and pepper flakes, and then cook them for 30 seconds; stir in the beans and cook them at Lo3 for 2 minutes. 4. Stop the process and stir in half the dill. 5. Taste and season the food with salt and black pepper, then transfer to a serving bowl. Top the dish with the feta and the remaining dill and drizzle with additional oil. 6. Serve the dish with lemon wedges.
Per Serving: Calories 70; Fat: 3.06g; Sodium: 318mg; Carbs: 9.11g; Fibre: 1.9g; Sugar: 3.8g; Protein: 2.87g

Turmeric Basmati Rice with Yellow Onion

Prep Time: 5 minutes | Cook Time: 9 minutes | Serves: 8

2 tablespoons unsalted butter
35 g peeled and diced yellow onion
400 g basmati rice

480 ml chicken stock
1 teaspoon ground turmeric
⅛ teaspoon salt

1. Move slider to AIR FRY/STOVETOP. Select SEAR/SAUTÉ and set to 3. Select START/STOP to begin cooking. Add butter to the pot and heat 30 seconds until melted. Place in the onion and cook for 5 minutes until onions are translucent. 2. Add the remaining ingredients. Press START/STOP to turn off the SEAR/SAUTÉ function and close the lid. 3. Move slider to PRESSURE. Ensure the pressure release valve is in the SEAL position. The temperature will default to HIGH, which is the correct setting. Set time to 3 minutes. Select START/STOP to begin cooking. 4. When cooking is complete, naturally release the pressure for 5 minutes. Then turn the pressure relief valve to the VENT position for quick pressure relief. Move slider to AIR FRY/ STOVETOP to unlock the lid, then carefully open it. 5. Ladle rice into eight bowls and serve warm.
Per Serving: Calories 210; Fat 12.54g; Sodium 289mg; Carbs 15.59g; Fibre 6.3g; Sugar 0.4g; Protein 17.08g

Greek Fried Rice with Eggs and Cucumber
Prep Time: 10 minutes | Cook Time: 5 minutes | Serves: 4

200 g long-grain white rice
1 can diced tomatoes, including juice
60 ml water
1 teaspoon salt
2 large eggs, whisked

75 g peeled and seeded diced English cucumber
30 g crumbled feta cheese
40 g sliced Kalamata olives
10 g chopped fresh mint leaves

1. Add the rice, water, tomatoes with juice, and salt in the pot. 2. Close the lid and move slider to PRESSURE. Ensure the pressure release valve is in the SEAL position. The temperature will default to HIGH, which is the correct setting. Set time to 3 minutes. Select START/STOP to begin cooking. 3. When cooking is complete, naturally release the pressure for 10 minutes. Then turn the pressure relief valve to the VENT position for quick pressure relief. Move slider to AIR FRY/ STOVETOP to unlock the lid, then carefully open it. 4. Make a well in the middle of the rice and add whisked eggs to the well. Stir eggs into rice and stir-fry 2 minutes. 5. Transfer rice mixture to a serving dish. Toss in cucumber, feta cheese, and olives. 6. Garnish with mint leaves and serve warm.
Per Serving: Calories 251; Fat 5.77g; Sodium 861mg; Carbs 42.4g; Fibre 3.1g; Sugar 3.46g; Protein 7.12g

Simple Asian Quinoa and Carrot Salad
Prep Time: 15 minutes | Cook Time: 1 minute | Serves: 3

180 g uncooked quinoa, rinsed
355 ml water
½ tsp sea salt, plus more to taste
60 ml avocado oil or extra-virgin olive oil
2 tbsp (30 ml) rice vinegar
2 tsp (10 ml) sesame oil
2 tsp (10 ml) soy sauce or tamari

½ tsp garlic powder
3 tbsp (24 g) diced green onion
130 g diced or matchstick-cut carrot
150 g seeded and diced red or orange pepper
10 g chopped fresh coriander
35 chopped almonds or peanuts (optional)

1. Combine the quinoa, water and salt in the pot. 2. Close the lid and move slider to PRESSURE. Ensure the pressure release valve is in the SEAL position. The temperature will default to HIGH, which is the correct setting. Set time to 1 minute. Select START/STOP to begin cooking. 3. When cooking is complete, naturally release the pressure for 15 minutes. Then turn the pressure relief valve to the VENT position for quick pressure relief. Move slider to AIR FRY/ STOVETOP to unlock the lid, then carefully open it. 4. In the meantime, make the dressing: In a small bowl, mix together the avocado oil, sesame oil, vinegar, soy sauce and garlic powder. Stir well. 5. Once the quinoa is completely done cooking, transfer to a big bowl. Mix in the carrot, green onion, pepper and coriander. Toss with the dressing. 6. Serve right away or store in the fridge for up to 5 days. Garnish with almonds or peanuts (if using) before serving.
Per Serving: Calories 608; Fat 33.95g; Sodium 966mg; Carbs 63.93g; Fibre 9.1g; Sugar 4.95g; Protein 16.75g

Savoury Cheese Mushroom Risotto
Prep Time: 15 minutes | Cook Time: 11 minutes | Serves: 4

4 tablespoons olive oil
4 tablespoons butter, divided
1 medium yellow onion, peeled and diced
4 cloves garlic, minced
200 g sliced mushrooms
300 g arborio rice

960 ml vegetable stock
100 g grated Parmesan cheese
1 teaspoon dried parsley
½ teaspoon salt
¼ teaspoon black pepper

1. Move slider to AIR FRY/STOVETOP. Select SEAR/SAUTÉ and set to 3. Select START/STOP to begin cooking. Heat oil and 2 tablespoons butter in the pot. Add onion and cook for 3 minutes. 2. Add garlic and cook for 30 seconds. 3. Stir in mushrooms and rice. Pour in stock and deglaze bottom of pot. Press START/STOP to turn off the SEAR/SAUTÉ function. 4. Close the lid and move slider to PRESSURE. Ensure the pressure release valve is in the SEAL position. The temperature will default to HIGH, which is the correct setting. Set time to 7 minutes. Select START/STOP to begin cooking. 5. When cooking is complete, turn the pressure relief valve to the VENT position for quick pressure relief. Move slider to the right to unlock the lid, then carefully open it. 6. Mix in remaining 2 tablespoons butter, Parmesan cheese, salt, dried parsley, and pepper. 7. Serve hot.
Per Serving: Calories 483; Fat 41.26g; Sodium 837mg; Carbs 29.26g; Fibre 9.9g; Sugar 1.68g; Protein 13.75g

Basil Green Beans with Tomatoes and Pine Nuts
Prep Time: 10 minutes | Cook Time: 5 minutes | Serves: 6

2 tablespoons olive oil
675 g cherry tomatoes, halved
2 medium garlic cloves, peeled and minced (2 teaspoons)
½ teaspoon table salt

675 g fresh green beans, trimmed
10 g loosely packed fresh basil leaves, finely chopped
2 tablespoons pine nuts

1. Move slider to AIR FRY/STOVETOP. Select SEAR/SAUTÉ and set to 3. Select START/STOP to begin cooking. 2. Warm the oil in the pot for a minute or two. Add the tomatoes, garlic, and salt. Cook, stirring frequently, until the tomatoes begin to break down and give off their liquid, 2 to 3 minutes. Stir in the green beans and turn off the SEAR/SAUTÉ function. 3. Close the lid and move slider to PRESSURE. Ensure the pressure release valve is in the SEAL position. Set the temperature to LOW and set time to 1 minute. Select START/STOP to begin cooking. 4. When cooking is complete, turn the pressure relief valve to the VENT position for quick pressure relief. Move slider to the right to unlock the lid, then carefully open it. 5. Stir in the basil and pine nuts, then set aside with the lid askew over the pot to blend the flavors for 5 minutes.
Per Serving: Calories 138; Fat 5.29g; Sodium 196mg; Carbs 23.39g; Fibre 4.6g; Sugar 15.43g; Protein 2.54g

Homemade Parmesan-Lemon Chicken Risotto

Prep Time: 15 minutes | Cook Time: 21 minutes | Serves: 8

4 tbsp (55 g) grass-fed butter or ghee, divided
455 g boneless, skinless chicken breast, cut into 2.5-cm cubes
1 medium yellow onion, diced
5 cloves garlic, finely chopped
120 ml dry white wine
2 tbsp (30 ml) fresh lemon juice
195 g uncooked arborio or other short-grain white rice
1 tsp sea salt
475 ml vegetable or chicken stock
60 ml heavy cream
75 g shredded Parmesan cheese, plus more for garnish
15 g finely chopped fresh flat-leaf parsley, plus more for garnish
Zest of 2 small lemons

1. Move slider to AIR FRY/STOVETOP. Select SEAR/SAUTÉ and set to 3. Select START/STOP to begin preheating. Allow unit to preheat for 5 minutes. After 5 minutes, add 2 tablespoons (28 g) butter to the pot. When the fat has melted, add the chicken and sauté, stirring occasionally, for 5 to 7 minutes, or until the pink colour is gone. Transfer to a plate and set aside. 2. Add the onion and sauté, stirring occasionally, for 7 minutes, or until caramelised. Then, add the garlic and sauté for 1 minute, stirring occasionally. Add wine and lemon juice to deglaze the pot, scraping up any browned bits with a wooden spoon. 3. Add the rice, then give everything a stir to combine, stirring for 1 minute. Press START/STOP to turn off the SEAR/SAUTÉ function. 4. Add the stock, salt, and sautéed the chicken, give everything a quick stir. 5. Close the lid and move slider to PRESSURE. Ensure the pressure release valve is in the SEAL position. The temperature will default to HIGH, which is the correct setting. Set time to 6 minutes. Select START/STOP to begin cooking. 6. When cooking is complete, naturally release the pressure for 10 minutes. Then turn the pressure relief valve to the VENT position for quick pressure relief. Move slider to AIR FRY/ STOVETOP to unlock the lid, then carefully open it. 7. Add the cream, Parmesan, the remaining 2 tablespoons of butter, parsley and lemon zest, then quickly stir until the cream and Parmesan are fully mixed in. Let the mixture rest for 10 minutes. 8. Serve immediately, garnished with shredded Parmesan and chopped fresh flat-leaf parsley.
Per Serving: Calories 308; Fat 10.88g; Sodium 1045mg; Carbs 37.59g; Fibre 2.1g; Sugar 5.28g; Protein 14.64g

Spicy Red Kidney Beans & Sausage Stew with Rice

Prep Time: 15 minutes | Cook Time: 12 minutes | Serves: 6

380 g uncooked brown rice
590 ml water
1 tsp salt, plus a pinch and more to taste
1 tsp extra-virgin olive oil
340 g andouille sausage, sliced
2 yellow onions, diced
1 celery rib, diced
1 pepper, seeded and diced
5 cloves garlic, grated
1 tsp smoked paprika
¼ tsp freshly ground black pepper, plus more to taste
¼ to ½ tsp cayenne pepper
½ tsp dried basil
½ tsp dried oregano
2 (430 g) cans red kidney beans, drained and rinsed, divided
120 ml chicken stock
3 dried bay leaves

1. Place the rice and water along with a pinch of salt in the pot, stir to mix well. 2. Close the lid and move slider to PRESSURE. Ensure the pressure release valve is in the SEAL position. The temperature will default to HIGH, which is the correct setting. Set time to 1 minute. Select START/STOP to begin cooking. 3. When cooking is complete, naturally release the pressure for 15 minutes. Then turn the pressure relief valve to the VENT position for quick pressure relief. Move slider to AIR FRY/ STOVETOP to unlock the lid, then carefully open it. 4. Fluff the rice with a fork and transfer the rice to a plate. Clean out the pot. 5. Add the olive oil to the pot. Move slider to AIR FRY/STOVETOP. Select SEAR/SAUTÉ and set to 3. Select START/STOP to begin cooking. Once the oil is shimmering, add the sausage and sauté for 3 minutes. 6. Stir in the onions, celery and pepper. Sauté for 2 minutes. 7. Press START/STOP, then stir in the garlic, paprika, cayenne, basil, oregano, the remaining salt, black pepper. 8. Puree 128 g of the kidney beans in a food processor until smooth. Add to the pot along with the remaining beans, stock and bay leaves. 9. Close the lid and move slider to PRESSURE. Ensure the pressure release valve is in the SEAL position. The temperature will default to HIGH, which is the correct setting. Set time to 5 minutes. Select START/STOP to begin cooking. 10. When the timer sounds, quick release the pressure. Open the lid and stir the sausage and beans. Add more black pepper and salt to taste, if needed. 11. Serve the beans and sausage over the brown rice.
Per Serving: Calories 483; Fat 17.68g; Sodium 943mg; Carbs 64.61g; Fibre 5.1g; Sugar 2.95g; Protein 19.42g

Stir-Fried Vegetables and Brown Rice

Prep Time: 10 minutes | Cook Time: 15 minutes | Serves: 2

3 tablespoons sesame oil, divided, plus more for greasing
150 g long-grain brown rice
180 ml water, plus 3 tablespoons
Salt
1 tablespoon cornflour
2 garlic cloves, crushed
1½ teaspoons peeled minced fresh ginger, divided
90 g broccoli florets
60 g julienned carrots
110 g snow peas, trimmed
3 fresh shiitake mushrooms, sliced
40 g drained sliced water chestnuts
2 to 3 tablespoons low-sodium soy sauce
40 g chopped onion

1. Grease the inside of the pressure cooker pot with sesame oil. 2. Add the rice, water and salt to the pot. Close the lid and move slider to PRESSURE. 3. Ensure the pressure release valve is in the SEAL position. The temperature will default to HIGH, which is the correct setting. Set time to 15 minutes. Select START/STOP to begin cooking. 4. When cooking is complete, naturally release the pressure for 10 minutes. Then turn the pressure relief valve to the VENT position for quick pressure relief. Move slider to AIR FRY/ STOVETOP to unlock the lid, then carefully open it. 5. While cooking the rice, prepare the vegetables. Mix together the cornflour, garlic, ½ teaspoon of ginger, and 2 tablespoons of sesame oil in a large bowl. Stir until well combined and the cornflour is dissolved. Add the broccoli, mushrooms, carrots, snow peas, and water chestnuts and toss to lightly coat. 6. In a wok, heat the remaining 1 tablespoon of sesame oil over medium heat. Turn the heat to medium-high and add the vegetables. Cook for 2 minutes, tossing constantly to prevent burning. 7. Stir in the soy sauce and remaining 3 tablespoons of water. Add the onion and remaining 1 teaspoon of ginger and season with salt. Cook, stirring constantly, until the vegetables are tender but still crisp, 1 to 2 minutes. 8. Divide the brown rice between two plates and top with the stir-fried vegetables.
Per Serving: Calories 503; Fat 22.74g; Sodium 779mg; Carbs 67.84g; Fibre 4.8g; Sugar 3.8g; Protein 8.53g

Herbed Black-Eyed Peas and Swiss Chard

Prep Time: 10 minutes | Cook Time: 13 minutes | Serves: 2

1 tablespoon oil
½ yellow onion, diced
2 garlic cloves, minced
240 ml chicken stock
225 g dried black-eyed peas
60 g chopped Swiss chard or kale
1½ teaspoons red pepper flakes
2 fresh thyme sprigs or ½ teaspoon dried thyme
½ tablespoon salt
¼ teaspoon freshly ground black pepper
1 tablespoon apple cider vinegar
1 to 2 teaspoons hot sauce (optional)

1. Move slider to AIR FRY/STOVETOP. Select SEAR/SAUTÉ and set to Lo1. Select START/STOP to begin preheating. Allow unit to preheat for 5 minutes. After 5 minutes, place in the onion to the pot. Cook, stirring frequently, for 2 minutes, or until softened. Place in the garlic and cook, stirring, until fragrant, about 1 minute. 2. Add the stock, peas, Swiss chard, thyme, red pepper flakes, salt, and pepper. Deglaze the pot by scraping all the flavourful brown bits up off the bottom of the pot with a wooden spoon, then mix well. Press START/STOP to turn off the SEAR/SAUTÉ function. 3. Close the lid and move slider to PRESSURE. Ensure the pressure release valve is in the SEAL position. The temperature will default to HIGH, which is the correct setting. Set time to 10 minutes. Select START/STOP to begin cooking. 4. When cooking is complete, quick release pressure for 10 minutes. Carefully open the lid. 5. Stir in the vinegar and hot sauce (if using). Adjust seasoning if desired. Serve.
Per Serving: Calories 208; Fat 8.78g; Sodium 1726mg; Carbs 25.66g; Fibre 5.3g; Sugar 12.89g; Protein 8.54g

Fresh Barley & Beans Taco Salad with Zesty Lime Vinaigrette

Prep Time: 15 minutes | Cook Time: 20 minutes | Serves: 6

180 g barley
240 ml water
1 teaspoon ground cumin
1 teaspoon chili powder
185 g prepared salsa
½ teaspoon fine sea salt
260 g cooked or canned black beans
2 romaine hearts, chopped
180 g shredded red cabbage
150 g cherry tomatoes, halved
60 g chopped green onions, tender white and green parts only
20 g chopped fresh coriander
50 g crumbled feta or shredded Cheddar cheese
Avocado slices, for garnish
Zesty Lime Vinaigrette:
60 ml extra-virgin olive oil
3 tablespoons raw apple cider vinegar
60 ml freshly squeezed lime juice
3 tablespoons pure maple syrup
1 clove garlic, minced
1 teaspoon ground cumin
⅛ teaspoon cayenne pepper
½ teaspoon fine sea salt
Freshly ground black pepper

1. Add the barley, water, chili powder, salsa, cumin, and salt to the pot and stir to well combine. Close the lid and move slider to PRESSURE. Ensure the pressure release valve is in the SEAL position. The temperature will default to HIGH, which is the correct setting. Set time to 20 minutes. Select START/STOP to begin cooking. 2. When cooking is complete, naturally release the pressure for 10 minutes. Then turn the pressure relief valve to the VENT position for quick pressure relief. Move slider to AIR FRY/ STOVETOP to unlock the lid, then carefully open it. 3. While the barley is cooking, prepare the vinaigrette. In a pint-sized mason jar, mix together the olive oil, lime juice, maple syrup, vinegar, garlic, cayenne, cumin, salt, and several grinds of pepper. Screw on the lid and shake vigorously to combine. Set aside. 4. Stir in the black beans to create the taco "meat." (If using canned beans, drain and rinse them first.) 5. To serve, place the romaine, tomatoes, cabbage, green onions, coriander, and barley and black bean mixture in a serving bowl. Drizzle the lime vinaigrette on top and sprinkle with the cheese and avocado slices, and serve right away.
Per Serving: Calories 372; Fat 13.02g; Sodium 714mg; Carbs 56.14g; Fibre 13.4g; Sugar 12.38g; Protein 11.67g

Traditional Hummus

Prep Time: 15 minutes | Cook Time: 50 minutes | Serves: 16

200 g dried chickpeas, rinsed and drained
½ teaspoon baking soda
Salt
180 g toasted tahini (see note), room temperature
3 tablespoons lemon juice
1 to 2 tablespoons extra-virgin olive oil
1 tablespoon chopped fresh flat-leaf parsley
½ teaspoon ground cumin
½ teaspoon sweet paprika

1. Combine the chickpeas, 2 teaspoons salt, baking soda and 1.4 L water in the pot. Close the lid and move slider to PRESSURE. Ensure the pressure release valve is in the SEAL position. The temperature will default to HIGH, which is the correct setting. Set time to 5 minutes. Select START/STOP to begin cooking. 2. When pressure cooking is complete, quick-release the steam by moving the pressure valve to Venting. Press START/STOP, then carefully open the pot. 3. Using potholders, carefully remove the pot from the housing and drain the chickpeas in a colander; return the pot to the housing. Rinse the chickpeas in cool water. Drain and return to the pot. Add water to the pot and distribute the chickpeas in an even layer. 4. Close the lid and still cook on high pressure for 25 minutes. When the timer beeps, naturally release the pressure for 20 minutes. Then turn the pressure relief valve to the VENT position for quick pressure relief. Move slider to AIR FRY/ STOVETOP to unlock the lid, then carefully open it. 5. Set a colander in a large bowl. Using potholders, carefully remove the pot from the housing and pour the chickpeas and liquid into the colander. 6. Reserve 180 ml of the cooking liquid, then discard the remainder. Let the chickpeas drain for about one minute, then transfer them, still warm, to a food processor. Add 1 teaspoon salt, then process for 3 minutes. Stop the machine and add the tahini. Continue to process until the mixture is lightened and very smooth, about 1 minute longer. Scrape the sides and bottom of the processor bowl. 7. With the machine running, pour in the reserved cooking liquid and the lemon juice, then process until combined, 45 to 60 seconds. Taste and season with salt. 8. Arrange the hummus onto a shallow serving bowl. Then, use the back of a spoon to swirl a well in the centre. Drizzle with the oil, then sprinkle with the parsley, cumin and paprika.
Per Serving: Calories 86; Fat 4.05g; Sodium 198mg; Carbs 9.73g; Fibre 2.6g; Sugar 1.45g; Protein 3.63g

Quick Spicy Lentil & Walnut Tacos

Prep Time: 15 minutes | Cook Time: 5 minutes | Serves: 6

185 g green or brown lentils
300 ml water
1 teaspoon ground cumin
1 teaspoon chili powder
1 yellow onion, chopped
One can fire-roasted tomatoes with green chiles
90 g walnut halves
Lettuce, tomatoes, green onions, and avocado, or your favourite taco toppings, for serving
1 teaspoon fine sea salt
12 taco shells, for serving

1. Add the lentils, water, chili powder and cumin to the pot. Stir well and ensure the lentils are covered in liquid, then sprinkle the onion and canned tomatoes (along with their juices) over the top, do not stir. 2. Close the lid and move slider to PRESSURE. Ensure the pressure release valve is in the SEAL position. The temperature will default to HIGH, which is the correct setting. Set time to 5 minutes. Select START/STOP to begin cooking. 3. Meanwhile, finely chop the walnuts, lettuce, green onions, fresh tomatoes, and avocado. 4. When the cooking cycle is complete, naturally release the pressure for 10 minutes. Then turn the pressure relief valve to the VENT position for quick pressure relief. Move slider to AIR FRY/ STOVETOP to unlock the lid, then carefully open it. 5. Use a fork to mash a lentil against the side of the pot to make sure it's tender. If the lentils aren't tender, secure the lid (be sure the sealing ring is properly seated in the lid) and cook at high pressure for 2 minutes more. 6. Let the pressure naturally release for 5 minutes before venting and opening the lid. 7. Stir in the salt and chopped walnuts. Taste and adjust the seasonings as needed. 8. To serve, spoon the taco "meat" into taco shells, and top with lettuce, tomato, green onion, and avocado. Store the leftover taco "meat" in an airtight container in the fridge for 5 days.
Per Serving: Calories 253; Fat 14.63g; Sodium 804mg; Carbs 27.64g; Fibre 3.5g; Sugar 1.55g; Protein 4.7g

Fantastic Braised Chickpeas with Swiss Chard

Prep Time: 15 minutes | Cook Time: 1 hour 10 minutes | Serves: 6

2 tablespoons extra-virgin olive oil, plus more to serve
2 tablespoons tomato paste
1 medium yellow onion, chopped
6 medium garlic cloves, smashed and peeled
1 tablespoon ground coriander
1 tablespoon cumin seeds
½ teaspoon ground allspice
½ teaspoon red pepper flakes
720 ml low-sodium chicken stock, or water
700 g can whole peeled tomatoes, crushed by hand
455 g dried chickpeas, rinsed and drained
1 bunch Swiss chard, stems finely chopped, leaves roughly chopped
Salt and ground black pepper
Lemon wedges, to serve

1. Move slider to AIR FRY/STOVETOP. Select SEAR/SAUTÉ and set to 3. Select START/STOP to begin cooking. Add the oil and heat until shimmering, then add the onion and cook, stirring occasionally, until softened, about 3 minutes. 2. Pour in the tomato paste and cook for about 2 minutes, stirring, until the paste begins to brown. Stir in the garlic, cumin, coriander, allspice and pepper flakes, then cook until fragrant, about 30 seconds. Stir in the stock, the tomatoes with their juices and the chickpeas, then distribute in an even layer. 3. Press START/STOP to turn off the SEAR/SAUTÉ function. 4. Close the lid and move slider to PRESSURE. Ensure the pressure release valve is in the SEAL position. The temperature will default to HIGH, which is the correct setting. Set time to 50 minutes. Select START/STOP to begin cooking. 5. When cooking is complete, naturally release the pressure for 15 minutes. Then turn the pressure relief valve to the VENT position for quick pressure relief. Move slider to AIR FRY/ STOVETOP to unlock the lid, then carefully open it. 6. Select SEAR/SAUTÉ and set the heat to Hi5, bring the mixture to a simmer. Cook for about 5 minutes and stir occasionally, until slightly thickened. Add the chard and continue to cook, stirring occasionally, until the chard is tender, about 5 minutes. 7. Press START/STOP to turn off the pot, then taste and season with salt and pepper. Serve with lemon wedges.
Per Serving: Calories 322; Fat 5.44g; Sodium 266mg; Carbs 54.52g; Fibre 11.8g; Sugar 13.22g; Protein 18.36g

Hearty Cranberry Beans with Spanish Chorizo & Red Cabbage

Prep Time: 15 minutes | Cook Time: 52 minutes | Serves: 6

455 g dried cranberry beans (see note), rinsed and drained
Salt and ground black pepper
½ teaspoon baking soda
2 tablespoons extra-virgin olive oil
150 g Spanish chorizo, casing removed, quartered lengthwise and sliced 1 cm thick
1 large yellow onion, finely chopped
1 tablespoon sweet paprika
1 teaspoon smoked paprika
½ teaspoon red pepper flakes
1 teaspoon dried oregano
1.5 L low-sodium chicken stock
½ small head red cabbage, cored and finely chopped

1. Combine together the beans, 2 teaspoons salt, the baking soda and 1.4 L water in the pot. Close the lid and move slider to PRESSURE. Ensure the pressure release valve is in the SEAL position. The temperature will default to HIGH, which is the correct setting. Set time to 5 minutes. Select START/STOP to begin cooking. 2. When cooking is complete, turn the pressure relief valve to the VENT position for quick pressure relief. Move slider to the right to unlock the lid, then carefully open it. 3. Using potholders, carefully remove the pot from the housing and drain the beans in a colander; return the pot to the housing. Rinse the beans under cool water; set aside. 4. Move slider to AIR FRY/STOVETOP. Select SEAR/SAUTÉ and set to 3. Select START/STOP to begin cooking. Add the oil and chorizo and cook, stirring occasionally, until the chorizo releases its fat and begins to brown, about 5 minutes. Add the onion and cook, stirring occasionally, until the onion is lightly browned, 6 to 8 minutes. Stir in both paprikas, the pepper flakes and oregano, then cook until fragrant, about 30 seconds. 5. Stir in the stock and beans, then distribute in an even layer. Press START/STOP to turn off the SEAR/SAUTÉ function. 6. Close the lid and move slider to PRESSURE. Ensure the pressure release valve is in the SEAL position. The temperature will default to HIGH, which is the correct setting. Set time to 25 minutes. Select START/STOP to begin cooking. 7. When the timer beeps, naturally release the pressure for 10 minutes. Then turn the pressure relief valve to the VENT position for quick pressure relief. Move slider to AIR FRY/ STOVETOP to unlock the lid, then carefully open it. 8. Stir the beans, then cook with SEAR/SAUTÉ function again. Stir in the cabbage and cook, stirring occasionally, until the cabbage is tender, 5 to 8 minutes. 9. Press START/STOP to turn off the pot. Let stand for 15 minutes, then taste and season with salt and pepper.
Per Serving: Calories 198; Fat 6.33g; Sodium 346mg; Carbs 30.68g; Fibre 2.4g; Sugar 16.57g; Protein 7.81g

Chinese Vegetable Fried Rice

Prep Time: 10 minutes | Cook Time: 10 minutes | Serves: 4

2 tablespoons olive oil
½ medium white onion, peeled and chopped
1 medium carrot, diced
2 large eggs, lightly beaten

400 g cooked white rice
105 g frozen peas
2 tablespoons soy sauce

1. Move slider to AIR FRY/STOVETOP. Select SEAR/SAUTÉ and set to 3. Select START/STOP to begin preheating. Allow unit to preheat for 2 minutes. After 2 minutes, add oil and heat it up. 2. Add onion and carrot to the pot. Cook for about 5 minutes until the vegetables are soft. Stir occasionally. 3. Move vegetables to side of pot and pour the beaten eggs into the empty spot in the pot. Scramble eggs in the pot for 3 minutes. 4. Pour in rice and peas. Stir and cook for another 2 minutes. 5. Mix in the soy sauce and turn off the SEAR/SAUTÉ function. 6. Serve immediately.
Per Serving: Calories 240; Fat 10.83g; Sodium 138mg; Carbs 29.88g; Fibre 2.3g; Sugar 2.93g; Protein 5.34g

Spanish Rice with Salsa

Prep Time: 15 minutes | Cook Time: 11 minutes | Serves: 6

2 tablespoons olive oil
360 ml dry white rice
2 tablespoons diced onion

480 ml chicken stock
215 g salsa

1. Move slider to AIR FRY/STOVETOP. Select SEAR/SAUTÉ and set to 3. Select START/STOP to begin preheating. Allow unit to preheat for 2 minutes. After 2 minutes, add oil and heat it up. Add in rice and onion. Sauté for 5 minutes, stirring occasionally. 2. Pour stock into the pot and deglaze bottom of the pot. Press START/STOP to turn off the SEAR/SAUTÉ function. 3. Add salsa and mix well. 4. Close lid and set pressure release to Sealing. 5. Close the lid and move slider to PRESSURE. Ensure the pressure release valve is in the SEAL position. The temperature will default to HIGH, which is the correct setting. Set time to 4 minutes. Select START/STOP to begin cooking. 6. When cooking is complete, allow pressure to release naturally for 10 minutes and then quick release remaining pressure, then carefully open it. 7. Fluff rice with a fork and serve.
Per Serving: Calories 353; Fat 10.59g; Sodium 636mg; Carbs 41.25g; Fibre 1.7g; Sugar 2g; Protein 21.47g

Cheesy Black Bean and Corn Quesadillas

Prep Time: 10 minutes | Cook Time: 10 minutes | Serves: 4

½ (375 g) can black beans
½ (375 g) can corn
½ (100 g) can mild diced green chilies

4 tablespoons unsalted butter, divided
8 (25 cm) flour tortillas
105 g grated Mexican-blend cheese

1. Combine together the black beans, corn, and green chilies in a medium bowl. 2. Move slider to AIR FRY/STOVETOP. Select SEAR/SAUTÉ and set to 3. Select START/STOP to begin preheating. Allow unit to preheat for 1 minute. After 1 minute, add 1 tablespoon butter. Once butter is melted, place one tortilla in the pot. 3. Spread one quarter of black bean mixture on top of tortilla. Add 100 g shredded cheese and top with another tortilla. Cook until bottom tortilla starts to brown, about 3 minutes. 4. Carefully flip quesadilla over and continue to cook until the other tortilla has started to brown and the cheese has melted, another 3 minutes. 5. Repeat with three remaining quesadillas, starting with 1 tablespoon butter for each quesadilla. 6. Cut each quesadilla into triangles and serve.
Per Serving: Calories 1166; Fat 46.95g; Sodium 1307mg; Carbs 130.28g; Fibre 20.8g; Sugar 9.7g; Protein 58.67g

Yummy Chipotle Black Beans with Bacon

Prep Time: 15 minutes | Cook Time: 60 minutes | Serves: 6

6 slices bacon, roughly chopped
1 large yellow onion, finely chopped
10 medium garlic cloves, finely chopped
1 tablespoon ground cumin
4 chipotle chilies in adobo, minced, plus 2 tablespoons adobo sauce
60 ml tequila (optional)

1.25 L low-sodium chicken stock
455 g dried black beans, rinsed and drained
Salt and ground black pepper
3 tablespoons lime juice, plus lime wedges to serve
1 tablespoon packed brown sugar
Chopped fresh coriander, to serve

1. Move slider to AIR FRY/STOVETOP. Select SEAR/SAUTÉ and set to 3. Select START/STOP to begin preheating. Allow unit to preheat for 2 minutes. After 2 minutes, add the bacon and cook for 5 to 8 minutes, stirring, until browned and crisp. 2. Using a slotted spoon, transfer to a paper towel–lined plate and set aside. Add the onion to the pot and cook, stirring occasionally, until lightly browned, 6 to 7 minutes. Stir in the garlic and cumin and cook until fragrant, about 30 seconds. 3. Place in the minced chipotle chilies and the tequila (if using) and cook for about 3 minutes, stirring occasionally, until most of the liquid has evaporated. Stir in the stock, beans and 1 teaspoon salt. Press START/STOP to turn off the SEAR/SAUTÉ function. 4. Close the lid and move slider to PRESSURE. Ensure the pressure release valve is in the SEAL position. The temperature will default to HIGH, which is the correct setting. Set time to 35 minutes. Select START/STOP to begin cooking. 5. When cooking is complete, naturally release the pressure for 20 minutes. Then turn the pressure relief valve to the VENT position for quick pressure relief. Move slider to AIR FRY/ STOVETOP to unlock the lid, then carefully open it. 6. Cook with SEAR/SAUTÉ function again and set the heat to Hi5, stirring occasionally, until the liquid is slightly thickened, about 5 minutes. 7. Stir in the adobo sauce, lime juice, sugar and reserved bacon. Taste and season with salt and pepper. 8. Serve sprinkled with coriander and with lime wedges on the side.
Per Serving: Calories 417; Fat 14.43g; Sodium 351mg; Carbs 52.36g; Fibre 10.9g; Sugar 5.81g; Protein 23.09g

Chapter 4 Soup and Salad

Rich Vegan Sweet Potato Soup 42

Creamy Cheddar Broccoli Soup 42

Vegetable and Sausage Soup 42

Mouthwatering Potpie Chicken Soup 42

Beef and Cabbage Rice Soup 43

Homemade Black Bean and Chorizo Soup... 43

Pinto Bean & Squash Soup with Tomato Salsa 43

Quick Stuffed Potato Soup 43

Creamy Mushroom Chicken Soup 44

Easy Chili Mac 44

Sweet Potato and Wild Rice Chowder 44

Hearty Pork and Pinto Bean Stew with Tomatoes 44

Perfect French Onion Soup 45

Smoked Salmon, Leek, and Potato Soup ... 45

Creamy Cheddar Broccoli and Potato Soup ... 45

Simple Spicy Black Bean Soup 45

Nutritious Lamb and Potato Soup 46

Persian Pearled Barley-Lentil Soup with Spinach 46

Thai Coconut Red Lentil Soup 46

Spicy Prawn Soup with White Beans 47

Herbed Kidney Bean and Sausage Soup with Cabbage 47

Thai-Style Curried Butternut Bisque 47

Black-Eyed Peas and Smoked Ham Soup ... 48

Creamy Cheese Tomato Soup with Basil ... 48

Coconut Prawn and Rice Soup 48

Rich Vegan Sweet Potato Soup

Prep Time: 15 minutes | Cook Time: 10 minutes | Serves: 6

4 tablespoons olive oil
1 large leek, white and light green parts only, finely chopped
2 cloves garlic, peeled and minced
½ teaspoon ground cumin
¼ teaspoon smoked paprika
¼ teaspoon ground allspice
¼ teaspoon ground cinnamon
900 g sweet potatoes, peeled and chopped
1.4 L vegetable stock
30 g thinly sliced green spring onions
½ teaspoon salt
½ teaspoon ground black pepper

1. Select SEAR/SAUTÉ. Select Lo3, and then press START/STOP to begin cooking. 2. When the pot is hot, heat the olive oil. Add the leek and garlic, and cook them for 3 minutes until tender; add cumin, paprika, allspice, and cinnamon, and cook them for 30 seconds until fragrant. 3. Stir in the sweet potatoes and stock, and stop the process. 4. Close the lid, turn the pressure release valve to SEAL position, and then move the slider to PRESSURE. Select HI and set the cooking time to 8 minutes. Press START/STOP to begin cooking. When finished, release the pressure naturally. 5. Remove lid and using an immersion blender, or work in batches in a blender, purée soup until smooth. Stir in spring onions, salt, and pepper. 6. Serve hot.
Per Serving: Calories 209; Fat: 9.26g; Sodium: 207mg; Carbs: 29.49g; Fibre: 3.8g; Sugar: 1.98g; Protein: 3.47g

Creamy Cheddar Broccoli Soup

Prep Time: 10 minutes | Cook Time: 25 minutes | Serves: 4

2 tablespoons butter
1 medium sweet onion, peeled and chopped
1 large carrot, peeled and chopped
2 cloves garlic, chopped
1 large bunch broccoli, coarsely chopped
120 ml chardonnay
720 ml chicken stock
1 teaspoon sea salt
½ teaspoon ground black pepper
Pinch of ground nutmeg
120 ml whole milk
100 g sharp Cheddar cheese

1. Select SEAR/SAUTÉ. Select Lo3, and then press START/STOP to begin cooking. 2. When the pot is hot, heat the butter; add onion, carrot, and garlic, and sauté them for 5 minutes until the onions are translucent; add broccoli and sauté them for 3 minutes until broccoli starts to become tender. 3. Add wine, stock, salt, pepper, and nutmeg, and simmer them at Lo1 for 10 minutes. Stop the process. 4. Close the lid, turn the pressure release valve to SEAL position, and then move the slider to PRESSURE. Select HI and set the cooking time to 10 minutes. Press START/STOP to begin cooking. When finished, release the pressure naturally. 5. Add milk and cheese. Purée the soup in the pot with an immersion blender. 6. Ladle into bowls and serve warm.
Per Serving: Calories 305; Fat: 18.58g; Sodium: 1584mg; Carbs: 18.23g; Fibre: 3.5g; Sugar: 11.36g; Protein: 13.15g

Vegetable and Sausage Soup

Prep Time: 15 minutes | Cook Time: 35 minutes | Serves: 4

1 tablespoon olive oil
1 small onion, peeled and diced
1 large carrot, peeled and diced
1 stalk celery, diced
1 small Russet potato, peeled and diced small
455 g smoked sausage, sliced
240 ml lager
720 ml chicken stock
1 tablespoon whole-grain mustard
1 (700 g) can diced tomatoes, including juice
1 small head cabbage, cored and thin chopped
½ teaspoon caraway seeds
½ teaspoon sea salt
½ teaspoon ground black pepper

1. Select SEAR/SAUTÉ. Select Lo3, and then press START/STOP to begin cooking. 2. When the pot is hot, heat olive oil; add onion, carrot, and celery, and sauté them for 3 to 5 minutes until onions are translucent; add potatoes and sausage, and cook them for 3 minutes until the potatoes start to brown. 3. Add lager and deglaze by scraping the brown bits from the edges of the pot; simmer them at Lo1 for 5 minutes. 4. Add stock, mustard, tomatoes, cabbage, caraway seeds, salt, and pepper, and stop the process. 5. Close the lid, turn the pressure release valve to SEAL position, and then move the slider to PRESSURE. Select HI and set the cooking time to 20 minutes. Press START/STOP to begin cooking. When finished, release the pressure naturally. 6. Ladle into bowls and serve warm.
Per Serving: Calories 507; Fat: 25.37g; Sodium: 2292mg; Carbs: 51.66g; Fibre: 12.5g; Sugar: 13.83g; Protein: 28.5g

Mouthwatering Potpie Chicken Soup

Prep Time: 15 minutes | Cook Time: 15 minutes | Serves: 6

3 tablespoons vegetable oil
2 stalks celery, chopped
1 medium onion, peeled and chopped
1 medium carrot, peeled and chopped
2 cloves garlic, peeled and minced
½ teaspoon salt
½ teaspoon ground black pepper
¼ teaspoon dried thyme
3 tablespoons all-purpose flour
720 ml chicken stock
420 g shredded cooked chicken breast
120 g heavy whipping cream
110 g frozen peas
12 round butter crackers, such as Ritz

1. Select SEAR/SAUTÉ. Select Lo3, and then press START/STOP to begin cooking. 2. When the pot is hot, heat the oil; add celery, onion, and carrot, and cook them for 8 minutes until tender; add garlic, salt, pepper, and cook them for 30 seconds until fragrant; sprinkle flour over the vegetables and cook for 1 minute until the flour is completely moistened; slowly whisk in stock, making sure to scrape any bits of the bottom of the pot. 3. Stop the process, and stir in the chicken. 4. Close the lid, turn the pressure release valve to SEAL position, and then move the slider to PRESSURE. Select HI and set the cooking time to 5 minutes. Press START/STOP to begin cooking. When finished, release the pressure quickly. 5. Open lid, stir soup well, and stir in cream and peas. Let stand on the Keep Warm setting for 10 minutes, or until peas are hot and tender. 6. Ladle the dish into bowls and top each bowl with 2 crackers. Serve immediately.
Per Serving: Calories 326; Fat: 16.87g; Sodium: 837mg; Carbs: 17.25g; Fibre: 1.9g; Sugar: 3.83g; Protein: 25.87g

Beef and Cabbage Rice Soup

Prep Time: 15 minutes | Cook Time: 15 minutes | Serves: 8

2 tablespoons vegetable oil
455 g 80% lean beef mince
1 medium yellow onion, peeled and chopped
1 medium carrot, peeled and chopped
1 large head cabbage, cored and chopped
3 cloves garlic, peeled and minced
1 tablespoon light brown sugar
960 ml chicken stock
1 (725 g) can tomato sauce
1 bay leaf
1 teaspoon dried oregano
½ teaspoon paprika
¼ teaspoon crushed red pepper flakes
½ teaspoon salt
½ teaspoon ground black pepper
100 g uncooked white rice

1. Select SEAR/SAUTÉ. Select Lo3, and then press START/STOP to begin cooking. 2. When the pot is hot, heat the oil; add beef mince and cook for 8 minutes until just starting to brown around the edges; add onion and carrot, and cook them for 5 minutes until tender; add the garlic and cabbage, and cook them for 1 minute until fragrant. 3. Stop the process and add the remaining ingredients. 4. Close the lid, turn the pressure release valve to SEAL position, and then move the slider to PRESSURE. Select HI and set the cooking time to 15 minutes. Press START/STOP to begin cooking. When finished, release the pressure naturally. 5. Discard bay leaf. Serve hot.
Per Serving: Calories 253; Fat: 10.46g; Sodium: 786mg; Carbs: 21.74g; Fibre: 4.4g; Sugar: 7.06g; Protein: 18.91g

Homemade Black Bean and Chorizo Soup

Prep Time: 35 minutes | Cook Time: 35 minutes | Serves: 4-6

2 tablespoons olive oil
1 large onion, chopped
1 medium green pepper
4 medium garlic cloves, chopped
2 teaspoons ground cumin
1.2 L store-bought chicken stock, or homemade
240 g dried black beans, picked over and rinsed
65 g sliced dried chorizo
Salt and freshly ground black pepper
1 tablespoon sherry vinegar or red wine vinegar
Optional Garnishes:
Chopped raw onions
Sour cream

1. Select SEAR/SAUTÉ. Select Lo3, and then press START/STOP to begin cooking. 2. When the pot is hot, heat the oil; add onions and peppers, and cook them for 5 minutes until tender. Add the garlic and cumin, and cook them for 45 seconds. 3. Stop the process, and add the stock, beans, chorizo, 1 teaspoon salt, and several grinds of pepper. 4. Close the lid, turn the pressure release valve to SEAL position, and then move the slider to PRESSURE. Select HI and set the cooking time to 30 minutes. Press START/STOP to begin cooking. When finished, release the pressure naturally. 5. Season the soup with the pepper and salt and serve with the optional garnishes, if desired.
Per Serving: Calories 290; Fat: 10.35g; Sodium: 922mg; Carbs: 35.41g; Fibre: 8.2g; Sugar: 3.4g; Protein: 15.33g

Pinto Bean & Squash Soup with Tomato Salsa

Prep Time: 35 minutes | Cook Time: 15 minutes | Serves: 4

160 g dried pinto beans
Salt
1 tablespoon olive oil
1 medium yellow onion, chopped
1 tablespoon chili powder
720 ml store-bought vegetable or chicken stock, or homemade
455 g peeled butternut squash cubes (2.5 cm cubes)
125 g frozen corn
220 g fresh tomato salsa

1. Place the beans in a large bowl, add cold water and 1 teaspoon salt, and then soak at room temperature for 8 hours. Or you can boil them in several cups of water with 1 teaspoon salt for 2 minutes. Remove them from the heat, cover, and set aside for 1 hour. 2. Drain and rinse the beans. 3. Select SEAR/SAUTÉ. Select Lo3, and then press START/STOP to begin cooking. 4. When the pot is hot, heat the oil, add onion and chili powder, and cook them for 4 minutes until tender. 5. Stop the process, and add drained beans, stock, squash, corn, and ½ teaspoon salt to the pot. 6. Close the lid, turn the pressure release valve to SEAL position, and then move the slider to PRESSURE. Select LO and set the cooking time to 6 minutes. Press START/STOP to begin cooking. When finished, release the pressure naturally. 7. Break up the largest chunks of squash, add salsa to the pot, and simmer them at Lo1 on SEAR/SAUTÉ mode for 2 minutes. 8. Serve and enjoy.
Per Serving: Calories 310; Fat: 6.11g; Sodium: 690mg; Carbs: 47.88g; Fibre: 10.9g; Sugar: 6.52g; Protein: 17.2g

Quick Stuffed Potato Soup

Prep Time: 20 minutes | Cook Time: 10 minutes | Serves: 4

1 tablespoon safflower oil
1 large yellow onion, chopped
1.2 kg russet potatoes (3 large), peeled and cut into 2.5 – 3 cm chunks
600 ml store-bought chicken or vegetable stock
Salt and freshly ground black pepper
120 g sour cream
150 g grated sharp cheddar cheese
4 slices thick-cut bacon, cooked and crumbled
4 green onions, thinly sliced

1. Select SEAR/SAUTÉ. Select Lo3, and then press START/STOP to begin cooking. 2. When the pot is hot, heat the oil, and then sauté the onion for 5 minutes until tender. 3. Stop the process, and add the potatoes, stock, and ¾ teaspoon salt to the pot. 4. Close the lid, turn the pressure release valve to SEAL position, and then move the slider to PRESSURE. Select HI and set the cooking time to 5 minutes. Press START/STOP to begin cooking. When finished, release the pressure quickly. 5. Remove the lid, add the sour cream and 75 g of the cheese, and stir gently with a rubber spatula until the cheese has melted and the largest chunks of potato are broken down into bite-size pieces. Season the dish with salt and pepper. 6. Serve garnished with the bacon, remaining cheese, and the green onions.
Per Serving: Calories 671; Fat: 36.17g; Sodium: 1176mg; Carbs: 64.77g; Fibre: 4.9g; Sugar: 4.37g; Protein: 24.03g

Creamy Mushroom Chicken Soup

Prep Time: 15 minutes | Cook Time: 25 minutes | Serves: 4

455 g chicken thighs cut in 1 cm cubes
1 teaspoon sea salt
½ teaspoon ground black pepper
2 tablespoons butter
1 small onion, peeled and diced
1 large carrot, peeled and diced
1 stalk celery, diced
200 g sliced mushrooms
960 ml chicken stock
2 teaspoons dried thyme
1 teaspoon dried oregano
1 teaspoon garlic powder
¼ teaspoon cayenne pepper
120 g heavy cream

1. Season the chicken thigh cubes with salt and pepper. Set aside. 2. Add the butter to the pot. Select SEAR/SAUTÉ. Select Lo3, and then press START/STOP to begin cooking. 3. When the butter melted, add the chicken, onion, carrot, celery, and mushrooms, and sauté them for 3 to 5 minutes until the onions are translucent. 4. Stop the process, and add the stock, thyme, oregano, garlic powder, and cayenne pepper. 5. Close the lid, turn the pressure release valve to SEAL position, and then move the slider to PRESSURE. Select HI and set the cooking time to 20 minutes. Press START/STOP to begin cooking. When finished, release the pressure quickly. 6. Stir in heavy cream. Ladle into bowls and serve warm.
Per Serving: Calories 517; Fat: 37.42g; Sodium: 2496mg; Carbs: 22.33g; Fibre: 1.2g; Sugar: 3.25g; Protein: 23.82g

Easy Chili Mac

Prep Time: 25 minutes | Cook Time: 15 minutes | Serves: 4

1 tablespoon olive oil
455 g 95% lean beef mince
1 medium yellow onion, chopped
1 can crushed fire-roasted tomatoes
1 can kidney beans, drained
100 g elbow macaroni
240 ml store-bought beef stock
2 tablespoons plus 1½ teaspoons mild chili powder
Salt and freshly ground black pepper
Optional Garnishes:
200 g grated cheddar
240 g sour cream or homemade yogurt

1. Add the oil to the pot. Select SEAR/SAUTÉ. Select Lo3, and then press START/STOP to begin cooking. 2. When the oil is hot, add the beef and onions and cook them for 10 minutes until they begin to brown, leaving the beef in fairly large (2.5 cm) chunks for the best texture. 3. Stop the process, and add the tomatoes, beans, macaroni, stock, chili powder, ½ teaspoon salt, and several grinds of pepper to the pot. 4. Close the lid, turn the pressure release valve to SEAL position, and then move the slider to PRESSURE. Select HI and set the cooking time to 5 minutes. Press START/STOP to begin cooking. When finished, release the pressure naturally. 5. Season the dish with salt and pepper, or garnish the dish with the garnishes if desired. Enjoy.
Per Serving: Calories 495; Fat: 20.78g; Sodium: 434mg; Carbs: 38.83g; Fibre: 6.1g; Sugar: 7.32g; Protein: 38.2g

Sweet Potato and Wild Rice Chowder

Prep Time: 20 minutes | Cook Time: 45 minutes | Serves: 4

1 (455 g) bag frozen corn
1 large (300 g) sweet potato, peeled and chopped
1 medium yellow onion, chopped
2 celery ribs, chopped
100 g wild rice
1 teaspoon poultry seasoning
Salt and freshly ground black pepper

1. Combine the stock, corn, sweet potato, onion, celery, wild rice, and poultry seasoning in the pot. 2. Close the lid, turn the pressure release valve to SEAL position, and then move the slider to PRESSURE. Select HI and set the cooking time to 40 minutes. Press START/STOP to begin cooking. When finished, release the pressure naturally. 3. Select SEAR/SAUTÉ. Select Lo1, and then press START/STOP to begin cooking. Simmer the dish for 5 minutes more until bubbly and thickened slightly 4. Season the dish with salt and pepper and serve.
Per Serving: Calories 308; Fat: 2.08g; Sodium: 75mg; Carbs: 64.18g; Fibre: 8g; Sugar: 11.02g; Protein: 9.25g

Hearty Pork and Pinto Bean Stew with Tomatoes

Prep Time: 20 minutes | Cook Time: 35 minutes | Serves: 6

455 g dried pinto beans, rinsed and drained
Salt and ground black pepper
½ teaspoon baking soda
1 teaspoon ground cumin
4 medium garlic cloves, thinly sliced
1 habanero chili, pierced a few times with a paring knife
1 tablespoon grated lime zest, plus 60 ml lime juice
2 tablespoons grated orange zest, plus 120 ml orange juice
700 g can diced fire-roasted tomatoes
3 tablespoons finely chopped coriander stems, plus 30 g lightly packed leaves, reserved separately
680 g boneless country-style pork ribs, trimmed and cut into 2.5 cm chunks
Sliced radishes, to serve

1. Stir together the beans, 2 teaspoons salt, the baking soda and 1.4 L water in the pot, then distribute in an even layer. 2. Close the lid, turn the pressure release valve to SEAL position, and then move the slider to PRESSURE. Select HI and set the cooking time to 5 minutes. Press START/STOP to begin cooking. When finished, release the pressure quickly. 3. Using potholders to carefully remove the pot from the unit and drain the beans in a colander; return the pot to the unit. 4. Rinse the beans under cool water and return to the pot. Stir in the cumin, garlic, habanero, lime zest and juice, orange zest and juice, the tomatoes with their juices, the coriander stems and the pork. Add 480 ml water; stir to combine, then distribute in an even layer. 5. Cook the dish at HI for 25 minutes on PRESSURE COOK mode, and release the pressure naturally. 6. Remove and discard the habanero. Let the dish stand for about 10 minutes, then taste and season with salt and pepper. Serve topped with the coriander leaves and sliced radishes.
Per Serving: Calories 491; Fat: 7.92g; Sodium: 358mg; Carbs: 63.44g; Fibre: 14.8g; Sugar: 12.43g; Protein: 41.65g

Perfect French Onion Soup

Prep Time: 10 minutes | Cook time: 30 minutes | Serves: 4

1 tablespoon olive oil
1.2 kg medium yellow onions, halved and sliced through root end
1 tablespoon balsamic vinegar
4 medium garlic cloves, chopped
1 teaspoon chopped fresh thyme, or ½ teaspoon dried
120 ml dry sherry or vermouth
1.68 L Homemade Beef Stock
Salt and freshly ground black pepper
125 g aged Gruyère cheese, grated, rind reserved
½ loaf French baguette

1. Put the oil in the pot, move slider to AIR FRY/STOVETOP. Select SEAR/SAUTÉ and set to Hi 5. When the oil is hot, add half of the onions and cook, stirring often, until they begin to brown, 8 minutes. 2. Add the remaining onions and vinegar and continue to cook, stirring occasionally, until there is a deep brown glaze on the bottom of the pot, 4 minutes. 3. Add the garlic and thyme and cook until fragrant, 45 seconds. Place in the vermouth and simmer for 1 minute, scraping up the browned residue from the base of the pot. Press START/STOP. 4. Add the stock, ½ teaspoon salt, and several grinds of pepper. Add the Gruyère rind to the pot. 5. Close the lid and move slider to PRESSURE, Ensuring the pressure release valve is in the SEAL position. The temperature will default to HIGH, which is the correct setting. Set time to 8 minutes. Select START/STOP to begin cooking. 6. When the cooking time is complete, release the pressure quickly by turning the pressure release valve to the VENT position. Move slider to the right to unlock the lid, then carefully open it. Discard the cheese rind and season the soup with salt and pepper. 7. Meanwhile, prepare the French baguette: Line a baking sheet with foil and adjust the oven rack so that it is 2 to 3 inches from the grilling element. 8. Cut the baguette at an angle into 2 cm-thick slices. Place the bread slices on the baking sheet. Carefully sprinkle 100 g of the grated cheese on the bread, and grill until the cheese is browned and bubbly, 3 minutes. 9. Ladle the soup into large soup bowls, top with the cheese toasts, and sprinkle the remaining cheese over the top. Serve.
Per Serving: Calories 753; Fat 45.52g; Sodium 1220mg; Carbs 75.27g; Fibre 6.9g; Sugar 23g; Protein 12.24g

Smoked Salmon, Leek, and Potato Soup

Prep Time: 10 minutes | Cook time: 15 minutes | Serves: 6

455 g leeks (3 large)
2 tablespoons butter
960 ml store-bought chicken or vegetable stock, or homemade
3 large russet potatoes, peeled and cut into 5 cm chunks
2 bay leaves
Salt and freshly ground black pepper
120 g whipping cream
250 g hot-smoked wild salmon, skin and bones discarded, at room temperature

1. Trim the toughest green part and root end from the leeks and discard. Halve the leeks lengthwise, rinse thoroughly under cold water to remove grit between the layers, and chop. 2. Add the butter to the pot, move slider to AIR FRY/STOVETOP. Select SEAR/SAUTÉ and set to 3. Open lid and select START/STOP to begin cooking. 3. When the butter has melted, place in the leeks. Cover with a regular pot lid and sauté, stirring occasionally, until the leeks are tender, 4 minutes. (The lid traps steam, melting the leeks without browning them.) Press START/STOP. 4. Add the stock, bay leaves, potatoes, and ½ teaspoon salt and stir to combine. 5. Close the lid and move slider to PRESSURE function. Ensuring the pressure release valve is in the SEAL position. The temperature will default to HIGH, which is the correct setting. Set time to 10 minutes. Select START/STOP to begin cooking. 6. When cooking is complete, release the pressure quickly by turning the pressure release valve to the VENT position. Move slider to the right to unlock the lid, then carefully open it. Using an immersion blender, blend the soup in the pot until mostly smooth. 7. Alternatively, blend the soup in batches in a standing blender with the lid slightly ajar and a towel draped over the lid to prevent splatters. Season with the pepper and salt, keeping in mind that the salmon is salty. 8. Divide the soup among six bowls. Flake the salmon and place small mounds of it on top of each bowl of soup.
Per Serving: Calories 430; Fat 16.37g; Sodium 801mg; Carbs 51.92g; Fibre 4.7g; Sugar 8.06g; Protein 20.83g

Creamy Cheddar Broccoli and Potato Soup

Prep Time: 10 minutes | Cook time: 15 minutes | Serves: 4

1 tablespoon olive oil
1 medium yellow onion, chopped
455 g broccoli crowns, florets left in 8 cm pieces, stems sliced
480 ml store-bought vegetable or chicken stock, or homemade
1 large russet potato, peeled and chopped
Salt and freshly ground black pepper
120 g whipping cream, warmed
50 g grated aged cheddar cheese
½ to ¾ teaspoon freshly grated nutmeg

1. Put the oil in the pot, move slider to AIR FRY/STOVETOP. Select SEAR/SAUTÉ and set to 3. Select START/STOP to begin preheating. When the oil is hot, add the onion and cook, stirring often, until beginning to brown, 4 minutes. Press START/STOP. 2. Add the broccoli, potatoes, ½ teaspoon salt, a few grinds of pepper, and stock and stir to combine. 3. Close the lid and move slider to PRESSURE function, Ensuring the pressure release valve is in the SEAL position. The temperature will default to HIGH, which is the correct setting. Set time to 10 minutes. Select START/STOP to begin cooking. 4. When the cooking time is up, let the pressure come down naturally for 10 minutes and then quick-release the remaining pressure. 5. Add the cream and cheese and whisk to combine and break up the vegetables. 6. Season the soup with the nutmeg and additional salt and pepper.
Per Serving: Calories 288; Fat 14.4g; Sodium 859mg; Carbs 32.08g; Fibre 5.6g; Sugar 6.43g; Protein 10.93g

Simple Spicy Black Bean Soup

Prep Time: 10 minutes | Cook time: 8 minutes | Serves: 4

690 g drained Simple Black Beans, plus 720 ml cooking liquid
1 chipotle chili in adobo, minced
20 g finely chopped fresh coriander
2 tablespoons lime juice
Salt and ground black pepper

1. In a large saucepan over medium, combine the beans, the 720 ml cooking liquid and the chipotle chili. Cook, stirring often, until heated through, 5 to 8 minutes. 2. Off heat, stir in the coriander and lime juice. Taste and season with salt and pepper.
Per Serving: Calories 236; Fat 1.06g; Sodium 23mg; Carbs 43.89g; Fibre 15.5g; Sugar 0.77g; Protein 15.63g

Nutritious Lamb and Potato Soup

Prep Time: 15 minutes | Cook Time: 32 minutes | Serves: 6

2 medium garlic cloves, peeled and minced (2 teaspoons)
1 teaspoon dried thyme
1 teaspoon dried oregano
½ teaspoon ground dried turmeric
¼ teaspoon grated nutmeg
½ teaspoon table salt
2 tablespoons olive oil
455 g boneless leg of lamb, any large pieces of fat removed, the meat cut into 2.5 cm pieces
1 medium red onion, chopped
2 L chicken stock
455 g medium parsnips, peeled and cut into 2.5 cm pieces
455 g small yellow potatoes such as Yukon Golds, none larger than a golf ball, each quartered
10 g loosely packed fresh coriander leaves, finely chopped

1. In a large bowl, mix together the lamb, garlic, thyme, turmeric, oregano, nutmeg, and salt until the meat is evenly coated. Set aside for 10 minutes. 2. Move slider to AIR FRY/STOVETOP. Select SEAR/SAUTÉ and set to 3. Select START/STOP to begin preheating. Allow unit to preheat for 2 minutes. After 2 minutes, warm the oil in the pot for one minute. Add the onion and cook, stirring frequently, until it just begins to soften, about 4 minutes. Add the lamb and every speck of its rub. Cook, stirring often, until the lamb loses its raw, pink colour, about 3 minutes. 3. Pour in the stock, press START/STOP to turn off the SEAR/SAUTÉ function, and scrape up any browned bits on the pot's bottom. 4. Close the lid and move slider to PRESSURE. Ensure the pressure release valve is in the SEAL position. The temperature will default to HIGH, which is the correct setting. Set time to 15 minutes. Select START/STOP to begin cooking. 5. When cooking is complete, turn the pressure relief valve to the VENT position for quick pressure relief. Move slider to the right to unlock the lid, then carefully open it. Stir in the parsnips and potatoes. Lock the lid back onto the pot. Still cook on high pressure for 7 minutes. 6. Again, use the quick-release method to bring the pot's pressure back to normal. Open the lid and stir in the coriander, then set the lid askew over the pot for 5 minutes to blend the flavours. Stir well before serving.
Per Serving: Calories 281; Fat 9.89g; Sodium 1496mg; Carbs 30.44g; Fibre 3.9g; Sugar 17.57g; Protein 19.48g

Persian Pearled Barley-Lentil Soup with Spinach

Prep Time: 20 minutes | Cook time: 6 hours 20 minutes | Serves: 4

2 tablespoons extra-virgin olive oil, plus more to serve
1 medium yellow onion, chopped
6 medium garlic cloves, finely chopped
2 medium carrots, peeled, quartered lengthwise and sliced 1 cm thick
2 tablespoons tomato paste
4 bay leaves
Salt and ground black pepper
1 tablespoon grated lime zest, plus 3 tablespoons lime juice, plus lime wedges to serve
160 g pearled barley
100 g brown or green lentils
1.5 L low-sodium vegetable stock
75 g lightly packed baby spinach, chopped
35 g lightly packed fresh coriander, chopped

1. Move slider to AIR FRY/STOVETOP. Select SEAR/SAUTÉ and set to Hi 5. Select START/STOP to begin preheating. 2. Add the oil and heat until shimmering. Add the onion, garlic, carrots, tomato paste, bay leaves and 1 teaspoon salt. Cook and stir occasionally, until the vegetables begin to brown, about 5 minutes. Stir in the lime zest and juice, lentils, barley and stock, scraping up any browned bits, then distribute in an even layer. Press START/STOP. 3. Close the lid and move slider to PRESSURE. Ensuring the pressure release valve is in the SEAL position. The temperature will default to HIGH, which is the correct setting. Set time to 15 minutes. Select START/STOP to begin cooking. 4. When cooking is complete, release the pressure quickly by turning the pressure release valve to the VENT position. Move slider to the right to unlock the lid, then carefully open it. 5. With the pot still on SEAR/SAUTÉ function, bring the mixture to a boil. Press START/STOP. 6. Lock the lid in place and move the pressure valve to Vent. Select Slow Cook and set the temperature to Lo. Set the cooking time for 6 hours; the soup is done when the barley and lentils are fully tender. Press START/STOP, then carefully open the pot. 7. Remove and discard the bay, then stir in the spinach and coriander. Taste and season with salt and pepper. 8. Serve drizzled with oil and with lime wedges on the side.
Per Serving: Calories 396; Fat 5.71g; Sodium 962mg; Carbs 74.66g; Fibre 17.5g; Sugar 12.12g; Protein 19.73g

Thai Coconut Red Lentil Soup

Prep Time: 10 minutes | Cook time: 25 minutes | Serves: 6

2 tablespoons olive oil
2 stalks celery, sliced
1 medium white onion, peeled and chopped
2 medium carrots, peeled and sliced
2 cloves garlic, minced
1 teaspoon minced ginger
1 tablespoon Thai red curry paste
½ teaspoon ground coriander
½ teaspoon ground cumin
¼ teaspoon cayenne pepper
¼ teaspoon smoked paprika
½ teaspoon salt
400 g dried green lentils
1 large russet potato, peeled and cubed
960 ml Roasted Vegetable Stock
1 can full-fat coconut milk
2 tablespoons fresh lime juice
2 tablespoons chopped fresh coriander
½ teaspoon black pepper

1. Move slider to AIR FRY/STOVETOP. Select SEAR/SAUTÉ and set to 3. Select START/STOP to begin preheating. 2. Heat the oil and add celery, onion, and carrots and cook until just tender, about 3 minutes. 3. Add garlic, ginger, cumin, curry paste, coriander, cayenne pepper, paprika, and salt. Cook until fragrant, about 30 seconds. Press the START/STOP button. 4. Add lentils, stock, potato, and coconut milk to pot and stir well. 5. Close the lid, move slider to PRESSURE. Ensuring the pressure release valve is in the SEAL position. The temperature will default to HIGH, which is the correct setting. Set time to 20 minutes. Select START/STOP to begin cooking. 6. When the time is up, let pressure release naturally, about 15 minutes. Remove lid and stir in lime juice. 7. Serve warm with coriander and black pepper for garnish.
Per Serving: Calories 349; Fat 22.6g; Sodium 595mg; Carbs 34.05g; Fibre 5.7g; Sugar 6.05g; Protein 8.6g

Spicy Prawn Soup with White Beans

Prep Time: 15 minutes | Cook Time: 35 minutes | Serves: 4

2 tablespoons unsalted butter
2 stalks celery, finely chopped
1 medium sweet onion, peeled and finely chopped
1 medium green pepper, seeded and finely chopped
1 clove garlic, peeled and minced
½ teaspoon seafood seasoning
½ teaspoon dried thyme
½ teaspoon ground black pepper
1 bay leaf
160 g dried cannellini beans, soaked overnight in water to cover and drained
960 ml chicken stock
455 g small peeled and deveined Prawn
125 g frozen or fresh corn kernels
¼ teaspoon hot sauce

1. Select SEAR/SAUTÉ. Select Lo3, and then press START/STOP to begin cooking. 2. When the pot is hot, melt the butter; add celery, onion, and green pepper and cook them for 5 minutes until just tender; add garlic, seafood seasoning, thyme, black pepper, and bay leaf, and cook them for 1 minute. 3. Stop the process, and add beans and stock to the pot. 4. Close the lid, turn the pressure release valve to SEAL position, and then move the slider to PRESSURE. Select HI and set the cooking time to 30 minutes. Press START/STOP to begin cooking. When finished, release the pressure naturally. 5. Open lid, remove bay leaf, and stir in prawn and corn. Simmer them at Lo1 on SEAR/SAUTÉ mode for 5 to 8 minutes until prawn are opaque. 6. Drizzle the dish with hot sauce before serving.
Per Serving: Calories 222; Fat: 6.32g; Sodium: 1618mg; Carbs: 21.48g; Fibre: 2.9g; Sugar: 7.73g; Protein: 20.09g

Herbed Kidney Bean and Sausage Soup with Cabbage

Prep Time: 15 minutes | Cook time: 45 minutes | Serves: 6

225 g Italian sausage
1 large yellow onion, peeled and chopped
180 g roughly chopped cabbage
2 cloves garlic, peeled and minced
1 teaspoon ground fennel
½ teaspoon dried oregano
1 teaspoon smoked paprika
455 g dried kidney beans, soaked overnight in water to cover and drained
4 sprigs fresh thyme
10 g roughly chopped fresh flat-leaf parsley
1.9 L water
½ teaspoon salt

1. Add sausage to the pot of your Ninja XL Pressure Cooker. Move slider to AIR FRY/STOVETOP. Select SEAR/SAUTÉ and set to Lo1. Select START/STOP to begin cooking, crumbling into 1 cm pieces, until sausage is browned, about 8 minutes. 2. Add onion and cook, stirring often, until tender, about 5 minutes. Add cabbage, garlic, oregano, fennel, and paprika and cook 2 minutes until garlic and spices are fragrant. 3. Add beans, thyme, and chopped parsley to pot and toss to coat in onion and spices. Add water, then press the START/STOP button. 4. Close the lid and move slider to PRESSURE. Ensuring the pressure release valve is in the SEAL position. 5. The temperature will default to HIGH, which is the correct setting. Set time to 30 minutes. Select START/STOP to begin cooking. 6. When the time is up, let pressure release naturally, about 15 minutes. Uncover, remove thyme sprigs, stir in salt, and serve hot.
Per Serving: Calories 167; Fat 11.05g; Sodium 553mg; Carbs 10.34g; Fibre 2.6g; Sugar 1.87g; Protein 9.37g

Thai-Style Curried Butternut Bisque

Prep Time: 10 minutes | Cook time: 20 minutes | Serves: 2-4

360 ml canned coconut milk (do not shake the can before opening)
1 tablespoon rapeseed oil
1 medium yellow onion, chopped
1 tablespoon red curry paste
1 medium butternut squash, seeded, peeled, and cut into large (4 cm) chunks
240 ml store-bought chicken or vegetable stock, or homemade
1 tablespoon fish sauce or soy sauce, plus more to taste
Salt and freshly ground black pepper
Optional Garnishes:
10 g fresh coriander leaves, chopped
30 g roasted unsalted peanuts, chopped

1. Set aside 2 tablespoons of the thick coconut milk from the top of the can for garnishing the soup. 2. Add oil to the pot. Move slider to AIR FRY/STOVETOP. Select SEAR/SAUTÉ and set to 3. Select START/STOP to begin preheating. Place in the onion when the oil is hot. Cook and stir often, until beginning to brown, 6 minutes. Add the curry paste and cook, stirring frequently, until fragrant, 20 seconds. Press START/STOP. 3. Add the squash, remaining coconut milk, the stock, and the fish sauce. Lock on the lid, select the PRESSURE function, Ensuring the pressure release valve is in the SEAL position. The temperature will default to HIGH, which is the correct setting. Set time to 10 minutes. Select START/STOP to begin cooking. 4. When the cooking time is up, quick-release the pressure. 5. Blend the soup with an immersion blender or in batches in a standing blender with the lid slightly ajar and a towel over the top to prevent splatters. 6. Season the soup with more fish sauce, salt, and pepper. 7. Garnish with swirls of the reserved coconut milk and the optional garnishes, if desired.
Per Serving: Calories 541; Fat 48g; Sodium 581mg; Carbs 24.63g; Fibre 6.9g; Sugar 12.24g; Protein 11.31g

Black-Eyed Peas and Smoked Ham Soup

Prep Time: 10 minutes | Cook time: 16 minutes | Serves: 6

2 tablespoons olive oil
2 stalks celery, chopped
1 medium carrot, peeled and chopped
1 medium yellow onion, peeled and chopped
2 cloves garlic, peeled and lightly crushed
½ teaspoon salt
300 g diced smoked ham
455 g dried black-eyed peas, soaked overnight in water to cover and drained
½ teaspoon dried thyme leaves
960 ml ham stock or chicken stock

1. Add oil to the pot. Move slider to AIR FRY/STOVETOP. Select SEAR/SAUTÉ and set to 3. Select START/STOP to begin preheating. 2. Once the oil is hot, add celery, carrot, and onion to pot. Cook until vegetables are very tender, about 5 minutes. 3. Add garlic and salt and cook until fragrant, about 30 seconds. Press the START/STOP button. 4. Add ham, thyme, black-eyed peas, and stock to pot. Close the lid and move slider to PRESSURE. Ensuring the pressure release valve is in the SEAL position. The temperature will default to HIGH, which is the correct setting. Set time to 10 minutes. Select START/STOP to begin cooking. 5. When the time is up, let pressure release naturally, about 15–20 minutes, then open lid and stir well. Serve hot.

Per Serving: Calories 112; Fat 6g; Sodium 922mg; Carbs 10.07g; Fibre 2.7g; Sugar 5.08g; Protein 5.13g

Creamy Cheese Tomato Soup with Basil

Prep Time: 10 minutes | Cook time: 10 minutes | Serves: 4

2 tablespoons olive oil (or the oil from the sun-dried tomato jar)
1 medium yellow onion, chopped
1 can San Marzano–style whole tomatoes, with their juice, roughly chopped
480 ml store-bought chicken or vegetable stock, or homemade
45 g chopped drained oil-packed sun-dried tomatoes
1 tablespoon sherry vinegar
50 g grated Parmigiano Reggiano cheese
120 g whipping cream
Salt and freshly ground black pepper
30 g fresh basil leaves, stacked, rolled into a tight cylinder, and thinly sliced crosswise into ribbons

1. Put the oil in the pot, move slider to AIR FRY/STOVETOP. Select SEAR/SAUTÉ and set to 3. Select START/STOP to begin preheating. When the oil is hot, add the onion and cook, stirring often, until tender, 4 minutes. Press START/STOP. 2. Add the tomatoes and juice, sun-dried tomatoes, stock, and vinegar. Close the lid and move slider to PRESSURE, Ensuring the pressure release valve is in the SEAL position. The temperature will default to HIGH, which is the correct setting. Set time to 5 minutes. Select START/STOP to begin cooking. 3. When cooking is complete, release the pressure quickly by turning the pressure release valve to the VENT position. Move slider to the right to unlock the lid, then carefully open it. 4.Blend the soup with an immersion blender until smooth. Or, in a blender with the lid slightly ajar, blend the soup in batches. Cover the lid with a towel to prevent the soup from splattering. Pour the soup back into the pot. 5. Add the cream and cheese and stir to combine. Season with the pepper and salt. Serve garnished with the basil.

Per Serving: Calories 308; Fat 20.44g; Sodium 995mg; Carbs 23.61g; Fibre 3.4g; Sugar 12.47g; Protein 8.61g

Coconut Prawn and Rice Soup

Prep Time: 10 minutes | Cook Time: 12 minutes | Serves: 6

1 L chicken stock
One can crushed tomatoes
1 medium yellow onion, chopped
240 ml regular or low-fat coconut milk
1 medium green pepper, stemmed, cored, and chopped
2 medium celery stalks, thinly sliced
100 g raw long-grain white rice, preferably jasmine or basmati
Up to 2 small jalapeño chiles, stemmed, seeded, and finely chopped
2 tablespoons packed fresh oregano leaves, minced
675 g medium prawn, peeled and deveined
10 g loosely packed fresh parsley leaves, chopped
2 teaspoons fresh lemon juice

1. Add the stock, tomatoes, coconut milk, onion, pepper, celery, rice, chiles, and oregano to the pot, stir to mix well. 2. Close the lid and move slider to PRESSURE. Ensure the pressure release valve is in the SEAL position. The temperature will default to HIGH, which is the correct setting. Set time to 10 minutes. Select START/STOP to begin cooking. 3. When cooking is complete, turn the pressure relief valve to the VENT position for quick pressure relief. Move slider to the right to unlock the lid, then carefully open it. 4. Move slider to AIR FRY/STOVETOP. Select SEAR/SAUTÉ and set to Lo1. Select START/STOP to begin cooking. 5. Stir the prawn, parsley, and lemon juice into the soup. Continue cooking, stirring often, until the prawn are pink and firm, about 2 minutes. Turn off the SEAR/SAUTÉ function and serve warm.

Per Serving: Calories 342; Fat 8.9g; Sodium 1377mg; Carbs 30.64g; Fibre 2.6g; Sugar 5.53g; Protein 34.11g

Chapter 5 Snacks and Starters

Crispy Cheese Beef Meatballs 50	Crunchy Dill Pickles with Ranch Dip 54
Broccoli, Potato, and Sausage Tots 50	Brie with Cherry Tomatoes 54
Pork Sausage-Stuffed Mushrooms 50	Coconut Chicken Bites 55
Chicken Wings with Honey-Orange Sauce... 50	Sesame Prawn Toasts 55
Easy Boiled Peanuts 51	Quick Avocado Fries with Salsa Fresca 55
Juicy Vinegary Beef Steak 51	Creamy Buffalo Cheese Chicken Dip 55
Classic Reuben Potato Skins 51	Mozzarella Sandwich with Puttanesca Sauce 56
Chinese Vegetable Spring Rolls 51	Spiced Lime Hummus........................... 56
Delicious Hoisin Meatballs with Sesame Seeds 52	Yummy Spicy Black Bean Dip 56
Dill Pickle Dijon Deviled Eggs 52	Cheese Chicken Nacho Scoops 57
Creamy Artichoke Crab Dip 52	Easy Peach Jam 57
Juicy Orange Pulled Pork Sliders 52	Sweet Potato Fries with Sriracha Ranch Sauce 57
Homemade Sour Cream Deviled Eggs with Olives 53	Beef Lentil Sliders 57
Flavourful Turkey Cabbage Dumplings 53	Red Pepper Hummus 58
Crispy Avocado Fries 53	Asian Chicken Coleslaw Noodles Wraps ... 58
Crispy Ranch Potato Chips 53	Savoury Ketchup................................. 58
Authentic Caribbean Chipotle Pork Sliders 54	Creamy Cheese Polenta 59
	Crispy Spicy Potato Chips 59
	Homemade Barbecue Sauce 59

Crispy Cheese Beef Meatballs

Prep Time: 15 minutes | Cook Time: 30 minutes | Serves: 8

320 g beef mince
60 g finely chopped pepperoni
2 large eggs
1 tablespoon Italian seasoning
2 cloves garlic, peeled and minced
50 g gluten-free bread crumbs
20 mini mozzarella balls, known as ciliegine
3 tablespoons olive oil, divided
480 g marinara sauce
480 ml water
20 fresh basil leaves

1. Combine the beef, pepperoni, eggs, Italian seasoning, garlic, and bread crumbs in a medium bowl. Form mixture into twenty meatballs. Press one mozzarella ball into the middle of each meatball, ensuring that meat completely surrounds mozzarella ball. 2. Select SEAR/SAUTÉ. Select Hi5, and then press START/STOP to begin cooking. 3. When the pot is hot, heat the oil for 30 seconds; add the meatballs around the edge of pot, and sear them for 4 minutes. You can cook the meatballs in batches. 4. Remove meatballs from the pot and set aside. 5. Discard extra juice and oil from the pot. 6. Add seared meatballs to a glass dish. Pour marinara sauce over meatballs. 7. Add water to the pot and place in the rack. Place the glass dish on top of the rack. 8. Close the lid, turn the pressure release valve to SEAL position, and then move the slider to PRESSURE. Select HI and set the cooking time to 20 minutes. Press START/STOP to begin cooking. When finished, release the pressure naturally. 9. Remove dish from the pot. 10. Garnish the meatballs with fresh basil leaves. Serve the meatballs with toothpicks so guests can easily retrieve meatballs.
Per Serving: Calories 232; Fat: 13.59g; Sodium: 614mg; Carbs: 15.09g; Fibre: 2.2g; Sugar: 2.84g; Protein: 13.68g

Broccoli, Potato, and Sausage Tots

Prep Time: 15 minutes | Cook Time: 40 minutes | Serves: 10

240 ml water
180 g fresh broccoli florets
295 g shredded russet potatoes, scrubbed
115 g breakfast pork sausage
1 shallot, peeled and finely minced
1 large egg
1 teaspoon dried oregano leaves
½ teaspoon salt

1. Add water to the pot and insert the basket. Add broccoli and potatoes to basket. 2. Close the lid, turn the pressure release valve to SEAL position, and then move the slider to PRESSURE. Select HI and set the cooking time to 2 minutes. Press START/STOP to begin cooking. When finished, release the pressure naturally. 3. Place parchment paper on a baking pan. 4. Transfer broccoli and potatoes to a food processor. Pulse them five times until smooth. 5. Transfer the broccoli-potato mixture to a medium bowl; add sausage, shallot, egg, oregano, and salt, and mix them until well combined. 6. Form the mixture into twenty tots and place on the prepared baking pan. 7. Add the baking pan to the pot. Close the lid and move slider to AIR FRY/STOVETOP, then use the dial to select BAKE/ROAST. Adjust the cooking temperature to 220°C and set the cooking time to 35 minutes. Press START/STOP to begin cooking. 8. Transfer tots to serving dish and serve warm.
Per Serving: Calories 69; Fat: 3.61g; Sodium: 214mg; Carbs: 6.11g; Fibre: 0.7g; Sugar: 0.43g; Protein: 3.3g

Pork Sausage-Stuffed Mushrooms

Prep Time: 10 minutes | Cook Time: 7 minutes | Serves: 10

1 tablespoon olive oil
115 g pork sausage meat
1 tablespoon peeled and finely diced yellow onion
1 tablespoon gluten-free bread crumbs
1 tablespoon prepared horseradish
2 tablespoons cream cheese, room temperature
1 teaspoon yellow mustard
¼ teaspoon garlic salt
240 ml water
200 g whole baby bella mushrooms (approximately 10), stemmed
2 tablespoons chopped fresh Italian flat-leaf parsley

1. Select SEAR/SAUTÉ. Select Hi5, and then press START/STOP to begin cooking. 2. When the pot is hot, heat the oil for 30 seconds; add sausage and onion, and cook them for 5 minutes until sausage is no longer pink. 3. Arrange the mixture to a small bowl and use paper towels to dab off excess oil and fat. 4. Add bread crumbs, horseradish, cream cheese, yellow mustard, and garlic salt. 5. Pour water into the pot. Stuff an equal amount of mixture into each mushroom cap and place in the basket. Insert the basket in pot. 6. Close the lid, turn the pressure release valve to SEAL position, and then move the slider to PRESSURE. Select LO and set the cooking time to 2 minutes. Press START/STOP to begin cooking. When finished, release the pressure quickly. 7. Transfer the mushrooms to a serving dish. Garnish the dish with chopped parsley. 8. Serve warm.
Per Serving: Calories 129; Fat: 5.59g; Sodium: 126mg; Carbs: 18.21g; Fibre: 2.8g; Sugar: 0.95g; Protein: 4.65g

Chicken Wings with Honey-Orange Sauce

Prep Time: 10 minutes | Cook Time: 10 minutes | Serves: 6

70 g honey
60 ml freshly squeezed orange juice
60 ml coconut aminos
1 tablespoon apple cider vinegar
2 tablespoons sriracha
3 cloves garlic, minced
½ teaspoon ground black pepper
900 g chicken wings
1 teaspoon sea salt
240 ml chicken stock

1. Whisk the honey, orange juice, coconut aminos, apple cider vinegar, sriracha, garlic, and black pepper in a large bowl. Set aside. 2. Season the chicken wings with salt. Set aside. 3. Add chicken stock to the pot and place in the basket. Add chicken wings to the basket. Stand up wings if necessary so as to not overcrowd them on top of each other. 4. Close the lid, turn the pressure release valve to SEAL position, and then move the slider to PRESSURE. Select HI and set the cooking time to 10 minutes. Press START/STOP to begin cooking. When finished, release the pressure naturally. 5. Toss the chicken wings in the sauce mixture. Serve.
Per Serving: Calories 247; Fat: 5.49g; Sodium: 676mg; Carbs: 14.27g; Fibre: 0.3g; Sugar: 13.12g; Protein: 33.84g

Easy Boiled Peanuts

Prep Time: 5 minutes | Cook Time: 55 minutes | Serves: 8

455 g raw, unsalted peanuts in the shell
1.4 L water

70 g Salt

1. Rinse and drain the peanuts, and then place them in the pot. 2. Add water and salt. 3. Close the lid, turn the pressure release valve to SEAL position, and then move the slider to PRESSURE. Select HI and set the cooking time to 55 minutes. Press START/STOP to begin cooking. When finished, release the pressure naturally. 4. Strain liquid and transfer peanuts to a serving dish with an additional bowl for the shells. Enjoy.
Per Serving: Calories 339; Fat: 29.12g; Sodium: 3550mg; Carbs: 12.65g; Fibre: 2.8g; Sugar: 5.95g; Protein: 12.59g

Juicy Vinegary Beef Steak

Prep Time: 10 minutes | Cook Time: 40 minutes | Serves: 8

2 tablespoons lime juice
2 tablespoons orange juice
1 tablespoon apple cider vinegar
2 tablespoons honey
1 teaspoon ground cumin
2 small jalapeños, seeded and diced

3 cloves garlic, minced
20 g chopped fresh corinader
3 tablespoons avocado oil, divided
900 g flank steak
360 ml beef stock

1. Combine lime juice, orange juice, apple cider vinegar, honey, cumin, jalapeños, garlic, corinader, and 2 tablespoons avocado oil in a small bowl. Spread mixture on all sides of the beef. 2. Cover the bowl and refrigerate for at least 1 hour or overnight if time allows. 3. Select SEAR/SAUTÉ. Select Hi5, and then press START/STOP to begin cooking. 4. When the pot is hot, heat 1 tablespoon oil; sear the meat for 4 to 5 minutes on each side. 5. Stop the process, and pour in the beef stock. 6. Close the lid, turn the pressure release valve to SEAL position, and then move the slider to PRESSURE. Select HI and set the cooking time to 35 minutes. Press START/STOP to begin cooking. When finished, release the pressure quickly. 7. Remove the meat to a serving platter. Thinly slice and serve.
Per Serving: Calories 245; Fat: 11.06g; Sodium: 122mg; Carbs: 10.59g; Fibre: 0.3g; Sugar: 5.31g; Protein: 25g

Classic Reuben Potato Skins

Prep Time: 15 minutes | Cook Time: 25 minutes | Serves: 10

4 tablespoons olive oil
900 g red potatoes (approximately 10), scrubbed
240 ml chicken stock
2 tablespoons unsalted butter, melted
100 g shredded Swiss cheese

250 g thick-sliced corned beef, chopped
60 g sauerkraut, drained
2 tablespoons Russian dressing, divided
2 teaspoons caraway seeds

1. Use a fork to pierce each potato four times. Set aside. 2. Select SEAR/SAUTÉ. Select Hi5, and then press START/STOP to begin cooking. 3. When the pot is hot, heat the oil for 30 seconds; add the potatoes to the pot, coat them with the oil on all sides, and sauté them for 5 minutes until browned. 4. Stop the process, and pour in the stock. 5. Close the lid, turn the pressure release valve to SEAL position, and then move the slider to PRESSURE. Select HI and set the cooking time to 7 minutes. Press START/STOP to begin cooking. When finished, release the pressure naturally. 6. Transfer the potatoes to a plate. Let them cool for 5 minutes until you can handle them. 7. Cut potatoes in half lengthwise. Scoop out approximately half of the potato, creating a boat. 8. Place boats on a baking sheet lined with parchment paper. Lightly brush potatoes with melted butter. 9. Add the baking sheet to the pot. Close the lid and move slider to AIR FRY/STOVETOP, then use the dial to select BAKE/ROAST. Adjust the cooking temperature to 180°C and set the cooking time to 5 minutes. Press START/STOP to begin cooking. 10. In a small bowl, combine Swiss cheese, corned beef, sauerkraut, and 1 tablespoon Russian dressing. 11. Distribute corned beef mixture among potato halves. Bake skins for an additional 5 minutes. 12. Take the potatoes out of and drizzle with the remaining Russian dressing. Garnish the dish with caraway seeds and serve.
Per Serving: Calories 264; Fat: 14.87g; Sodium: 207mg; Carbs: 16.64g; Fibre: 1.8g; Sugar: 1.94g; Protein: 16.5g

Chinese Vegetable Spring Rolls

Prep Time: 15 minutes | Cook Time: 10 minutes | Serves: 6

90 g shredded cole slaw mix (cabbage and carrots)
2 green onions, thinly sliced
110 g sliced canned bamboo shoots
10 g chopped fresh corinader
2 cloves garlic, peeled and minced
25 g sliced shiitake mushrooms
1 teaspoon honey

1 teaspoon soy sauce
1 teaspoon rice wine vinegar
½ teaspoon fish sauce
½ teaspoon sriracha
¼ teaspoon white pepper
12 (20 cm) spring roll wrappers
480 ml water, divided

1. Combine the cole slaw mix, green onions, bamboo shoots, corinader, garlic, mushrooms, honey, soy sauce, rice wine vinegar, fish sauce, sriracha, and white pepper in a medium bowl. 2. Select SEAR/SAUTÉ. Select Hi5, and then press START/STOP to begin cooking. 3. When the pot is hot, sauté the mixture for 3 to 5 minutes until cabbage is limp. Arrange the mixture to a bowl and set aside. 4. Working one at a time, dip the spring roll wrappers in 120 ml water and place them on a flat surface. 5. Top each wrapper with an equal amount of the cabbage mixture, making a row down the centre. Roll up the wrappers, tuck in the ends, and place side by side in the basket. 6. Add 360 ml water to the pot and place in the basket. 7. Close the lid, turn the pressure release valve to SEAL position, and then move the slider to PRESSURE. Select HI and set the cooking time to 2 minutes. Press START/STOP to begin cooking. When finished, release the pressure naturally. 8. Serve warm.
Per Serving: Calories 213; Fat: 1.34g; Sodium: 429mg; Carbs: 42.56g; Fibre: 2.5g; Sugar: 3.45g; Protein: 7.56g

Delicious Hoisin Meatballs with Sesame Seeds

Prep Time: 15 minutes | Cook Time: 20 minutes | Serves: 6

240 ml dry red wine
3 tbsp. hoisin sauce
2 tbsp. soy sauce
1 large egg, lightly beaten
4 green onions, chopped
40 g finely chopped onion
10 g minced fresh coriander

2 garlic cloves, minced
½ tsp. salt
½ tsp. pepper
455 g minced beef
455 g minced pork
Sesame seeds

1. Add the wine, hoisin sauce and soy sauce to the pot, stir well. Move slider to AIR FRY/STOVETOP. Select SEAR/SAUTÉ and set to Hi5. Select START/STOP to begin preheating. Bring to a boil. Reduce the heat to Lo1; simmer until liquid is reduced slightly. Press START/STOP to turn off the SEAR/SAUTÉ function. 2. In a big bowl, mix together the next seven ingredients. Add beef and pork; mix lightly but thoroughly. Shape into 4 cm meatballs; place in the pot. 3. Close the lid and move the slider to PRESSURE. Ensure the pressure release valve is in the SEAL position. The temperature will default to HIGH, which is the correct setting. Set time to 10 minutes. Select START/STOP to begin cooking. 4. When cooking is complete, turn the pressure release valve to the vent position for a quick pressure release. Move slider to the right to unlock the lid, then carefully open it. 5. Sprinkle with sesame seeds.
Per Serving: Calories 457; Fat 26.6g; Sodium 517mg; Carbs 8.98g; Fibre 1.4g; Sugar 5.48g; Protein 41.41g

Dill Pickle Dijon Deviled Eggs

Prep Time: 15 minutes | Cook Time: 4 minutes | Serves: 6

240 ml cold water
12 large eggs
160 g mayonnaise
4 tsp. dill pickle relish
2 tsp. snipped fresh dill

2 tsp. Dijon mustard
1 tsp. coarsely ground pepper
¼ tsp. garlic powder
⅛ tsp. paprika or cayenne pepper

1. Pour water into the pressure cooker pot. Place the Deluxe Reversible Rack in the lower position in the pot; set eggs on the rack. 2. Close the lid and move the slider to PRESSURE. Ensure the pressure release valve is in the SEAL position. The temperature will default to HIGH, which is the correct setting. Set time to 4 minutes. Select START/STOP to begin cooking. 3. When cooking is complete, naturally release the pressure for 5 minutes. Then quick release pressure by turning the pressure release valve to the VENT position. Move slider to AIR FRY/ STOVETOP to unlock the lid, then carefully open it. Immediately place the eggs in a bowl of ice water to cool. 4. Cut eggs lengthwise in half. Remove yolks, reserving the whites. In a bowl, mash yolks. Stir in all remaining ingredients except paprika. Spoon or pipe into egg whites. 5. Refrigerate, covered, at least 30 minutes before serving. Sprinkle with paprika.
Per Serving: Calories 205; Fat 17.77g; Sodium 271mg; Carbs 4.08g; Fibre 0.7g; Sugar 1.51g; Protein 7.25g

Creamy Artichoke Crab Dip

Prep Time: 10 minutes | Cook Time: 10 minutes | Serves: 8

400 g cream cheese, room temperature
20 g sour cream, room temperature
65 g minced onion
75 g seeded and finely diced red pepper
½ teaspoon Worcestershire sauce
2 teaspoons prepared horseradish
1 teaspoon Old Bay Seasoning

1 teaspoon sriracha
130 g diced canned artichoke hearts
330 g lump crabmeat
2 teaspoons lemon zest
¼ teaspoon ground black pepper
25 g freshly grated Parmesan cheese, divided
480 ml water

1. Cream together cream cheese and sour cream in a medium bowl until smooth. Add remaining ingredients except 10 g Parmesan cheese and 480 ml water and combine. 2. Spoon them into a glass dish. Sprinkle top with remaining cheese. 3. Pour 480 ml water in the pot and place in the rack. Place the dish on the rack. 4. Close the lid, turn the pressure release valve to SEAL position, and then move the slider to PRESSURE. Select HI and set the cooking time to 10 minutes. Press START/STOP to begin cooking. When finished, release the pressure quickly. 5. Serve warm.
Per Serving: Calories 197; Fat: 16.8g; Sodium: 309mg; Carbs: 6.81g; Fibre: 1.3g; Sugar: 2.92g; Protein: 6.01g

Juicy Orange Pulled Pork Sliders

Prep Time: 15 minutes | Cook Time: 50 minutes | Serves: 24

1 boneless pork shoulder roast, halved
2 garlic cloves, minced
½ tsp. lemon-pepper seasoning
1 can unsweetened crushed pineapple, undrained

120 ml orange juice
1 jar mango salsa
24 whole wheat dinner rolls, split

1. Rub the roast with garlic and lemon pepper. Transfer to the pot and top with pineapple and orange juice. 2. Close the lid and move the slider to PRESSURE. Ensure the pressure release valve is in the SEAL position. The temperature will default to HIGH, which is the correct setting. Set time to 50 minutes. Select START/STOP to begin cooking. 3. When cooking is complete, turn the pressure release valve to the vent position for a quick pressure release. Move slider to the right to unlock the lid, then carefully open it. 4. A thermometer inserted in pork should read at least 60°C. 5. Remove the roast and let it cool slightly. Skim the fat from cooking juices. Shred pork with 2 forks. Return pork and cooking juices to the pressure cooker. Stir in salsa; heat through. Serve with rolls.
Per Serving: Calories 545; Fat 5.27g; Sodium 197mg; Carbs 100.97g; Fibre 3.6g; Sugar 87.31g; Protein 25.42g

Homemade Sour Cream Deviled Eggs with Olives

Prep Time: 10 minutes | Cook Time: 5 minutes | Serves: 16

8 large eggs
60 g fat-free mayonnaise
60 g reduced-fat sour cream
2 tbsp. soft bread crumbs
1 tbsp. prepared mustard

¼ tsp. salt
Dash white pepper
4 pimiento-stuffed olives, sliced
Paprika, optional

1. Add 240 ml water to the pot and place the bottom layer of the Deluxe Reversible Rack in the lower position in the pot. Place the eggs on the rack. 2. Close the lid and move the slider to PRESSURE. Ensure the pressure release valve is in the SEAL position. The temperature will default to HIGH, which is the correct setting. Set time to 5 minutes. Select START/STOP to begin cooking. 3. When cooking is complete, naturally release the pressure for 5 minutes. Then quick release pressure by turning the pressure release valve to the VENT position. Move slider to AIR FRY/ STOVETOP to unlock the lid, then carefully open it. 4. Immediately place eggs in a bowl of ice water to cool. Remove shells. 5. Cut eggs lengthwise in half. Remove yolks; refrigerate 8 yolk halves for another use. Set whites aside. 6. Mash the remaining yolks in a small bowl. Stir in sour cream, mayonnaise, bread crumbs, mustard, salt and pepper. Stuff or pipe into egg whites. 7. Garnish with sliced olives. If desired, sprinkle with paprika.
Per Serving: Calories 50; Fat 2.59g; Sodium 97mg; Carbs 4.47g; Fibre 0.4g; Sugar 0.59g; Protein 2.12g

Flavourful Turkey Cabbage Dumplings

Prep Time: 20 minutes | Cook Time: 7 minutes | Serves: 5

45 g finely shredded Chinese or napa cabbage
2 tbsp. minced fresh coriander
2 tbsp. minced chives
1 large egg, lightly beaten
4 tsp. rice vinegar
2 garlic cloves, minced
1½ tsp. sesame oil
½ tsp. salt

½ tsp. ground ginger
½ tsp. Chinese five-spice powder
¼ tsp. grated lemon zest
¼ tsp. pepper
350 g lean minced turkey
30 pot sticker or gyoza wrappers
9 Chinese or napa cabbage leaves
Sweet chili sauce, optional

1. Mix up the first 12 ingredients in a large bowl. Add turkey; mix lightly but thoroughly. 2. Place 1 tbsp. filling in centre of each pot sticker wrapper. Moisten wrapper edge with water. Fold the wrapper over filling and seal edges, pleating the front side several times to form a pleated pouch. 3. Stand dumplings on a work surface to flatten bottoms; curve slightly to form crescent shapes, if desired. 4. Add 240 ml water to the pot. Then place the bottom layer of the Deluxe Reversible Rack in the lower position in the pot. Line the tray with 3 cabbage leaves. Arrange 10 dumplings over cabbage (do not stack). 5. Close the lid and move the slider to PRESSURE. Ensure the pressure release valve is in the SEAL position. The temperature will default to HIGH, which is the correct setting. Set time to 7 minutes. Select START/STOP to begin cooking. 6. When cooking is complete, quick-release pressure. A thermometer inserted in dumpling should read at least 75°C. 7. Transfer dumplings to a serving plate; keep warm. Discard cabbage and cooking juices. Repeat with additional water, remaining cabbage and dumplings. If desired, serve with the chili sauce.
Per Serving: Calories 707; Fat 10.94g; Sodium 1396mg; Carbs 116.55g; Fibre 4.8g; Sugar 2.47g; Protein 33.15g

Crispy Avocado Fries

Prep Time: 10 minutes | Cook Time: 10 minutes | Serves: 2

1 large egg
2 tablespoons whole milk
40g crushed chili corn chips

1 medium avocado, halved, peeled, pitted, and sliced into 12 "fries"
Cooking oil

1. Place the Cook & Crisp Basket in your Pressure Cooker Steam Fryer. 2. Mix egg and milk in a suitable bowl. Add chili corn chip crumbs to a separate shallow dish. 3. Dip avocado slices into egg mixture. Dredge in chip crumbs to coat. 4. Place half of avocado slices in Cook & Crisp Basket greased with cooking oil. 5. Put on the Smart Lid on top of the Ninja Foodi Steam Fryer. 6. Move the Lid Slider to the "Air Fry/ Stovetop". Select the "Air Fry" mode for cooking. 7. Adjust the cooking temperature to 190°C. 8. Cook for 5 minutes. Arrange onto serving plate and repeat with the remaining avocado slices. 9. Serve fries warm.
Per Serving: Calories 275; Fat: 2.2g; Sodium 486mg; Carbs: 27.3g; Fibre: 0.4g; Sugars 17.5g; Protein 36.3g

Crispy Ranch Potato Chips

Prep Time: 10 minutes | Cook Time: 16 minutes | Serves: 2

1 teaspoon dry ranch seasoning mix
½ teaspoon salt
¼ teaspoon black pepper

300g sliced scrubbed fingerling potatoes
2 teaspoons olive oil

1. Place the Cook & Crisp Basket in your Pressure Cooker Steam Fryer. 2. Mix ranch seasoning mix, salt, and pepper in a suitable bowl. Set aside ½ teaspoon for garnish. 3. Toss sliced potatoes with oil in a suitable bowl. Sprinkle with seasoning mix, except reserved ½ teaspoon, to coat. 4. Place chips in ungreased Cook & Crisp Basket. Put on the Smart Lid on top of the Ninja Foodi Steam Fryer. Move the Lid Slider to the "Air Fry/Stovetop". Select the "Air Fry" mode for cooking. 5. Adjust the cooking temperature to 200°C. 6. Cook for 3 minutes. Shake basket. Cook an additional 3 minutes. 7. basket. Cook for 5 minutes. Shake basket once more. Cook an additional 5 minutes. 8. Transfer chips to a suitable bowl. Garnish with remaining seasoning, then let rest 15 minutes before serving.
Per Serving: Calories 385; Fat: 13.2g; Sodium 929mg; Carbs: 31.6g; Fibre: 4.2g; Sugars 2.6g; Protein 36.4g

Chapter 5 Snacks and Starters | 53

Authentic Caribbean Chipotle Pork Sliders

Prep Time: 15 minutes | Cook Time: 75 minutes | Serves: 20

1 large onion, quartered
1 boneless pork shoulder roast
2 chipotle peppers in adobo sauce, finely chopped
3 tbsp. adobo sauce
80 g honey barbecue sauce
Coleslaw:
180 g red cabbage, finely chopped
1 medium mango, peeled and chopped
75 g pineapple tidbits, drained
25 g chopped fresh coriander

60 ml water
4 garlic cloves, minced
1 Tbsp. ground cumin
1 tsp. salt
¼ tsp. pepper

1 tbsp. lime juice
¼ tsp. salt
⅛ tsp. pepper
20 Hawaiian sweet rolls, split and toasted

1. Place onion in the bottom of the pot. Cut roast in half; place over onion. In a small bowl, mix together the barbecue sauce, chipotle peppers, adobo sauce, water, cumin, garlic, salt and pepper; pour over meat. 2. Close the lid and move the slider to PRESSURE. Ensure the pressure release valve is in the SEAL position. The temperature will default to HIGH, which is the correct setting. Set time to 75 minutes. Select START/STOP to begin cooking. 3. When cooking is complete, naturally release the pressure for 10 minutes. Then quick release pressure by turning the pressure release valve to the VENT position. Move slider to AIR FRY/ STOVETOP to unlock the lid, then carefully open it. 4. Remove roast and let cool slightly. Skim fat from cooking juices. If desired, select SEAR/SAUTÉ setting, and adjust for Hi5 heat. Cook the juices until slightly thickened. 5. Shred pork with two forks. Return pork to pressure cooker; stir to heat through. 6. For the coleslaw, combine the cabbage, pineapple, mango, coriander, lime juice, salt and pepper in a big bowl. Place some pork mixture on each roll bottom; top with 2 tbsp. coleslaw. Replace tops.
Per Serving: Calories 405; Fat 14.48g; Sodium 819mg; Carbs 38.82g; Fibre 2.3g; Sugar 25.55g; Protein 29.51g

Crunchy Dill Pickles with Ranch Dip

Prep Time: 10 minutes | Cook Time: 8 minutes | Serves: 4

4 to 6 dill pickles, sliced in half or quartered lengthwise
60g plain flour
2 eggs, beaten
100g plain breadcrumbs
Light Ranch Dip:
60ml reduced-fat: mayonnaise
55g buttermilk
60g non-fat: Greek yogurt
1 tablespoon chopped fresh chives

1 teaspoon salt
⅛ teaspoon cayenne pepper
2 tablespoons fresh dill leaves, dried well
Vegetable oil, in a spray bottle

1 tablespoon chopped fresh parsley
1 tablespoon lemon juice
Salt and black pepper

1. Place the Cook & Crisp Basket in your Pressure Cooker Steam Fryer. 2. Set up your dredging station using three shallow dishes. Add the flour in the first shallow dish. Place the eggs into the second dish. Mix the breadcrumbs, salt, cayenne and fresh dill in a food processor and process until everything is mixed and the crumbs are very fine. Place the crumb mixture in the third dish. 3. Coat the pickles pieces by dredging them first in the flour, then the egg, and then the breadcrumbs, pressing the crumbs on gently with your hands. Set the coated pickles on the Cook & Crisp Basket and grease them on all sides with vegetable oil. 4. Put on the Smart Lid on top of the Ninja Foodi Steam Fryer. 5. Move the Lid Slider to the "Air Fry/Stovetop". Select the "Air Fry" mode for cooking. 6. Cook one layer of pickles at a time at 200°C for 8 minutes, turning them over halfway through the cooking process and spraying again. 7. While the pickles are cooking, make the light ranch dip by mixing everything in a suitable bowl. 8. Serve the pickles warm with the dip on the side.
Per Serving: Calories 353; Fat: 18.5g; Sodium 682mg; Carbs: 2.3g; Fibre: 0.8g; Sugars 1g; Protein 45.8g

Brie with Cherry Tomatoes

Prep Time: 10 minutes | Cook Time: 15 minutes | Serves: 8

1 baguette
680g red and yellow cherry tomatoes
1 tablespoon olive oil
Salt and black pepper
1 teaspoon balsamic vinegar

1 tablespoon chopped fresh parsley
1 (200g) wheel of Brie cheese
Olive oil
½ teaspoon Italian seasoning
1 tablespoon chopped fresh basil

1. Place the Cook & Crisp Basket in your Pressure Cooker Steam Fryer. 2. Start by making the crostini. Slice the baguette diagonally into 1 cm slices and brush the slices with olive oil on both sides. Transfer them into the Cook & Crisp Basket. 3. Put on the Smart Lid on top of the Ninja Foodi Steam Fryer. Move the Lid Slider to the "Air Fry/Stovetop". Select the "Air Fry" mode for cooking. 4. Air fry the baguette slices at 175°C in batches for around 6 minutes or until browned on all sides. Set the bread aside on your serving platter. 5. Toss the cherry tomatoes in a suitable bowl with the olive oil, black pepper and salt. Put on the Smart Lid on top of the Ninja Foodi Steam Fryer. Move the Lid Slider to the "Air Fry/Stovetop". Select the "Air Fry" mode for cooking. 6. Air fry the cherry tomatoes at 175°C for around 3 to 5 minutes, shaking the basket a few times during the cooking process. The tomatoes should be soft and some of them will burst open. Toss the warm tomatoes with the balsamic vinegar and fresh parsley and set aside. 7. Cut a circle of parchment paper the same size as your wheel of Brie cheese. Brush both sides of the Brie wheel with the olive oil and sprinkle with the Italian seasoning, if using. 8. Place the circle of parchment paper on one side of the Brie and transfer the Brie to the Ninja Foodi Pressure Steam Fryer basket, parchment side down. Put on the Smart Lid on top of the Ninja Foodi Steam Fryer. Move the Lid Slider to the "Air Fry/Stovetop". Select the "Air Fry" mode for cooking. 9. Air Fry the brie at 175°C for 10 minutes. Carefully remove the Brie before the rind cracks and the cheese starts to leak out. 10. Transfer the wheel to your serving platter and top with the roasted tomatoes. Sprinkle with basil and serve with the toasted bread slices.
Per Serving: Calories 476; Fat: 37.7g; Sodium 742mg; Carbs: 15.3g; Fibre: 6g; Sugars 5g; Protein 24.8g

Coconut Chicken Bites

Prep Time: 5 minutes | Cook Time: 20 minutes | Serves: 4

2 teaspoons garlic powder
2 eggs
Salt and black pepper to the taste
70g coconut flakes
Cooking spray
455g chicken breasts, skinless, boneless and cubed

1. Place the Cook & Crisp Basket in your Pressure Cooker Steam Fryer. 2. Put the coconut in a suitable bowl and mix the eggs with garlic powder, black pepper and salt in a second one. Dredge the chicken cubes in eggs and then in coconut and arrange them all in the Cook & Crisp Basket. Grease with cooking spray. 3. Put on the Smart Lid on top of the Ninja Foodi Steam Fryer. 4. Move the Lid Slider to the "Air Fry/Stovetop". Select the "Air Fry" mode for cooking. 5. Air Fry at 185°C for around 20 minutes. Arrange the chicken bites on a platter and serve as an appetizer.
Per Serving: Calories 339; Fat: 14g; Sodium 556mg; Carbs: 44.6g; Fibre: 6.4g; Sugars 3.8g; Protein 10.5g

Sesame Prawn Toasts

Prep Time: 10 minutes | Cook Time: 8 minutes | Serves: 6

225g raw prawns, peeled and de-veined
1 egg (or 2 egg whites)
2 spring onions, more for garnish
2 teaspoons grated fresh ginger
1 teaspoon soy sauce
½ teaspoon toasted sesame oil
2 tablespoons chopped fresh coriander or parsley
1 to 2 teaspoons sriracha sauce
6 slices thinly-sliced white sandwich bread (Pepperidge Farm®)
65g sesame seeds
Thai chili sauce

1. Place the Cook & Crisp Basket in your Pressure Cooker Steam Fryer. 2. Mix the prawns, egg, spring onions, fresh ginger, soy sauce, sesame oil, coriander (or parsley) and sriracha sauce in a food processor and process into a chunky paste, scraping down the sides of the food processor bowl as necessary. 3. Cut the crusts off the sandwich bread and generously spread the prawns paste onto each slice of bread. Place the sesame seeds on a plate and invert each prawns toast into the sesame seeds to coat, pressing down gently. Cut each slice of bread into 4 triangles. 4. Transfer one layer of prawn toast triangles to the Cook & Crisp Basket. 5. Put on the Smart Lid on top of the Ninja Foodi Steam Fryer. 6. Move the Lid Slider to the "Air Fry/Stovetop". Select the "Air Fry" mode for cooking. 7. Cook on the "Air Fry" mode at 200°C for 6 to 8 minutes, or until the sesame seeds are toasted on top. 8. Serve warm with a little Thai chili sauce and some sliced spring onions as garnish.
Per Serving: Calories 223; Fat: 10.6g; Sodium 646mg; Carbs: 4.1g; Fibre: 2.4g; Sugars 1.6g; Protein 29.5g

Quick Avocado Fries with Salsa Fresca

Prep Time: 10 minutes | Cook Time: 6 minutes | Serves: 6

60g flour
2 teaspoons salt
2 eggs, beaten
110g panko breadcrumbs
⅛ teaspoon cayenne pepper
¼ teaspoon smoked paprika (optional)
2 large avocados, just ripe
Vegetable oil, in a spray bottle
Quick Salsa Fresca:
150g cherry tomatoes
1 tablespoon-sized chunk of shallot or red onion
2 teaspoons fresh lime juice
1 teaspoon chopped fresh coriander or parsley
Salt and black pepper

1. Place the Cook & Crisp Basket in your Pressure Cooker Steam Fryer. 2. Set up your dredging station with three shallow dishes. Place the flour and salt in the first shallow dish. Place the eggs into the second dish. Mix the breadcrumbs, cayenne pepper and paprika (if using) in the third dish. 3. Cut the avocado in half around the pit and separate the two sides. Slice the avocados into long strips while still in their skin. Run a spoon around the slices, separating them from the avocado skin. Try to keep the slices whole, but don't worry if they break – you can still coat. 4. Coat the avocado slices by dredging them first in the flour, then the egg and then the breadcrumbs, pressing the crumbs on gently with your hands. Set the coated avocado fries on the Cook & Crisp Basket and grease them on all sides with vegetable oil. 5. Put on the Smart Lid on top of the Ninja Foodi Steam Fryer. 6. Move the Lid Slider to the "Air Fry/Stovetop". Select the "Air Fry" mode for cooking. 7. Air-fry the avocado fries, one layer at a time, at 200°C for 6 minutes, turning them over halfway through the cooking time and spraying again if necessary. When the fries are nicely browned on all sides, season with salt and remove. 8. While the avocado fries are cooking, make the salsa fresca by combining everything in a food processor. Pulse several times until the salsa is a chunky purée. 9. Serve the fries warm with the salsa on the side for dipping.
Per Serving: Calories 282; Fat: 15.4g; Sodium 646mg; Carbs: 16.4g; Fibre: 7g; Sugars 6.5g; Protein 22.5g

Creamy Buffalo Cheese Chicken Dip

Prep Time: 10 minutes | Cook Time: 15 minutes | Serves: 6

360 ml water
225 g boneless, skinless chicken breast
200 g cream cheese, cut into cubes
150 g shredded Cheddar cheese, divided
120 ml ranch dressing
5 tablespoons butter
2 tablespoons Worcestershire sauce
1 tablespoon red wine vinegar

1. Pour water into the pot. Then place the bottom layer of the Deluxe Reversible Rack in the lower position in the pot. 2. In a metal bowl, mix together the chicken, cream cheese, 50 g Cheddar cheese, butter, Worcestershire, ranch dressing, and vinegar. 3. Cover the bowl with a paper towel and piece of foil, crimped around the edges. Create a foil sling and lower bowl onto the rack in the pot. 4. Close the lid and move slider to PRESSURE. Ensure the pressure release valve is in the SEAL position. The temperature will default to HIGH, which is the correct setting. Set time to 15 minutes. Select START/STOP to begin cooking. 5. When cooking is complete, naturally release the pressure for 10 minutes. Then turn the pressure relief valve to the VENT position for quick pressure relief. Move slider to AIR FRY/ STOVETOP to unlock the lid, then carefully open it. 6. Carefully lift bowl out of the pot with the foil sling. Remove paper towel and foil from bowl. 7. Remove chicken from bowl and shred with two forks. 8. While dip is still hot, mix in shredded chicken and remaining Cheddar cheese. Stir until combined and cheese is melted.
Per Serving: Calories 466; Fat 41.02g; Sodium 761mg; Carbs 11.86g; Fibre 0.6g; Sugar 4.94g; Protein 13.34g

Mozzarella Sandwich with Puttanesca Sauce

Prep Time: 10 minutes | Cook Time: 8 minutes | Serves: 8

8 slices of sliced white bread (Pepperidge Farm®)
200g mozzarella cheese, sliced
60g plain flour
3 eggs, beaten
170g seasoned panko breadcrumbs
Puttanesca Sauce:
2 teaspoons olive oil
1 anchovy, chopped
2 cloves garlic, minced
1 (350g) can petite diced tomatoes
120ml chicken stock or water
45g Kalamata olives, chopped

½ teaspoon garlic powder
½ teaspoon salt
Black pepper
Olive oil, in a spray bottle

2 tablespoons capers
½ teaspoon dried oregano
¼ teaspoon crushed red pepper flakes
Salt and black pepper
1 tablespoon fresh parsley, chopped

1. Place the Cook & Crisp Basket in your Pressure Cooker Steam Fryer. 2. Start by making the puttanesca sauce. Heat the olive oil in a suitable saucepan on the stovetop. Stir in anchovies and garlic and sauté for around 3 minutes. Stir in the chicken stock, tomatoes, olives, oregano, capers, and crushed red pepper flakes and simmer for around 20 minutes. Season with the black pepper and salt and stir in the parsley. 3. Cut the bread crust. Place four slices of the bread on a cutting board. Lay the cheese on four slices of bread. Lay the remaining four slices of bread on top of the cheese to make small sandwiches, then cut each sandwich into 4 triangles. 4. Set up your dredging station using three shallow dishes. Add the flour in the first shallow dish, the eggs in the second dish and in the third dish, mix the garlic powder, panko breadcrumbs, salt and black pepper. 5. Dredge each little triangle in the flour first and then dip them into the egg. 6. Allow the excess egg to drip off and then press the triangles into the breadcrumb mixture, pressing the crumbs on with your hands so they adhere. Arrange the coated triangles in the freezer for around 2 hours, until the cheese is frozen. 7. Grease all sides of the mozzarella triangles with the oil and arrange a single layer of triangles into the Ninja Foodi Pressure Steam Fryer basket. Put on the Smart Lid on top of the Ninja Foodi Steam Fryer. Move the Lid Slider to the "Air Fry/Stovetop". Select the "Air Fry" mode for cooking. Air fry in batches at 200°C for 5 minutes. 8. Serve with the warm puttanesca sauce.
Per Serving: Calories 371; Fat: 4.9g; Sodium 1207mg; Carbs: 57.5g; Fibre: 25g; Sugars 7g; Protein 25.6g

Spiced Lime Hummus

Prep Time: 10 minutes | Cook Time: 30 minutes | Serves: 6

Garnish:
1 Roma tomato, seeded and small-diced
1 tablespoon red onion, peeled and finely diced
2 tablespoons chopped fresh coriander
1 teaspoon lime juice
Hummus:
90 g dried chickpeas
480 ml water
1 tablespoon tahini paste
2 cloves garlic, peeled and minced
1 tablespoon lime juice

1 clove garlic, peeled and minced
⅛ teaspoon cayenne pepper
⅛ teaspoon salt

1 teaspoon lime zest
¼ teaspoon ground cumin
¼ teaspoon chili powder
¼ teaspoon salt
2 tablespoons olive oil

1. In small bowl, mix the garnish ingredients. Refrigerate covered until ready to use. 2. Add chickpeas and water to the pot. 3. Close the lid and move slider to PRESSURE. Make sure the pressure release valve is in the SEAL position. The temperature will default to HIGH, which is the correct setting. Set time to 30 minutes. Select START/STOP to begin cooking. 4. When cooking is complete, naturally release the pressure for 5 minutes. Then turn the pressure relief valve to the VENT position for quick pressure relief. Move slider to AIR FRY/ STOVETOP to unlock the lid, then carefully open it. 5. Drain the pot and reserve water. 6. Transfer chickpeas to a food processor. Add the tahini paste, garlic, lime juice, lime zest, chili powder, cumin, salt, and olive oil. If consistency is too thick, slowly add reserved water, 1 tablespoon at a time. 7. Transfer the hummus to a serving dish. Garnish with tomato mixture and serve.
Per Serving: Calories 122; Fat 6.29g; Sodium 159mg; Carbs 13.41g; Fibre 2.5g; Sugar 3.26g; Protein 3.94g

Yummy Spicy Black Bean Dip

Prep Time: 15 minutes | Cook Time: 39 minutes | Serves: 6

1 tablespoon olive oil
1 small red onion, peeled and diced
3 cloves garlic, peeled and minced
185 g dried black beans, rinsed
360 ml chicken stock
2 teaspoons chili powder

2 teaspoons ground cumin
1 teaspoon salt
¼ teaspoon cayenne pepper
1 can diced green chiles, including juice
1 can diced tomatoes, including juice
120 g sour cream

1. Move slider to AIR FRY/STOVETOP. Select SEAR/SAUTÉ and set to Lo1. Select START/STOP to begin preheating. Allow unit to preheat for 5 minutes. After 5 minutes, heat the oil for 30 seconds. Add onion to the pot and sauté for 5 minutes until the onions are translucent. Add garlic. Heat for an additional minute. 2. Add black beans, chili powder, cumin, stock, salt, cayenne pepper, green chiles with juice, and tomatoes with juice to the pot and stir to combine. 3. Close the lid and move slider to PRESSURE. Ensure the pressure release valve is in the SEAL position. The temperature will default to HIGH, which is the correct setting. Set time to 30 minutes. Select START/STOP to begin cooking. 4. When cooking is complete, turn the pressure relief valve to the VENT position for quick pressure relief. Move slider to the right to unlock the lid, then carefully open it. 5. Use an immersion blender to blend the dip in the pot until smooth. With dip still in pot, press the SEAR/SAUTÉ button and set to 3, heat for 3 minutes, stirring several times. 6. Transfer the dip to a serving dish. Garnish with sour cream and serve.
Per Serving: Calories 278; Fat 9.45g; Sodium 817mg; Carbs 27.36g; Fibre 7.4g; Sugar 3.18g; Protein 21.94g

Cheese Chicken Nacho Scoops

Prep Time: 15 minutes | Cook Time: 12 minutes | Serves: 16

455 g boneless skinless chicken breasts
120 ml reduced-sodium chicken stock
2 tbsp. lime juice
2 tsp. chili powder
125 g frozen petite corn, thawed
300 g chunky salsa

155 g finely shredded cheddar cheese
1 medium sweet red pepper, finely chopped
4 green onions, thinly sliced
Baked tortilla chip scoops
Minced fresh coriander

1. Place chicken in the pot; add stock, lime juice and chili powder. Close the lid and move slider to PRESSURE. Make sure the pressure release valve is in the SEAL position. The temperature will default to HIGH, which is the correct setting. Set time to 7 minutes. Select START/STOP to begin cooking. 2. When cooking is complete, turn the pressure relief valve to the VENT position for quick pressure relief. Move slider to the right to unlock the lid, then carefully open it. 3. Remove the chicken and discard the cooking juices. Shred the chicken with 2 forks; return to pressure cooker. Move slider to AIR FRY/STOVETOP. Select SEAR/SAUTÉ and set to Lo1. Select START/STOP to begin cooking. 4. Add corn and salsa; cook and stir until heated through, about 5 minutes. Press START/STOP to turn off the SEAR/SAUTÉ function. 5. Transfer to a large bowl; stir in cheese, red pepper and green onions. Serve with tortilla scoops; sprinkle with coriander.
Per Serving: Calories 155; Fat 5.58g; Sodium 307mg; Carbs 15.59g; Fibre 2.3g; Sugar 2.18g; Protein 10.83g

Easy Peach Jam

Prep Time: 15 minutes | Cook Time: 1 minute | Serves: 16

1 kg chopped peaches, peeled and pitted
800 g sugar

1 packet pectin
1 tablespoon lemon juice

1. In a big bowl, mash the chopped peaches with a potato masher. Place the mashed peaches inside your pressure cooker pot. 2. Pour sugar over the peaches and let sit for 2-3 minutes until the juices have been released. 3. Mix in pectin and lemon juice. 4. Close the lid and move slider to PRESSURE. Make sure the pressure release valve is in the SEAL position. The temperature will default to HIGH, which is the correct setting. Set time to 1 minute. Select START/STOP to begin cooking. 5. When cooking is complete, turn the pressure relief valve to the VENT position for quick pressure relief. Move slider to the right to unlock the lid, then carefully open it. 6. Spoon into pint-sized canning jars, leaving 2.5 cm of space between jam and lid. 7. Let cool and then refrigerate or freeze.
Per Serving: Calories 171; Fat 0.1g; Sodium 6mg; Carbs 44.66g; Fibre 1.3g; Sugar 42.79g; Protein 0.45g

Sweet Potato Fries with Sriracha Ranch Sauce

Prep Time: 10 minutes | Cook Time: 13 minutes | Serves: 2

Sriracha Ranch Dipping Sauce:
60 g mayonnaise
2 tablespoons sour cream
2 teaspoons sriracha
1 teaspoon chopped fresh dill
1 clove garlic, peeled and minced
½ teaspoon lemon juice
¼ teaspoon salt

Sweet Potato Fries:
1 large sweet potato, peeled, trimmed, and cut into 1 cm sticks
2 tablespoons olive oil
1 teaspoon salt
½ teaspoon ground black pepper
½ teaspoon garlic powder
240 ml water

1. Line a baking sheet with parchment paper, set aside. 2 In a small bowl, combine the Sriracha Ranch Dipping Sauce ingredients. Refrigerate covered until ready to use. 2. Place sweet potato sticks in a medium bowl and toss with oil, salt, garlic powder and pepper. 3. Add water to the pot and place the bottom layer of the Cook & Crisp Basket in the lower position in the pot. Add fries to the basket. 4. Move slider to STEAMCRISP. set temperature to 220°C and set time to 3 minutes. Press START/STOP to begin cooking. 5. When cooking is complete, transfer the fries to the prepared baking sheet and scatter evenly. Drain off the pot. Arrange the basket inside and place the baking sheets on the basket. 6. Move slider to AIR FRY/STOVETOP. Select BROIL. BAKE/ROAST, set temperature to 200°C, and set time to 10 minutes. Select START/STOP to begin cooking. Bake until crisp and browned, tossing once halfway through cooking. 7. Transfer fries to serving dish. Serve warm with chilled dipping sauce.
Per Serving: Calories 328; Fat 24.64g; Sodium 1770mg; Carbs 23.58g; Fibre 3.9g; Sugar 6.97g; Protein 4.72g

Beef Lentil Sliders

Prep Time: 15 minutes | Cook Time: 25 minutes | Serves: 15

180 g dried yellow lentils
480 ml beef stock
225 g 80/20 beef mince
40 g finely chopped old-fashioned oats

2 large eggs
2 tablespoons peeled and finely diced yellow onion
2 teaspoons sriracha
½ teaspoon salt

1. Add lentils and stock to the pot. Close the lid. 2. Close the lid and move slider to PRESSURE. Make sure the pressure release valve is in the SEAL position. The temperature will default to HIGH, which is the correct setting. Set time to 15 minutes. Select START/STOP to begin cooking. 3. When cooking is complete, naturally release the pressure for 10 minutes. Then turn the pressure relief valve to the VENT position for quick pressure relief. Move slider to AIR FRY/ STOVETOP to unlock the lid, then carefully open it. 4. Drain liquid from the pot and transfer lentils to a medium bowl. Using the back of a wooden spoon, smash most of the lentils, leaving the consistency somewhat chunky. Add beef, onion, oats, eggs, sriracha, and salt. Form mixture into fifteen slider patties. 5. Cook on stovetop over medium-high heat for 5 minutes on each side. 6. Transfer the patties to serving dish and serve warm.
Per Serving: Calories 75; Fat 4.62g; Sodium 177mg; Carbs 4.13g; Fibre 0.8g; Sugar 0.47g; Protein 5.58g

Red Pepper Hummus

Prep Time: 10 minutes | Cook Time: 30 minutes | Serves: 6

90 g dried chickpeas
480 ml water
150 g jarred roasted red peppers with liquid, chopped and divided
1 tablespoon tahini paste
2 cloves garlic, peeled and minced
1 tablespoon lemon juice
1 teaspoon lemon zest

¼ teaspoon ground cumin
¼ teaspoon smoked paprika
⅛ teaspoon cayenne pepper
¼ teaspoon salt
1 teaspoon sesame oil
1 tablespoon olive oil

1. Add chickpeas and water to the pot. Drain the liquid from jar of roasted peppers into pot. Set aside drained peppers. 2. Close the lid and move slider to PRESSURE. Make sure the pressure release valve is in the SEAL position. The temperature will default to HIGH, which is the correct setting. Set time to 30 minutes. Select START/STOP to begin cooking. 3. When cooking is complete, naturally release the pressure for 5 minutes. Then turn the pressure relief valve to the VENT position for quick pressure relief. Move slider to AIR FRY/ STOVETOP to unlock the lid, then carefully open it. 4. Drain the pot, reserving liquid in a small bowl. 5. Transfer chickpeas to a food processor. Add all but ¼ chopped red peppers, garlic, tahini paste, lemon juice, lemon zest, cumin, cayenne pepper, smoked paprika, salt, sesame oil, and olive oil. If consistency is too thick, slowly add reserved liquid, 1 tablespoon at a time. 6. Transfer the hummus to a serving dish. Garnish with remaining chopped roasted red peppers and serve.
Per Serving: Calories 108; Fat 4.82g; Sodium 423mg; Carbs 13.27g; Fibre 2.5g; Sugar 2.8g; Protein 3.93g

Asian Chicken Coleslaw Noodles Wraps

Prep Time: 15 minutes | Cook Time: 10 minutes | Serves: 4

900 g boneless skinless chicken breast halves
60 ml reduced-sodium soy sauce
6 tbsp. water, divided
60 g ketchup
55 g honey
2 tbsp. minced fresh gingerroot

2 tbsp. sesame oil
1 small onion, finely chopped
2 tbsp. corn flour
12 round rice papers
270 g broccoli coleslaw mix
95 g crispy chow mein noodles

1. Place chicken in the pot. In a small bowl, combine the soy sauce, ketchup, 60 ml water, honey, ginger and oil; stir in the onion. Pour over the chicken. 2. Close the lid and move slider to PRESSURE. Make sure the pressure release valve is in the SEAL position. The temperature will default to HIGH, which is the correct setting. Set time to 7 minutes. Select START/STOP to begin cooking. 3. When cooking is complete, turn the pressure relief valve to the VENT position for quick pressure relief. Move slider to the right to unlock the lid, then carefully open it. 4. Insert a thermometer into the chicken and it should read at least 75°C. Remove chicken; shred with 2 forks. Set aside. 5. In a small bowl, mix corn flour and remaining 2 tbsp water until smooth; gradually stir into the pressure cooker. 6. Move slider to AIR FRY/STOVETOP. Select SEAR/SAUTÉ and set to Lo1. Select START/STOP to begin cooking. Simmer, stirring constantly, until thickened, 1-2 minutes. Remove the sauce from the pressure cooker. Toss the shredded chicken with 180 g sauce; reserve remaining sauce for serving. 7. Fill a large shallow dish partway with water. Dip a rice paper wrapper into water just until pliable, about 45 seconds (do not soften completely); allow excess water to drip off. 8. Place wrapper on a flat surface. Layer coleslaw, chicken mixture and 1 tbsp. noodles across bottom third of wrapper. 9. Fold in both sides of wrapper; fold bottom over filling, then roll up tightly. Place on a serving plate, seam side down. Repeat with remaining ingredients. Serve with reserved sauce.
Per Serving: Calories 642; Fat 15.13g; Sodium 1080mg; Carbs 67.69g; Fibre 2.7g; Sugar 22.3g; Protein 56.91g

Savoury Ketchup

Prep Time: 15 minutes | Cook Time: 20 minutes | Serves: 16

900 g plum tomatoes, roughly chopped
5 pitted dates
6 tablespoons distilled white vinegar
1 tablespoon gluten-free vegan Worcestershire sauce
1 tablespoon paprika
1 teaspoon onion powder
1 teaspoon salt (optional)

½ teaspoon mustard powder
¼ teaspoon celery seed
¼ teaspoon garlic powder
Pinch of ground cloves
2 tablespoons water
1 tablespoon corn flour

1. Mix together the tomatoes, dates, Worcestershire sauce, paprika, vinegar, onion powder, salt (if using), celery seed, garlic powder, mustard powder, and cloves in the pot. Using a potato masher, mash the tomatoes until they have released much of their liquid. 2. Close the lid and move slider to PRESSURE. Make sure the pressure release valve is in the SEAL position. The temperature will default to HIGH, which is the correct setting. Set time to 5 minutes. Select START/STOP to begin cooking. 3. When cooking is complete, turn the pressure relief valve to the VENT position for quick pressure relief. Move slider to the right to unlock the lid, then carefully open it. 4. Move slider to AIR FRY/STOVETOP. Select SEAR/SAUTÉ and set to Lo1. Select START/STOP to begin cooking. Simmer about 10 minutes, until reduced, stirring frequently. 5. In a small bowl, mix together the water and corn flour and add to the simmering ketchup, stirring until thickened, 2 to 4 minutes more. Strain the ketchup through a fine-mesh sieve. The ketchup will thicken as it cools. Store in the fridge for up to 6 months in a covered container.
Per Serving: Calories 63; Fat 0.15g; Sodium 167mg; Carbs 15.92g; Fibre 0.9g; Sugar 14.18g; Protein 0.38g

Creamy Cheese Polenta

Prep Time: 15 minutes | Cook Time: 10 minutes | Serves: 4

946 ml filtered water
120 ml chicken or vegetable stock
160 g polenta (not quick-cooking)
1 tsp sea salt
½ tsp dried thyme

55 g grass-fed butter
60 ml heavy cream
170 g shredded Parmesan cheese, plus more for garnish
30 g shredded mild cheddar cheese

1. Move slider to AIR FRY/STOVETOP. Select SEAR/SAUTÉ and set to 3. Select START/STOP to begin cooking. 2. Add the water, polenta, stock, salt and thyme in the pot, whisking to mix the polenta into the water, about 1 minute. Press START/STOP to turn off the SEAR/SAUTÉ function. 3. Close the lid and move slider to PRESSURE. Make sure the pressure release valve is in the SEAL position. The temperature will default to HIGH, which is the correct setting. Set time to 9 minutes. Select START/STOP to begin cooking. 4. When cooking is complete, turn the pressure relief valve to the VENT position for quick pressure relief. Move slider to the right to unlock the lid, then carefully open it. 5. Add the butter, cream and shredded cheeses, stirring until fully incorporated. 6. Transfer to a serving bowl and garnish with grated or shredded Parmesan cheese.
Per Serving: Calories 395; Fat 30.05g; Sodium 1729mg; Carbs 16.18g; Fibre 2.2g; Sugar 1.79g; Protein 15.72g

Crispy Spicy Potato Chips

Prep Time: 10 minutes | Cook Time: 17 minutes | Serves: 2

½ teaspoon smoked paprika
¼ teaspoon chili powder
¼ teaspoon garlic powder
⅛ teaspoon onion powder
⅛ teaspoon cayenne pepper

⅛ teaspoon light brown sugar
1 teaspoon salt
1 medium russet potato, scrubbed and sliced into ¼ cm-thick circles
2 teaspoons olive oil

1. Place the Cook & Crisp Basket in your Pressure Cooker Steam Fryer. 2. In a suitable bowl, mix up the smoked paprika, garlic powder, chili powder, onion powder, cayenne pepper, brown sugar, and ½ teaspoon salt. Set aside. 3. In a separate large bowl, toss chips with olive oil and ½ teaspoon salt. 4. Place chips in ungreased Cook & Crisp Basket. Put on the Smart Lid on top of the Ninja Foodi Steam Fryer. Move the Lid Slider to the "Air Fry/Stovetop". Select the "Air Fry" mode for cooking. 5. Adjust the cooking temperature to 200°C. 6. Cook for 6 minutes. Shake basket, then cook an additional 5 minutes. Shake basket once more. Cook for an additional 6 minutes. 7. Transfer chips to bowl with seasoning mix and toss. Let rest 15 minutes before serving.
Per Serving: Calories 342; Fat: 13.7g; Sodium 678mg; Carbs: 32.3g; Fibre: 4.5g; Sugars 22.1g; Protein 26.7g

Homemade Barbecue Sauce

Prep Time: 15 minutes | Cook Time: 9 minutes | Serves: 12

2 tablespoons minced onion
2 garlic cloves, minced
1 teaspoon smoked paprika
1 teaspoon ground allspice
240 ml water

1 can no-salt-added tomato sauce
55 g maple syrup
2 tablespoons stone-ground mustard
2 tablespoons apple cider vinegar
½ teaspoon salt (optional)

1. Move slider to AIR FRY/STOVETOP. Select SEAR/SAUTÉ and set to 3. Select START/STOP to begin preheating. Allow unit to preheat for 2 minutes. After 2 minutes, sauté the onion for 2 minutes, adding some water as needed to prevent sticking, until slightly browned. Add the garlic, paprika, and allspice and stir for 30 seconds, until fragrant. Stir in the water, scraping up any browned bits from the bottom of the pot. Add the tomato sauce, maple syrup, mustard, vinegar, and salt (if using). Whisk to combine. Press START/STOP to turn off the SEAR/SAUTÉ function. 2. Close the lid and move slider to PRESSURE. Make sure the pressure release valve is in the SEAL position. The temperature will default to HIGH, which is the correct setting. Set time to 4 minutes. Select START/STOP to begin cooking. 3. When the timer beeps, quick-release the pressure and carefully open the lid. If the sauce is not thick enough for your taste, select the SEAR/SAUTÉ function and allow the sauce to reduce, stirring frequently, until it reaches your desired consistency. 4. Store in the fridge for up to 4 weeks in a covered container.
Per Serving: Calories 31; Fat 0.52g; Sodium 102mg; Carbs 6.56g; Fibre 1g; Sugar 5.1g; Protein 0.66g

Chapter 6 Poultry Mains

Herbed Pomegranate Chicken Chunks	61	Italian Herbed Turkey Breast	65
Creamy Mushroom and Chicken	61	Asian-Spiced Duck Breast	65
Mouthwatering Spiced Chicken Wings	61	BBQ Chicken Patties	65
Cheesy Chicken Artichoke Casserole	62	Flavourful Creamy Chicken and Brown Rice	66
Lemony Garlic Chicken Breasts	62	Spicy Turkey Sweet Potato Boats	66
Herbed Whole Chicken	62	Chicken & Quinoa Bowls	66
Buffalo Chicken Lettuce Wraps	62	Italian Duck Breasts with Tomatoes	67
Chicken and Italian Sausage Ragu	63	Delicious Chicken Puttanesca	67
Hearty Chicken Sausage Gumbo	63	Faux-Tisserie Chicken	67
Rich Thai Orange Chicken	63	Healthy Pesto Chicken Quinoa	67
Coconut Chicken and Mushroom Stroganoff	64	Cheese Sausage–Stuffed Peppers	68
Tasty Jerk-Spiced Chicken Wings	64	Chicken, Mushrooms and Rice Bowls	68
Crispy Crusted Chicken Tenders	64	Yummy Chicken & Sausage Jambalaya	68
Simple Air-Fried Chicken Breasts	64	Aromatic Chicken Vindaloo	69
Spicy Chicken Thighs	65	Spicy Broiled Chicken Breasts	69
Spicy Air-Fried Chicken Legs	65		

Herbed Pomegranate Chicken Chunks

Prep Time: 15 minutes | Cook Time: 30 minutes | Serves: 4

2 tbsp (28 g) grass-fed butter, ghee or avocado oil
905 g boneless, skinless chicken thighs, quartered
1 medium yellow onion, thinly sliced
5 cloves garlic, finely chopped
1 tsp sea salt
1 tsp chili powder
¼ tsp ground cloves
¼ tsp ground allspice
¼ tsp ground cinnamon
¼ tsp ground cardamom
60 ml sugar-free 100% pomegranate juice
2 large celery ribs with leaves, thinly sliced
15 g finely chopped fresh flat-leaf parsley, plus more for garnish
1 tbsp (2 g) finely chopped fresh rosemary
1 tbsp (2 g) finely chopped fresh mint
2 tsp (2 g) finely chopped fresh thyme leaves
60 ml honey
1 tbsp (15 ml) quality blackstrap molasses
175 ml chicken or vegetable stock
87 g pomegranate arils, for garnish

1. Place your healthy fat of choice in the pot. Move slider to AIR FRY/STOVETOP. Select SEAR/SAUTÉ and set to 3. Select START/STOP to begin cooking. Once the fat has melted, add the chicken and brown for about 3½ minutes on each side. You may need to do this in two batches if the chicken is too cramped in the pot. Remove the chicken and arrange onto a plate. Set aside. 2. Add the onion to the pot and sauté for 5 minutes, stirring occasionally, or until fragrant. Then, add the garlic, chili powder, salt, cloves, cinnamon, allspice, and cardamom and sauté for 1 minute, stirring occasionally. Add the pomegranate juice and deglaze the pot, scraping up any browned bits with a wooden spoon. Press START/STOP. 3. Add the celery, parsley, thyme, mint, rosemary, honey, molasses, browned chicken and stock, stirring well and ensuring the chicken is submerged in the liquid. 4. Close the lid and move the slider to PRESSURE. Ensure the pressure release valve is in the SEAL position. The temperature will default to HIGH, which is the correct setting. Set time to 12 minutes. Select START/STOP to begin cooking. 5. When cooking is complete, naturally release the pressure for 15 minutes. Then quick release pressure by turning the pressure release valve to the VENT position. Move slider to AIR FRY/ STOVETOP to unlock the lid, then carefully open it. 6. With tongs or a large slotted spoon, arrange the chicken onto a plate or cutting board. Chop the chicken into bite-size chunks, then set aside. 7. Move slider to AIR FRY/STOVETOP. Select SEAR/SAUTÉ and set to 3. Select START/STOP to begin cooking. Allow the liquid to come to a simmer, then simmer for about 5 minutes, or until the liquid slightly thickens. Press START/STOP. Add the chicken, give the mixture a stir, taste for seasoning and adjust the salt to taste. Let it rest for 10 minutes. 8. Serve immediately, garnished with fresh pomegranate arils and chopped fresh flat-leaf parsley.
Per Serving: Calories 775; Fat 30.15g; Sodium 1481mg; Carbs 83.34g; Fibre 6.5g; Sugar 41.07g; Protein 43.4g

Creamy Mushroom and Chicken

Prep Time: 15 minutes | Cook Time: 15 minutes | Serves: 6

4 tablespoons salted butter
455 g baby bella mushrooms, sliced
1 large shallot, diced
1 yellow pepper, diced
1.3 kg boneless, skinless chicken breasts, cut into bite-size pieces
240 ml chicken stock
1 teaspoon garlic powder
1 teaspoon seasoned salt
1 teaspoon black pepper
120 g heavy cream
1 package Boursin spread (any flavour) or 100 g cream cheese, cut into chunky cubes
110 g frozen peas
1 jar roasted red peppers, drained and sliced into 1 cm strips
2 tablespoons cornflour
100 g grated Parmesan cheese
Canned biscuits of your choice, cooked according to package instructions, for serving

1. Place the butter in the pot. Move slider to AIR FRY/STOVETOP. Select SEAR/SAUTÉ and set to Hi5. Select START/STOP to begin cooking. Once the butter's melted, add the mushrooms, shallot, and pepper and sauté for 3 minutes until slightly softened. 2. Add the chicken and sauté for 2–3 minutes, until the chicken is lightly seared and the edges are pinkish-white in colour, but not yet fully cooked. Stir in the chicken stock, garlic powder, seasoned salt, and pepper. Press START/STOP to turn off the SEAR/SAUTÉ function. 3. Close the lid and move the slider to PRESSURE. Ensure the pressure release valve is in the SEAL position. The temperature will default to HIGH, which is the correct setting. Set time to 4 minutes. Select START/STOP to begin cooking. 4. Quick release the pressure when done. Press START/STOP. 5. Mix the cornflour with 2 tablespoons water to form a slurry. Set aside. 6. Stir in the cream, Boursin (or cream cheese), frozen peas, and roasted red peppers and let sit for a minute, stirring occasionally (the residual heat will thaw the peas). 7. Select SEAR/SAUTÉ and set to Hi5. Select START/STOP to begin cooking. Once the sauce is bubbling, immediately stir in the cornflour slurry and Parmesan and let bubble for 30 seconds before turning the pot off by pressing START/STOP again. 8. Serve over biscuits.
Per Serving: Calories 887; Fat 28.67g; Sodium 1621mg; Carbs 122.05g; Fibre 14g; Sugar 17.43g; Protein 44.51g

Mouthwatering Spiced Chicken Wings

Prep Time: 15 minutes | Cook Time: 10 minutes | Serves: 6

1.5 kg chicken wings, cut into their three parts, any flappers removed and discarded
3 tablespoons dried spice blend
240 ml liquid (Choose from water, beer, white wine, stock, or unsweetened apple cider)
Up to 1 teaspoon table salt (optional)
200 g coating mixture (such as barbecue sauce, chutney, French dressing, honey mustard, Ranch dressing)

1. In a large bowl, mix together the chicken wing pieces, the dried spice blend, and the salt (if using). Toss well until the chicken pieces are well coated in the spice blend. 2. Pour the liquid into the pot. Then place the Cook & Crisp Basket in the pot. Pile all the coated wings onto the basket. 3. Close the lid and move the slider to PRESSURE. Ensure the pressure release valve is in the SEAL position. The temperature will default to HIGH, which is the correct setting. Set time to 5 minutes. Select START/STOP to begin cooking. 4. When cooking is complete, naturally release the pressure for 10 minutes. Then quick release pressure by turning the pressure release valve to the VENT position. Move slider to AIR FRY/STOVETOP to unlock the lid, then carefully open it. 5. Use kitchen tongs or a big spoon to transfer the hot chicken wings to a large bowl. Add the coating mixture and toss well. 6. Turn the coated chicken back to the basket in the pot. Move slider in the AIR FRY/STOVETOP position. Select BROIL and set time to 5 minutes. Select START/ STOP to begin cooking, turning once. Serve warm.
Per Serving: Calories 394; Fat 9.8g; Sodium 1033mg; Carbs 18.69g; Fibre 2.1g; Sugar 8.5g; Protein 55.18g

Cheesy Chicken Artichoke Casserole

Prep Time: 15 minutes | Cook Time: 25 minutes | Serves: 6

900 g boneless, skinless chicken breasts, each breast sliced crosswise into fillets about 1 cm thick
60 g plain flour (seasoned with a pinch each of garlic powder, salt, and pepper)
60 ml extra-virgin olive oil
4 tablespoons salted butter, divided
2 large shallots, diced
3 cloves garlic, minced or pressed
120 ml dry white wine (like a chardonnay)
Juice of 1 lemon
180 ml garlic stock (e.g. Garlic Better Than Bouillon) or chicken stock
2 teaspoons dried oregano, plus more for topping
½ teaspoon Salt
½ teaspoon black pepper
1 tablespoon cornflour
1 can artichoke hearts, drained and quartered
25 g Italian or garlic-and-herb breadcrumbs
25 g grated Parmesan cheese

1. Dredge the chicken on both sides in the flour mixture and set aside. 2. Pour the olive oil and 2 tablespoons of the butter into the pot. 3. Move slider to AIR FRY/STOVETOP. Select SEAR/SAUTÉ and set to Hi5. Select START/STOP to begin cooking. Heat about 3 minutes, until the butter's melted. 4. Working in batches, sear the chicken for 1 minute per side until very lightly browned, take the chicken out of with tongs, and set aside on a plate. Leave any excess oil in the pot for more flavour. 5. Add the remaining 2 tablespoons of butter, scraping up any browned bits from the bottom of the pot. Add the shallots and sauté for about 2 minutes, until beginning to brown, then add the garlic and sauté for 1 more minute. Pour in the wine and lemon juice and bring to a simmer. 6. Add the stock, Salt, oregano, and pepper and stir well, letting the bottom of the pot one last scrape for good measure. Return the chicken to the pot. 7. Close the lid and move the slider to PRESSURE. Ensure the pressure release valve is in the SEAL position. The temperature will default to HIGH, which is the correct setting. Set time to 5 minutes. Select START/STOP to begin cooking. Quick release the pressure when done. 8. Mix the cornflour with 1 tablespoon water to form a slurry. Close the lid and let stand for 10 minutes. 9. Transfer the chicken to a casserole dish that fits the pot. Move slider to AIR FRY/STOVETOP. Select SEAR/SAUTÉ and set to Hi5. Select START/STOP to begin cooking. 10. Once the sauce bubbles, immediately add the cornflour slurry and stir for 30 seconds, as the sauce thickens. Once the bubbles die down, the sauce will thicken. Stir in the artichokes and then pour the sauce on top of the chicken in the casserole dish. 11. Mix the breadcrumbs and Parmesan, sprinkle evenly over the chicken and top with a few more shakes of oregano. 12. Place the deluxe reversible rack in the pot in the higher broil position. Place the casserole on the rack. 13. Close lid and move slider in the AIR FRY/STOVETOP position. Select BROIL and set time to 3 minutes. Select START/ STOP to begin cooking. 14. Remove and serve immediately over rice or angel-hair pasta (cooked separately), if needed. And of course, dip some Italian or French bread in that remarkable sauce.
Per Serving: Calories 487; Fat 21.01g; Sodium 962mg; Carbs 54.84g; Fibre 6g; Sugar 9.39g; Protein 21.7g

Lemony Garlic Chicken Breasts

Prep Time: 15 minutes | Cook Time: 7 minutes | Serves: 2

120 ml water
2 lemons (zest from 1, juice from both)
2 cloves garlic, crushed
1 tsp dried oregano
455 g boneless, skinless chicken breast

1. Pour the water into the pot. Add the lemon zest and juice, garlic and oregano, then add the chicken to the pot. 2. Close the lid and move the slider to PRESSURE. Ensure the pressure release valve is in the SEAL position. The temperature will default to HIGH, which is the correct setting. Set time to 7 minutes. Select START/STOP to begin cooking. 3. When the timer beeps, quick release the pressure and carefully open the lid. Carefully remove the chicken, slice and serve.
Per Serving: Calories 411; Fat 13.06g; Sodium 608mg; Carbs 52.03g; Fibre 3.8g; Sugar 13.42g; Protein 21.43g

Herbed Whole Chicken

Prep Time: 15 minutes | Cook Time: 36 minutes | Serves: 6

2 tablespoons olive oil
2 tablespoons dried herbs blend
1 teaspoon Salt
One whole chicken, any giblets or neck removed
480 ml chicken stock or water

1. Use a fork to mash or mix the oil, dried herbs, and salt in a small bowl until uniform. Rub this mixture all over the outside of the chicken. 2. Pour the stock or water into the pot. Then place the bottom layer of the Deluxe Reversible Rack in the lower position in the pot. 3. Place chicken on the rack. Close the lid and move the slider to PRESSURE. Ensure the pressure release valve is in the SEAL position. The temperature will default to HIGH, which is the correct setting. Set time to 36 minutes. Select START/STOP to begin cooking. 4. When cooking is complete, turn it off and let its pressure return to normal naturally, about 1 hour. 5. Open the lid. Cool the chicken in the pot for a few minutes, then use large kitchen tongs and a large metal spatula to transfer the bird to a nearby cutting board. 6. Cool for another 5 to 10 minutes, then carve the chicken as desired.
Per Serving: Calories 314; Fat 15.91g; Sodium 804mg; Carbs 2.24g; Fibre 0g; Sugar 0g; Protein 38.02g

Buffalo Chicken Lettuce Wraps

Prep Time: 20 minutes | Cook Time: 15 minutes | Serves: 4

120 ml chicken stock
905 g boneless, skinless chicken breast
120 g buffalo wing sauce
50 g chopped celery
30 g crumbled blue cheese
2 green onions, chopped
8 large lettuce leaves
Ranch or blue cheese dressing, for drizzling

1. Pour the chicken stock into the pot, and then add the chicken breast. 2. Close the lid, turn the pressure release valve to SEAL position, and then move the slider to PRESSURE. Select HI and set the cooking time to 6 minutes. Press START/STOP to begin cooking. When finished, release the pressure naturally. 3. Mix together the wing sauce, blue cheese, celery, and green onions in a medium bowl. 4. Remove the chicken from the pot, chop the chicken and mix it with the sauce mixture. 5. Divide the buffalo chicken among the lettuce leaves, then drizzle with dressing.
Per Serving: Calories 720; Fat: 18.22g; Sodium: 1279mg; Carbs: 110.47g; Fibre: 22.7g; Sugar: 55.86g; Protein: 37.9g

Chicken and Italian Sausage Ragu

Prep Time: 30 minutes | Cook Time: 15 minutes | Serves: 4

2 tablespoons olive oil
200 g spicy Italian sausage
1 medium yellow onion, chopped
1 red or green pepper, chopped
1 tablespoon balsamic vinegar
240 g thin marinara sauce
60 ml store-bought chicken stock, or homemade
300 g boneless, skinless chicken thighs, fat trimmed, cut into 5 cm pieces
Salt and freshly ground black pepper
90 g polenta (not quick-cooking)
Optional Garnish:
50 g shaved Parmesan cheese curls

1. Add 1 tablespoon of the oil to the pot. Select SEAR/SAUTÉ. Select Lo3, and then press START/STOP to begin cooking. 2. When the oil is hot, add the sausages and cook them for 3 minutes until browned. Add the onion and pepper, and cook then for 4 minutes until tender. Stop the process. 3. Add the vinegar, scraping up the browned bits on the bottom of a suitable baking pan. Add the marinara sauce and stock and stir to combine. Season the chicken all over with salt and pepper. Add it to the pot and stir to combine. 4. Place the rack in the pot over the chicken. Place 680 ml warm water, the remaining 1 tablespoon oil, and ½ teaspoon salt in the pan. Gradually whisk in the polenta. Tent the pan tightly with foil and place on the rack. 5. Close the lid, turn the pressure release valve to SEAL position, and then move the slider to PRESSURE. Select HI and set the cooking time to 8 minutes. Press START/STOP to begin cooking. When finished, release the pressure naturally. 6. Remove the lid, and blot the top of the foil on the baking dish with a paper towel to remove any water. Carefully take the baking dish out of the pot, remove the foil, and stir the polenta. 7. Remove the rack from the pot. 8. Serve the polenta in shallow bowls, topped with the chicken ragu and garnished with the cheese curls, if desired.
Per Serving: Calories 436; Fat: 23.04g; Sodium: 881mg; Carbs: 39.18g; Fibre: 6.2g; Sugar: 11.49g; Protein: 20.92g

Hearty Chicken Sausage Gumbo

Prep Time: 30 minutes | Cook Time: 25 minutes | Serves: 8

60 ml vegetable oil
30 g plain flour
4 stalks celery, chopped
1 large yellow onion, peeled and diced
1 large green pepper, seeded and diced
110 g sliced fresh okra
4 cloves garlic, peeled and minced
1 can diced tomatoes
½ teaspoon dried thyme
½ teaspoon Creole seasoning
3 bay leaves
2 tablespoons fileé powder
2 teaspoons Worcestershire sauce
1 teaspoon hot sauce
960 ml chicken stock
455 g smoked sausage, sliced
280 g shredded cooked chicken
¼ teaspoon salt
¼ teaspoon ground black pepper
500 g cooked long-grain rice

1. Add the oil to the pot. Select SEAR/SAUTÉ. Select Lo3, and then press START/STOP to begin cooking. 2. When the oil is hot, add flour and cook for 15 minutes until flour is medium brown in color; add celery, onion, green pepper, okra, garlic, and tomatoes, and cook them for 8 minutes until tender; add thyme, Creole seasoning, bay leaves, fileé, Worcestershire sauce, hot sauce, and stock and stir them well, making sure nothing is stuck to the bottom of the pot. 3. Add sausage to the pot and stop the process. 4. Close the lid, turn the pressure release valve to SEAL position, and then move the slider to PRESSURE. Select HI and set the cooking time to 8 minutes. Press START/STOP to begin cooking. When finished, release the pressure quickly. 5. Open lid, discard bay leaves, and stir in chicken, salt, and black pepper. Let stand on Keep Warm setting for 10 minutes. 6. Serve the dish hot over rice.
Per Serving: Calories 624; Fat: 37.51g; Sodium: 1195mg; Carbs: 28.47g; Fibre: 4.9g; Sugar: 3.34g; Protein: 45.17g

Rich Thai Orange Chicken

Prep Time: 20 minutes | Cook Time: 20 minutes | Serves: 4-6

2 tbsp. grass-fed butter, ghee or avocado oil
1 large shallot, thinly sliced
5 cloves garlic, finely chopped
2.5-cm chunk fresh ginger, peeled and finely minced or grated
¾ tsp. sea salt
¼ tsp. red pepper flakes (optional)
60 ml honey
175 ml freshly squeezed orange juice
60 ml cider vinegar
2 tbsp coconut aminos
2 tsp. Asian fish sauce
905 g boneless, skinless chicken breast
25 g fresh Thai basil leaves, plus more for garnish
25 g finely chopped fresh mint

1. Add the healthy fat of choice to the pot. 2. Select SEAR/SAUTÉ. Select Lo3, and then press START/STOP to begin cooking. 3. When the fat is melted, add the shallot and sauté for 3 minutes or until fragrant; add the garlic and ginger and sauté them for 2 minutes. 4. Stop the process, and add the salt, red pepper flakes (optional), honey, orange juice, vinegar, coconut aminos, fish sauce and chicken to the pot, and give the mixture a stir, making sure the chicken is submerged in the liquid. 5. Close the lid, turn the pressure release valve to SEAL position, and then move the slider to PRESSURE. Select HI and set the cooking time to 9 minutes. Press START/STOP to begin cooking. When finished, release the pressure naturally. 6. Arrange the chicken onto a plate or cutting board. Cut the chicken into bite-size chunks, and then set aside. 7. Simmer the liquid in the pot at Lo2 on SEAR/SAUTÉ mode for 5 minutes or until the liquid slightly thickens. 8. Stop the process, and add the shredded chicken, Thai basil and mint to the pot, then stir them a few times until the fresh herbs have wilted into the sauce, then allow the mixture to rest for 10 minutes. 9. Garnish the dish with fresh Thai basil leaves and enjoy.
Per Serving: Calories 368; Fat: 11.97g; Sodium: 864mg; Carbs: 48.52g; Fibre: 2.6g; Sugar: 22.8g; Protein: 16.49g

Coconut Chicken and Mushroom Stroganoff

Prep Time: 20 minutes | Cook Time: 25 minutes | Serves: 4

2 tbsp. avocado oil or olive oil
675 g chicken breast, cut into 2.5- to 5-cm chunks
2 tbsp cornflour plus more if needed
340 g Portobello mushrooms, sliced
3 cloves garlic, minced
2 tbsp coconut aminos or soy sauce

1 tbsp cider vinegar
175 ml chicken stock
120 ml full-fat canned coconut milk or coconut cream
Salt
Cooked rice, cauliflower rice or pasta, for serving
3 tbsp. (8 g) chopped fresh basil or (12 g) parsley, for garnish (optional)

1. In a resealable plastic bag, toss the chicken and cornflour together. Shake it up so that the chicken is completely covered. 2. Add the oil to the pot. Select SEAR/SAUTÉ. Select Lo3, and then press START/STOP to begin cooking. 3. When the oil is hot, place in the chicken chunks and cook them for 1 to 2 minutes on each side or until they are slightly browned. 4. Stop the process, and then toss in the mushrooms and garlic. 5. In a small bowl, stir together the coconut aminos, vinegar and chicken stock. Pour on top of the chicken mixture. 6. Close the lid, turn the pressure release valve to SEAL position, and then move the slider to PRESSURE. Select HI and set the cooking time to 7 minutes. Press START/STOP to begin cooking. When finished, release the pressure naturally. 7. If the sauce seems too thin, add another tablespoon of tapioca starch to the coconut milk. Pour the coconut milk into the pot and mix until well incorporated. 8. Cook the food at Lo3 on SEAR/SAUTÉ again for another 10 minutes or until the mixture is creamy. 9. Season the mixture with salt and stop the process. 10. Spoon the mixture on top of rice, cauliflower rice or pasta and serve immediately, garnished with the fresh basil or parsley.
Per Serving: Calories 746; Fat: 34.43g; Sodium: 482mg; Carbs: 73.07g; Fibre: 10.7g; Sugar: 3.06g; Protein: 46.66g

Tasty Jerk-Spiced Chicken Wings

Prep Time: 10 minutes | Cook Time: 16 minutes | Serves: 8

1 teaspoon salt
120ml red wine vinegar
5 tablespoon lime juice
4 chopped spring onions
1 tablespoon grated ginger
2 tablespoon brown sugar
1 tablespoon chopped thyme
1 teaspoon white pepper

1 teaspoon cayenne pepper
1 teaspoon cinnamon
1 tablespoon allspice
1 Habanero pepper, chopped
6 chopped garlic cloves
2 tablespoon low-sodium soy sauce
2 tablespoons olive oil
1.8kg of chicken wings

1. Place the Cook & Crisp Basket in your Pressure Cooker Steam Fryer. 2. Mix all the recipe ingredients except wings in a suitable bowl. 3. Pour the prepared marinade into a gallon bag and add chicken wings. Chill 2 to 24 hours to marinate. 4. Place all the chicken wings into a strainer to drain excess liquids. 5. Pour half of the wings into your Ninja Foodi Pressure Steam Fryer. 6. Put on the Smart Lid on top of the Ninja Foodi Steam Fryer. 7. Move the Lid Slider to the "Air Fry/Stovetop". Select the "Air Fry" mode for cooking. 8. Adjust the cooking temperature to 200°C. 9. Cook for 14 to 16 minutes, making sure to shake halfway through the cooking process. 10. Remove and repeat the process with remaining wings.
Per Serving: Calories: 483; Fat: 7.9g; Sodium: 704mg; Carbs: 6g; Fibre: 3.6g; Sugar 6g; Protein 21g

Crispy Crusted Chicken Tenders

Prep Time: 10 minutes | Cook Time: 10 minutes | Serves: 4

675g chicken tenders
1 tablespoon olive oil
1 egg, whisked
1 teaspoon fresh parsley, minced

1 teaspoon garlic, minced
Sea salt and black pepper, to taste
100g breadcrumbs

1. Place the Cook & Crisp Basket in your Pressure Cooker Steam Fryer. 2. Pat the chicken dry with kitchen towels. 3. In a suitable bowl, mix the oil, egg, parsley, garlic, salt, and black pepper. 4. Dip the prepared chicken tenders into the egg mixture. Then, roll the chicken over the breadcrumbs. 5. Put on the Smart Lid on top of the Ninja Foodi Steam Fryer. 6. Move the Lid Slider to the "Air Fry/Stovetop". Select the "Air Fry" mode for cooking. 7. Cook the chicken tenders at 180°C for around 10 minutes, shaking the Cook & Crisp Basket halfway through the cooking time. 8. Serve.
Per Serving: Calories: 302; Fat: 7g; Sodium: 224mg; Carbs: 6g; Fibre: 6g; Sugar 2g; Protein 22g

Simple Air-Fried Chicken Breasts

Prep Time: 10 minutes | Cook Time: 12 minutes | Serves: 4

455g chicken breasts raw, boneless and skinless
1 tablespoon butter, room temperature
1 teaspoon garlic powder
Salt and black pepper, to taste

1 teaspoon dried parsley flakes
1 teaspoon smoked paprika
½ teaspoon dried oregano

1. Place the Cook & Crisp Basket in your Pressure Cooker Steam Fryer. 2. Pat the chicken dry with kitchen towels. Toss the chicken breasts with the remaining ingredients. 3. Put on the Smart Lid on top of the Ninja Foodi Steam Fryer. 4. Move the Lid Slider to the "Air Fry/Stovetop". Select the "Air Fry" mode for cooking. 5. Cook the prepared chicken at 195°C for around 12 minutes, turning them over halfway through the cooking time. Serve.
Per Serving: Calories: 227; Fat:13.4g; Carbs: 0.2g; Proteins: 23.4g; Sugars: 0.2g; Fibre: 1g

Spicy Chicken Thighs

Prep Time: 10 minutes | Cook Time: 22 minutes | Serves: 4

455g chicken thighs, bone-in
Sea salt and black pepper, to taste
2 tablespoons olive oil

1 teaspoon stone-mustard
60ml hot sauce

1. Place the Cook & Crisp Basket in your Pressure Cooker Steam Fryer. 2. Pat the chicken dry with kitchen towels. Toss the chicken with the remaining ingredients. 3. Put on the Smart Lid on top of the Ninja Foodi Steam Fryer. 4. Move the Lid Slider to the "Air Fry/Stovetop". Select the "Air Fry" mode for cooking. 5. Cook the prepared chicken at 195°C for around 22 minutes, turning them over halfway through the cooking time. 6. Serve.
Per Serving: Calories: 317; Fat:25.4g; Carbs: 1.5g; Proteins: 19.1g; Sugars: 0.6g; Fibre: 1g

Spicy Air-Fried Chicken Legs

Prep Time: 10 minutes | Cook Time: 30 minutes | Serves: 4

4 chicken legs, bone-in
2 tablespoons sesame oil
Salt and black pepper, to taste
½ teaspoon mustard seeds

1 teaspoon cayenne pepper
½ teaspoon onion powder
½ teaspoon garlic powder

1. Place the Cook & Crisp Basket in your Pressure Cooker Steam Fryer. 2. Dry the chicken with paper towels. Toss the bone-in chicken legs with the remaining ingredients. 3. Put on the Smart Lid on top of the Ninja Foodi Steam Fryer. 4. Move the Lid Slider to the "Air Fry/Stovetop". Select the "Air Fry" mode for cooking. 5. Cook the prepared chicken at 195°C for around 30 minutes, turning them over halfway through the cooking time. 6. Serve.
Per Serving: Calories: 387; Fat:18.1g; Carbs: 1.9g; Proteins: 51.1g; Sugars: 0.6g; Fibre: 0.4g

Italian Herbed Turkey Breast

Prep Time: 10 minutes | Cook Time: 1 hour | Serves: 4

1 tablespoon butter
Salt and black pepper, to taste
1 teaspoon cayenne pepper

1 teaspoon Italian herb mix
455g turkey breast, bone-in

1. Place the Cook & Crisp Basket in your Pressure Cooker Steam Fryer. 2. In a suitable mixing bowl, mix the butter, salt, black pepper, cayenne pepper, and herb mix. 3. Rub the mixture all over the turkey breast. 4. Put on the Smart Lid on top of the Ninja Foodi Steam Fryer. 5. Move the Lid Slider to the "Air Fry/Stovetop". Select the "Air Fry" mode for cooking. 6. Cook the turkey breast at 175°C for around 1 hour, turning them over every 20 minutes. 7. Serve.
Per Serving: Calories: 210; Fat:10.1g; Carbs: 1.3g; Proteins: 25.1g; Sugars: 0.6g; Fibre: 0.4g

Asian-Spiced Duck Breast

Prep Time: 10 minutes | Cook Time: 30 minutes | Serves: 3

455g duck breast
1 tablespoon Hoisin sauce
1 tablespoon Five-spice powder

Sea salt and black pepper, to taste
¼ teaspoon cinnamon

1. Place the Cook & Crisp Basket in your Pressure Cooker Steam Fryer. 2. Toss the duck breast with the remaining ingredients. 3. Put on the Smart Lid on top of the Ninja Foodi Steam Fryer. 4. Move the Lid Slider to the "Air Fry/Stovetop". Select the "Air Fry" mode for cooking. 5. Cook the duck breast at 165°C for about 15 minutes, flipping them over halfway through the cooking time. 6. Turn the heat to 175°C; continue to cook for about 15 minutes or until cooked through. 7. Serve.
Per Serving: Calories: 345; Fat:23.2g; Carbs: 5.7g; Proteins: 27.1g; Sugars: 2.3g; Fibre: 0.8g

BBQ Chicken Patties

Prep Time: 10 minutes | Cook Time: 17 minutes | Serves: 3

340g chicken, ground
10g tortilla chips, crushed
25g Parmesan cheese, grated
1 egg, beaten

2 tablespoons onion, minced
2 garlic cloves, minced
1 tablespoon BBQ sauce

1. Place the Cook & Crisp Basket in your Pressure Cooker Steam Fryer. 2. Mix all the recipe ingredients until everything is well mixed. Form the mixture into three patties. 3. Put on the Smart Lid on top of the Ninja Foodi Steam Fryer. 4. Move the Lid Slider to the "Air Fry/Stovetop". Select the "Air Fry" mode for cooking. 5. Cook the burgers at 195°C for about 17 minutes or until cooked through; make sure to turn them over halfway through the cooking time. 6. Serve.
Per Serving: Calories: 373; Fat:23.8g; Carbs: 7g; Proteins: 27g; Sugars: 0.7g; Fibre: 0.9g

Flavourful Creamy Chicken and Brown Rice

Prep Time: 15 minutes | Cook Time: 25 minutes | Serves: 4

1 tablespoon extra-virgin olive oil
1 yellow onion, chopped
200 g cremini mushrooms, roughly chopped
2 cloves garlic, minced
200 g long-grain brown rice, rinsed
300 ml water
1 teaspoon dried thyme
1 teaspoon fine sea salt
455 g boneless, skinless chicken breasts
Freshly ground black pepper
110 g fresh or frozen peas
1 tablespoon freshly squeezed lemon juice
60 ml full-fat canned coconut milk

1. Move slider to AIR FRY/STOVETOP. Select SEAR/SAUTÉ and set to 3. Select START/STOP to begin preheating. Allow unit to preheat for 2 minutes. After 2 minutes, add the olive oil to the pot. When the oil is hot, add the onion, garlic and mushrooms and sauté until softened, about 5 minutes. 2. Add the brown rice, thyme, water, and ½ teaspoon of the salt and stir well, scraping the bottom of the pot with a spatula to make sure nothing has stuck. Place the chicken breasts on top of the rice mixture and season with the remaining ½ teaspoon salt and several grinds of pepper. Press START/STOP to turn off the SEAR/SAUTÉ function. 3. Close the lid and move slider to PRESSURE. Ensure the pressure release valve is in the SEAL position. The temperature will default to HIGH, which is the correct setting. Set time to 10 minutes. Select START/STOP to begin cooking. 4. When cooking is complete, turn the pressure relief valve to the VENT position for quick pressure relief. Move slider to the right to unlock the lid, then carefully open it. 5. Use tongs to transfer the chicken to a cutting board to rest for 5 minutes. If using fresh peas, add them now, scattering them over the rice. Close the lid again, making sure the sealing ring is properly placed. Still cook on high pressure for 8 minutes more. While the rice cooks, cut the chicken into bite-sized pieces. 6. When cooking is complete, naturally release the pressure for 10 minutes. Then turn the pressure relief valve to the VENT position for quick pressure relief. Move slider to AIR FRY/ STOVETOP to unlock the lid, then carefully open it. 7. Stir the chicken into the rice, along with the lemon juice and coconut milk. If using frozen peas, add them now. Taste and adjust the seasoning as needed, then serve immediately. 8. Store the leftovers in an airtight container in the fridge for 3 or 4 days.

Per Serving: Calories 633; Fat 15.94g; Sodium 933mg; Carbs 108.46g; Fibre 11.9g; Sugar 9.3g; Protein 21.37g

Spicy Turkey Sweet Potato Boats

Prep Time: 25 minutes | Cook Time: 30 minutes | Serves: 4

1 tablespoon extra-virgin olive oil
1 yellow onion, chopped
455 g minced turkey
1 teaspoon chili powder
1½ teaspoons fine sea salt
120 ml water
1 green pepper, seeded and chopped
120 g tomato paste
1 butternut squash (about 455 g), peeled and cut into 2.5 cm cubes, or 200 g frozen butternut squash pieces
2 tablespoons pure maple syrup
1½ tablespoons spicy brown mustard
Freshly ground black pepper
2 small sweet potatoes, pierced with a fork to vent
Chopped green onions, tender white and green parts only, for garnish
Chopped fresh flat-leaf parsley, for garnish

1. Move slider to AIR FRY/STOVETOP. Select SEAR/SAUTÉ and set to 3. Select START/STOP to begin preheating. Allow unit to preheat for 2 minutes. After 2 minutes, heat the olive oil in the pot. Add the onion, turkey, chili powder, and 1 teaspoon of the salt and sauté until the turkey is browned and cooked through, breaking it up with a wooden spoon as you stir, about 8 minutes. Press START/STOP to turn off the SEAR/SAUTÉ function. 2. Add the water and scrape up any browned bits stuck to the bottom of the pot. Without stirring, add the pepper, butternut squash cubes, maple syrup, tomato paste, mustard, remaining ½ teaspoon salt, and several grinds of pepper. 3. Arrange the Deluxe Reversible Rack on top of the filling and place the sweet potatoes on the rack. 4. Close the lid and move slider to PRESSURE. Ensure the pressure release valve is in the SEAL position. The temperature will default to HIGH, which is the correct setting. Set time to 20 minutes. Select START/STOP to begin cooking. 5. When cooking is complete, naturally release the pressure for 10 minutes. Then turn the pressure relief valve to the VENT position for quick pressure relief. Move slider to AIR FRY/ STOVETOP to unlock the lid, then carefully open it. 6. Use oven mitts to lift the rack and potatoes out of the pot. Stir the filling, using a wooden spoon to mash up the squash. Cook on SEAR/SAUTÉ function and set to 3, simmer away excess liquid until the sauce is to your liking. Adjust the seasoning as needed. 7. Carefully slice the hot sweet potatoes in half lengthwise and spoon filling over each half. Garnish with the parsley and green onions and serve immediately. 8. Store the leftover filling in an airtight container in the fridge for 3 or 4 days.

Per Serving: Calories 710; Fat 54.87g; Sodium 1078mg; Carbs 30.01g; Fibre 4.4g; Sugar 17.8g; Protein 25.17g

Chicken & Quinoa Bowls

Prep Time: 25 minutes | Cook Time: 15 minutes | Serves: 4

2 teaspoons taco seasoning
6 to 8 boneless, skinless chicken thighs, fat trimmed
2 tablespoons olive oil
180 g fresh refrigerated tomato salsa
240 ml plus 1 tablespoon store-bought chicken stock, or homemade
145 g red quinoa, rinsed
1 can black beans, drained and rinsed,
Salt and freshly ground black pepper
215 g prepared guacamole
Optional toppings
Shredded cheddar cheese
Sour cream
Sliced olives

1. Rub the taco seasoning into the chicken thighs. 2. Select SEAR/SAUTÉ. Select Lo3, and then press START/STOP to begin cooking. 3. When the pot is hot, heat the oil, and brown the chicken thighs for 3 minutes on one side only until golden brown. You can cook them in batches. 4. Stop the process, and drain off the fat in the pot and return the pot to the unit. 5. Add ½ of the salsa and 60 ml of the stock to the pot and scrape up the browned bits on the bottom of the pot. Add the chicken and any accumulated juices to the pot. Spoon the remaining salsa over the chicken. 6. Place the rack in the pot over the chicken. 7. Combine the quinoa and remaining plus 1 tablespoon stock in a baking pan; spoon the beans over the quinoa mixture, but don't stir them in. Place the pan on the rack. 8. Close the lid, turn the pressure release valve to SEAL position, and then move the slider to PRESSURE. Select HI and set the cooking time to 12 minutes. Press START/STOP to begin cooking. When finished, release the pressure naturally. 9. Fluff the quinoa-bean mixture with a fork and season with salt and pepper. 10. Divide the quinoa among bowls and top with the chicken and some of the cooking liquid from the pot. 11. Top the dish with the guacamole and sprinkle with the optional toppings, if using, and serve.

Per Serving: Calories 937; Fat: 65.62g; Sodium: 659mg; Carbs: 31.42g; Fibre: 8g; Sugar: 2.13g; Protein: 54.98g

Italian Duck Breasts with Tomatoes

Prep Time: 15 minutes | Cook Time: 15 minutes | Serves: 4

900 g. duck breasts, halved
2 tbsp. olive oil
½ tbsp. Italian seasoning
½ tsp. ground black pepper
¼ tsp. salt
2 cloves garlic, minced

120 ml chicken stock
180 g heavy cream
70 g sun-dried tomatoes, chopped
30 g spinach, chopped
5 g parmesan cheese, grated

1. Combine the oil, Italian seasoning, pepper, salt, and garlic in a bowl. 2. Rub all sides of the duck breasts with the spice mix. 3. Select SEAR/SAUTÉ. Select Lo3, and then press START/STOP to begin cooking. 4. When the pot is hot, cook the duck breasts on both sides until they have turned golden brown. 5. Stop the process and pour in the chicken stock. 6. Close the lid, turn the pressure release valve to SEAL position, and then move the slider to PRESSURE. Select HI and set the cooking time to 4 minutes. Press START/STOP to begin cooking. When finished, release the pressure quickly. 7. Stir in the heavy cream, tomatoes, spinach, and cheese, and then cook them at HI on PRESSURE mode for 5 minutes; release the pressure quickly. 8. Serve and enjoy.
Per Serving: Calories 507; Fat: 28.8g; Sodium: 652mg; Carbs: 9.11g; Fibre: 1.3g; Sugar: 4.1g; Protein: 51.21g

Delicious Chicken Puttanesca

Prep Time: 20 minutes | Cook Time: 10 minutes | Serves: 4

2 small boneless, skinless chicken breasts
Salt and freshly ground black pepper
2 tablespoons olive oil
300 g dry penne pasta
600 ml store-bought chicken or vegetable stock, or homemade

1 can diced tomatoes with Italian herbs, with juices
75 g oil-cured black or Kalamata olives
4 oil-packed rolled anchovies with capers, plus 1 tablespoon oil from the jar
Pinch of red pepper flakes

1. Pat the chicken dry with paper towels. Season the chicken all over with salt and several grinds of pepper. 2. Select SEAR/SAUTÉ. Select Lo3, and then press START/STOP to begin cooking. 3. When the pot is hot, heat the oil; add the chicken breasts and cook them for 3 minutes on each side until golden brown. 4. Stop the process, and add penne, stock, tomatoes, olives, anchovies and oil, red pepper flakes, and several grinds of pepper. Stir everything together and place the chicken breasts on top of the pasta mixture. 5. Close the lid, turn the pressure release valve to SEAL position, and then move the slider to PRESSURE. Select LO and set the cooking time to 6 minutes. Press START/STOP to begin cooking. When finished, release the pressure quickly. 6. Transfer the chicken to a cutting board and chop it into bite-size pieces. Return the chicken to the pot and stir to combine. 7. Loosely cover the pot with the lid and let stand for 5 minutes; the liquid will thicken upon standing. Enjoy.
Per Serving: Calories 974; Fat: 61.53g; Sodium: 1354mg; Carbs: 96.66g; Fibre: 13.1g; Sugar: 3.83g; Protein: 14.65g

Faux-Tisserie Chicken

Prep Time: 20 minutes | Cook Time: 10 minutes | Serves: 4-6

1 (1.7 kg) whole roasting chicken, neck and giblets in cavity removed and reserved
455 g red potatoes cut into 3 cm chunks
2 large carrots, peeled and cut into 2.5 cm pieces
2 tablespoons olive oil

4 teaspoons lemon pepper seasoning (not salt-free)
Optional Gravy
1½ tablespoons plain flour
1½ tablespoons butter, at room temperature
Salt and freshly ground black pepper

1. Place the rack in the pot and add 240 ml water. Place the neck and giblets (if you have them) in the water. 2. Toss the vegetables with 1 tablespoon olive oil and 1 teaspoon lemon pepper seasoning. Stuff half the potatoes and carrots into the chicken cavity; do not pack them in or they will not cook evenly. 3. Tuck the wings behind the chicken's back and tie the drumsticks together with butcher's twine. Season the outside of the chicken with the remaining lemon pepper seasoning. 4. Place the chicken breast-side up on the rack. Place the remaining carrots and potatoes around the chicken. Drizzle with the remaining 1 tablespoon oil. 5. Close the lid, turn the pressure release valve to SEAL position, and then move the slider to PRESSURE. Select HI and set the cooking time to 28 minutes. Press START/STOP to begin cooking. When finished, release the pressure quickly. 6. An instant-read thermometer should read 70°C when inserted into the breast. 7. For crispy skin, preheat the broiler and adjust the oven rack. Transfer the chicken on the rack to a foil-lined baking sheet. Place the loose vegetables in a serving bowl and cover with foil. 8. Broil the chicken, rotating the pan once, until the skin on top is browned, about 6 minutes. Carve the chicken and serve with the vegetables and a little of the cooking liquid.
Per Serving: Calories 777; Fat: 45.15g; Sodium: 251mg; Carbs: 14.32g; Fibre: 2g; Sugar: 2.11g; Protein: 74.14g

Healthy Pesto Chicken Quinoa

Prep Time: 20 minutes | Cook Time: 5 minutes | Serves: 5

175 g uncooked quinoa, rinsed
355 ml chicken stock
½ tsp. salt, plus more to taste
455 g chicken breast, cut into bite-size pieces

175 g homemade or store-bought pesto, divided (see note)
150 g sliced cherry tomatoes
35 g fresh Parmesan cheese, for garnish
Mixed greens, for serving

1. Combine the quinoa, chicken stock, salt, chicken breast and half of the pesto in the pot. 2. Close the lid, turn the pressure release valve to SEAL position, and then move the slider to PRESSURE. Select HI and set the cooking time to 1 minute. Press START/STOP to begin cooking. When finished, give a natural pressure release. 3. Open the lid and fluff the quinoa with a fork. 4. Serve with sliced tomatoes, remaining pesto, Parmesan cheese and additional salt, if needed. 5. Alternatively, this recipe can be made ahead and stored in the fridge. 6. Serve warm or at room temperature over a bed of greens.
Per Serving: Calories 355; Fat: 13.22g; Sodium: 519mg; Carbs: 30.14g; Fibre: 3.1g; Sugar: 4.85g; Protein: 27.9g

Cheese Sausage-Stuffed Peppers

Prep Time: 30 minutes | Cook Time: 35 minutes | Serves: 4

125 g dry quinoa, rinsed and drained
420 ml store-bought chicken stock, or homemade
Salt and freshly ground black pepper
455 g raw Italian chicken or turkey sausages, casings removed
20 g chopped fresh basil
4 medium peppers, top ½ cm of stem end removed, seeds discarded
240 g thin jarred marinara sauce
120 g grated mozzarella cheese

1. Place the quinoa 240 ml of the stock, a pinch of salt, and a few grinds of pepper in the pot. 2. Close the lid, turn the pressure release valve to SEAL position, and then move the slider to PRESSURE. Select HI and set the cooking time to 1 minute. Press START/STOP to begin cooking. When finished, release the pressure naturally. 3. Pour the quinoa into a large bowl and fluff with a fork. Let it cool for 5 minutes. 4. Rinse out the pot and return it to the unit. Add the sausage and basil to the quinoa and mix well to combine. Stuff the quinoa mixture into the peppers. 5. In a small bowl, combine the remaining 18 ml stock with the marinara sauce. Pour 300 ml of the mixture into the pot. 6. Place the rack in the pot and set the peppers on top. Spoon the remaining sauce over the peppers and sprinkle with the cheese. 7. Close the lid, turn the pressure release valve to SEAL position, and then move the slider to PRESSURE. Select HI and set the cooking time to 15 minutes. Press START/STOP to begin cooking. When finished, release the pressure naturally. 8. Carefully lift the rack from the pot and transfer the peppers to dinner plates. Spoon the sauce over the peppers. 9. Serve and enjoy.

Per Serving: Calories 382; Fat: 12.94g; Sodium: 1690mg; Carbs: 34.54g; Fibre: 5.4g; Sugar: 10.35g; Protein: 32.64g

Chicken, Mushrooms and Rice Bowls

Prep Time: 35 minutes | Cook Time: 22 minutes | Serves: 4

5 dried shiitake mushrooms
Boiling water
455 g boneless, skinless chicken thighs, trimmed and cut into 2.5 cm pieces
3 tablespoons oyster sauce
2 tablespoons soy sauce, plus more to serve
2 teaspoons finely grated fresh ginger
2 teaspoons white sugar
Salt and ground black pepper
185 g long-grain white rice, rinsed and drained
2 teaspoons grapeseed or other neutral oil
240 ml low-sodium chicken stock
3 spring onions, cut into 2.5 cm lengths on the diagonal

1. Place the shiitakes in a small heat-safe bowl and cover with boiling water. Soak until softened, about 30 minutes. Remove the shiitakes, reserving 60 ml of the liquid. Remove and discard the stems; thinly slice the caps. 2. Meanwhile, in a medium bowl, mix together the chicken, soy sauce, oyster sauce, sugar, ginger, ½ teaspoon each salt and pepper. Set aside. 3. Stir together the rice and oil in the pot. Stir in the stock, the reserved mushroom liquid and the sliced mushroom caps. Add the chicken and its marinade in an even layer over the top; do not stir. 4. Close the lid and move the slider to PRESSURE. Make sure the pressure release valve is in the SEAL position. The temperature will default to HIGH, which is the correct setting. Set time to 10 minutes. Select START/STOP to begin cooking. 5. When cooking is complete, turn the pressure release valve to the vent position for a quick pressure release. Move slider to the right to unlock the lid, then carefully open it. 6. Move slider to AIR FRY/STOVETOP. Select SEAR/SAUTÉ and set to 3. Select START/STOP to begin cooking. Cook until you hear sizzling, 9 to 12 minutes. Press START/STOP to turn off the pot. 7. Using potholders, carefully remove the insert from the housing. Scatter the spring onions over the rice, cover with a kitchen towel and let stand for 10 minutes. 8. Fluff the mixture, stirring in the spring onions and chicken. Taste and season with additional soy sauce and pepper.

Per Serving: Calories 450; Fat 10.93g; Sodium 816mg; Carbs 70.84g; Fibre 3.3g; Sugar 10.51g; Protein 16.42g

Yummy Chicken & Sausage Jambalaya

Prep Time: 15 minutes | Cook Time: 17 minutes | Serves: 6

2 tsp (10 ml) extra-virgin olive oil
455 g andouille sausage, cut into 6-mm thick slices
2 boneless, skinless chicken breasts, cut into bite-size pieces
1 yellow onion, chopped
1 red pepper, seeded and chopped
2 celery ribs, chopped
3 cloves garlic, minced
2 tsp (5 g) Cajun or Creole seasoning
½ tsp coarse salt
1 tsp Italian seasoning
475 ml low-sodium chicken stock
300 g uncooked long-grain white rice
1 (411 g) can fire-roasted diced tomatoes, undrained

1. Move slider to AIR FRY/STOVETOP. Select SEAR/SAUTÉ and set to 3. Select START/STOP to begin preheating. Heat the oil in the pot, add the sausage and chicken, cooking until they're browned, about 4 to 5 minutes. Remove the sausage and chicken and set aside. 2. Add the onion, pepper and celery to the pot. Cook until the onion is soft, about 5 minutes, stirring often. Add the garlic, salt, Cajun seasoning and Italian seasoning and cook for an additional 1 minute. Add the chicken stock, stirring well to scrape up any browned bits from the bottom. Press START/STOP to turn off the SEAR/SAUTÉ function. 3. Add the rice, then add the sausage and chicken back to the pot on top of the rice. Pour the fire-roasted tomatoes over all. 4. Close the lid and move the slider to PRESSURE. Make sure the pressure release valve is in the SEAL position. The temperature will default to HIGH, which is the correct setting. Set time to 5 minutes. Select START/STOP to begin cooking. 5. When cooking is complete, turn the pressure release valve to the vent position for a quick pressure release. Move slider to the right to unlock the lid, then carefully open it. Gently stir and serve immediately.

Per Serving: Calories 440; Fat 17.65g; Sodium 1143mg; Carbs 52.9g; Fibre 5.2g; Sugar 3.66g; Protein 20.97g

Aromatic Chicken Vindaloo

Prep Time: 15 minutes | Cook Time: 15 minutes | Serves: 4

2 tbsp (30 ml) avocado oil or extra-virgin olive oil
1 large yellow onion, diced
1 (15-cm) piece fresh ginger, peeled and chopped
6 cloves garlic, minced
1 hot red chili pepper, seeded and chopped
1 (411-g) can diced tomatoes
2 tbsp (32 g) tomato paste
80 ml white wine vinegar
295 ml chicken stock
1 tbsp (6 g) garam masala
2 tsp (4 g) ground coriander
2 tsp (4 g) ground turmeric
1 tsp mustard powder
1 tsp ground cinnamon
1½ tsp (9 g) sea salt, plus more to taste
905 g raw chicken breast, cut into 2.5- to 5-cm pieces
4 medium Yukon gold potatoes, cut into chunks
Cooked rice, for serving (optional)
Chopped fresh coriander, for garnish

1. Move slider to AIR FRY/STOVETOP. Select SEAR/SAUTÉ and set to 3. Select START/STOP to begin preheating. Allow unit to preheat for 5 minutes. After 5 minutes, add oil to the pot, then add the onion, ginger, garlic and chili pepper. Sauté for 3 to 4 minutes, or until fragrant and lightly browned. Select START/STOP. 2. Transfer the onion mixture to a blender. Add the tomatoes, tomato paste, chicken stock, garam masala, coriander, vinegar, mustard powder, turmeric, cinnamon and salt. Blend until smooth, 1 to 2 minutes. 3. Clean the pot to ensure no onion mixture is sticking to the bottom. Return the pot to its base and pour the sauce into the pot. Add the chicken and potatoes. 4. Close the lid and move the slider to PRESSURE. Make sure the pressure release valve is in the SEAL position. The temperature will default to HIGH, which is the correct setting. Set time to 10 minutes. Select START/STOP to begin cooking. 5. Use a quick release, and open the lid once the steam is completely released. 6. Serve plain or over a bed of rice. Season with additional salt to taste and garnish with fresh coriander.

Per Serving: Calories 829; Fat 29.61g; Sodium 1299mg; Carbs 81.43g; Fibre 12.3g; Sugar 10.67g; Protein 59.14g

Spicy Broiled Chicken Breasts

Prep Time: 15 minutes | Cook Time: 13 minutes | Serves: 4

240 ml water or chicken stock
905 g chicken breasts, skin-on
2 tsp (5 g) smoked paprika
½ tsp cayenne pepper
¼ tsp garlic powder
1 tsp onion powder
¼ tsp coarse salt
¼ tsp freshly ground black pepper
55 g unsalted butter, melted

1. Pour the water or chicken stock into the pot, then add the chicken breasts. 2. Close the lid and move the slider to PRESSURE. Make sure the pressure release valve is in the SEAL position. The temperature will default to HIGH, which is the correct setting. Set time to 8 minutes. Select START/STOP to begin cooking. 3. When cooking is complete, turn the pressure release valve to the vent position for a quick pressure release. Move slider to the right to unlock the lid, then carefully open it. Pour the water out of the pot and transfer the chicken to a plate, set aside. 4. Place the deluxe reversible rack in the pot in the higher broil position. Place the chicken on the rack. 5. Close lid and move slider in the AIR FRY/STOVETOP position. Select BROIL and set time to 5 minutes. Select START/ STOP to begin cooking. 6. Broil until the chicken is browned and crispy. 7. In a small bowl, mix together the paprika, garlic, cayenne, and onion powders, salt and black pepper, then stir in the melted butter. Brush the breasts liberally with the butter mixture and serve immediately.

Per Serving: Calories 485; Fat 29.3g; Sodium 406mg; Carbs 4.4g; Fibre 0.7g; Sugar 0.31g; Protein 48.61g

Chapter 7 Beef, Pork, and Lamb

Wonderful Pulled Beef Brisket 71	Spicy Baby Back Ribs 76
Delicious Miso Pork Ramen 71	Tangy Pork Ragù................................. 77
Tangy Shredded Beef with Pineapple 71	BBQ Pulled Pork Sandwiches 77
Classic Beef Burgundy 72	Tasty Beef Enchiladas........................... 77
Sweet-and-Sour Beef Short Ribs 72	Pork and Vegetables Skewers 77
Barbecued Apricot Pulled Pork 72	Homemade Mongolian Beef 78
Savoury Cheese Steak Mushroom Sloppy Joes 73	Italian Pot Roast Ragù 78
Wholesome Pork and Chicken Noodles 73	Limey Steak Salad 78
Refreshing Carnitas Tacos with Avocado Crema 73	Simple Beef Dinner Rolls 78
	Tender and Juicy Filet Mignon 79
Fresh Salsa Verde Pulled Pork 74	Garlic Beef Shoulder 79
Homemade Chipotle Pulled Pork 74	Italian Herbed Pork Cut 79
Juicy Smoked Brisket Skewers 74	Mustard Sausage with Fennel 79
Smoky Corned Beef with Original Potatoes 74	Spiced Pork Patties 79
Easy Egg Salad Sandwiches 75	Comforting Lamb and Vegetables Casserole 80
Cheesy Beef Sandwiches 75	Palatable Pork Chops with Apples 80
Italian-Flavoured Pork Loin 75	Spicy Pork Chops with Creamy Mushroom Gravy 80
Authentic Pepperoncini Pot Roast 75	
Tender Pork Chops with Onion Gravy 76	Healthy Spiced Pork Strips with Lettuce ... 81
Perfect Mexican Beef Casserole 76	Delicious Pork and Cabbage Stew 81
Hearty Lamb Ragù 76	

Wonderful Pulled Beef Brisket

Prep Time: 20 minutes | Cook Time: 1 hour 40 minutes | Serves: 8

1 (350 g) can diced tomatoes
120 ml bold red wine, such as Zinfandel or Syrah
2 tablespoons balsamic vinegar
65 g frozen pearl onions (do not thaw)
8 baby carrots
8 pitted prunes
6 large pitted green olives, sliced
1 tablespoon fresh thyme leaves
2 medium garlic cloves, peeled and minced (2 teaspoons)
½ teaspoon table salt
½ teaspoon ground black pepper
1 (1.3 kg) beef brisket, preferably the flat cut, trimmed and cut in half widthwise

1. Mix the tomatoes, wine, and vinegar in the pot. Stir in the carrots, pearl onions, prunes, olives, thyme, salt, garlic, and pepper. Pour the meat into the sauce, and then turn the cut over to coat both sides. 2. Close the lid, turn the pressure release valve to SEAL position, and then move the slider to PRESSURE. Select HI and set the cooking time to 90 minutes. Press START/STOP to begin cooking. When finished, release the pressure naturally. 3. Transfer the brisket (whole or in pieces) to a cutting board. Skim excess surface fat from the sauce in the pot with a flatware tablespoon. 4. Bring the sauce in the pot to a simmer at Lo2 on SEAR/SAUTÉ mode; cook the sauce until it looks like a loose and wet barbecue sauce, stirring a few times, 5 to 10 minutes. 5. Shred the meat with two forks. When the sauce has reached the right consistency, stir in the shredded brisket and cook them for 1 minute until coated, stirring often. 6. Stop the process, place the lid askew over the insert and set aside for 5 minutes to blend the flavours and let the meat continue to absorb the sauce. 7. Serve and enjoy.
Per Serving: Calories 381; Fat: 25.81g; Sodium: 2272mg; Carbs: 10.4g; Fibre: 1.6g; Sugar: 3.42g; Protein: 25.64g

Delicious Miso Pork Ramen

Prep Time: 45 minutes | Cook Time: 25 minutes | Serves: 4

4 large eggs
675 g pork shoulder, cut into 4 large pieces
Salt and freshly ground black pepper
1 tablespoon rapeseed oil
1.4 L store-bought chicken stock, or homemade
4 green onions, thinly sliced, white and green parts separated
3 tablespoons red or white miso
2 (75 g) packages dried ramen noodles (seasoning packet discarded)
2 heads baby bok choy, split lengthwise
Optional Garnishes:
Nori seaweed sheets
Canned bamboo shoots
Shichimi togarashi (spicy Japanese chili and sesame seed seasoning)

1. Place the eggs on a rack set in the pot and add 240 ml cold water. 2. Close the lid, turn the pressure release valve to SEAL position, and then move the slider to PRESSURE. Select HI and set the cooking time to 3 minutes. Press START/STOP to begin cooking. When finished, release the pressure quickly. 3. Put the eggs in an ice bath for a few minutes to keep them from overcooking. Discard the ice water, peel the eggs, and cut them in half lengthwise; set aside. 4. Season the pork all over with salt and pepper and drizzle with the oil. 5. Select SEAR/SAUTÉ. Select Lo3, and then press START/STOP to begin cooking. 6. When the pot is hot, cook the pork for 6 minutes until browned on all over. 7. Stop the process, and add the stock and white parts of the green onions. 8. Close the lid, turn the pressure release valve to SEAL position, and then move the slider to PRESSURE. Select HI and set the cooking time to 35 minutes. Press START/STOP to begin cooking. When finished, release the pressure quickly. 9. Transfer the pork to a cutting board. Using a sharp carving knife, slice the pork against the grain into very thin slices. 10. Bring the stock in the pot to a simmer at Lo3 on SEAR/SAUTÉ mode; use a ladle to skim some of the foam/fat that rises to the surface. Whisk in the miso. 11. Place in the noodles and bok choy and simmer for 3 minutes until just tender. Stop the process. 12. Ladle the soup into large bowls. Top the dish with the pork, eggs, green onions, and any optional garnishes.
Per Serving: Calories 679; Fat: 43g; Sodium: 1898mg; Carbs: 20.04g; Fibre: 2.2g; Sugar: 5.29g; Protein: 50.81g

Tangy Shredded Beef with Pineapple

Prep Time: 35 minutes | Cook Time: 55 minutes | Serves: 6-8

1 large pineapple, trimmed: top, bottom and outer skin removed
240 ml cider vinegar
80 ml coconut aminos
80 ml pure maple syrup or honey
1 tsp. sea salt
45 g grass-fed butter, ghee or avocado oil
905 g to 1.4 kg grass-fed beef roast; e.g., chuck or rump
5 cloves garlic, chopped
1½ tsp. dried thyme

1. Slice the pineapple in half, and cut the halves in half. Remove the inner core and discard, and then cut the pineapple flesh into 2.5- to 4-cm chunks. 2. Add the pineapple chunks into a blender, then add the vinegar, coconut aminos, your sweetener of choice and the salt. Blend them on low speed for 20 seconds or until pureed and no pineapple chunks remain. Set aside. 3. Select SEAR/SAUTÉ. Select Lo3, and then press START/STOP to begin cooking. 4. When the pot is hot, melt the healthy fat of your choice; add the roast and brown for about 3½ minutes per side. Transfer the roast to a plate. 5. Pour the garlic and thyme into the pot and sauté for 2 minutes until fragrant, stirring occasionally. Add the pureed pineapple, giving the mixture a quick stir and scraping up any browned bits with a wooden spoon. 6. Stop the process, and place the browned roast in the pot. 7. Close the lid, turn the pressure release valve to SEAL position, and then move the slider to PRESSURE. Select HI and set the cooking time to 35 minutes. Press START/STOP to begin cooking. When finished, release the pressure naturally. 8. Carefully remove the roast, place on a large plate or cutting board and pull apart into shredded pieces. Return the shredded beef to the pot. 9. Cook them at HI on PRESSURE mode for 5 minutes, and then release the pressure quickly. 10. To reduce the sauce, press sauté and allow the sauce and shredded beef to simmer at Lo3 on SEAR/SAUTÉ mode for 5 to 10 minutes to thicken. 11. Once the sauce has reduced, allow the shredded beef to sit and rest in the pot for about 15 minutes before serving. 12. Serve immediately or refrigerate for later use.
Per Serving: Calories 129; Fat: 3.15g; Sodium: 308mg; Carbs: 24.86g; Fibre: 1.8g; Sugar: 19.4g; Protein: 1.05g

Classic Beef Burgundy

Prep Time: 35 minutes | Cook Time: 55 minutes | Serves: 6

Nonstick cooking spray, for pot
4 slices thick bacon
905 g top sirloin steak, trimmed of fat, sliced into chunks
1 medium white onion, diced
2 cloves garlic, minced
260 g peeled and chopped carrot
280 g sliced mushrooms
35 g cornflour
700 ml beef stock, divided
240 ml high-quality red wine (Burgundy or a bold cabernet)
1 tbsp. tomato paste
2 tbsp. honey or (30 g) dark brown sugar
1 sprig rosemary
2 bay leaves
Salt
Freshly ground black pepper
Mashed potatoes or cooked rice, for serving (optional)

1. In a small bowl, whisk together the cornflour with about 120 ml of the beef stock. Set aside. 2. Select SEAR/SAUTÉ. Select Lo3, and then press START/STOP to begin cooking. 3. When the pot is hot, spray the bottom of the pot with nonstick cooking spray, then add the bacon, and cook for 2 to 3 minutes per side. Arrange the bacon onto a paper towel–lined plate, but reserve the rendered fat in the pot. 4. Add the steak and onion to the bacon fat in the pot, and cook them for 6 to 8 minutes until the steak is browned. 5. Stop the process, and toss in the garlic, carrot and mushrooms. Pour the beef stock mixture over the veggies and beef, and then add the remaining stock to the pot. Add the wine, tomato paste, honey, rosemary and bay leaves. 6. Close the lid, turn the pressure release valve to SEAL position, and then move the slider to PRESSURE. Select HI and set the cooking time to 40 minutes. Press START/STOP to begin cooking. When finished, release the pressure naturally. 7. Before serving, remove the bay leaf and rosemary sprig and season with the black pepper and salt. 8. Serve the dish warm over mashed potatoes or rice, or enjoy as a stew.
Per Serving: Calories 462; Fat: 28.92g; Sodium: 530mg; Carbs: 11.01g; Fibre: 2.7g; Sugar: 5.16g; Protein: 37.27g

Sweet-and-Sour Beef Short Ribs

Prep Time: 15 minutes | Cook Time: 65 minutes | Serves: 6

1 tablespoon mild smoked paprika
2 teaspoons dried oregano
2 teaspoons dried thyme
1 teaspoon ground dried mustard
1 teaspoon onion powder
½ teaspoon table salt
½ teaspoon ground black pepper
1.3 kg boneless beef short ribs
360 ml water
2 tablespoons vegetable, corn, or rapeseed oil
1 tablespoon granulated white sugar
1 tablespoon apple cider vinegar

1. In a large bowl, mix the smoked paprika, oregano, mustard, thyme, onion powder, salt, and pepper. Add the short ribs and toss they are evenly and thoroughly coated. 2. Pour the water into the pot. Then place the Cook & Crisp Basket in the lower position in the pot. Pile the coated short ribs into the basket. 3. Close the lid and move the slider to PRESSURE. Ensure the pressure release valve is in the SEAL position. The temperature will default to HIGH, which is the correct setting. Set time to 45 minutes. Select START/STOP to begin cooking. 4. When cooking is complete, naturally release the pressure for 20 minutes. Then quick release pressure by turning the pressure release valve to the VENT position. Move slider to AIR FRY/ STOVETOP to unlock the lid, then carefully open it. 5. Use kitchen tongs to transfer the short ribs to a nearby bowl. Pour any liquid in the pot into a second bowl, then clean and dry the pot before returning it to the pressure cooker. 6. Move slider to AIR FRY/STOVETOP. Select SEAR/SAUTÉ and set to 3. Select START/STOP to begin cooking. 7. Warm the rapeseed oil in the pot for a minute or two. Add about a third of short ribs and cook, turning occasionally, until crisped on all sides, about 6 minutes. Transfer these to a serving platter and brown the remaining two batches in the same way. 8. Once all the meat is on the platter, pour the reserved liquid into the pot and bring it to a full simmer. Stir in the sugar and vinegar. 9. Continue cooking, stirring often, until this liquid has reduced to a thick glaze, about 6 minutes. Press START/STOP to turn off the SEAR/SAUTÉ function. Then smear and spread this glaze over the short ribs before serving.
Per Serving: Calories 480; Fat 28.62g; Sodium 443mg; Carbs 3.03g; Fibre 0.7g; Sugar 1.69g; Protein 53.7g

Barbecued Apricot Pulled Pork

Prep Time: 15 minutes | Cook Time: 60 minutes | Serves: 8

3 tbsp (43 g) grass-fed butter, ghee or avocado oil
1 (905 g to 1.4 kg) pork roast
1 small yellow onion, thinly sliced
5 cloves garlic, chopped
½ tsp chopped fresh thyme leaves
½ tsp chopped fresh rosemary leaves
250 g sugar-free homemade or store-bought barbecue sauce
120 ml cider vinegar
255 g sugar-free all-fruit apricot jam
60 ml pure maple syrup or honey
1 tsp sea salt

1. Place your healthy fat of choice in the pot. Move slider to AIR FRY/STOVETOP. Select SEAR/SAUTÉ and set to 3. Select START/STOP to begin cooking. 2. Once the fat has melted, add the roast and brown for about 3½ minutes on each side. Remove the roast and transfer to a plate. Set aside. 3. Add the onion, garlic, thyme and rosemary to the pot and sauté, stirring occasionally, for 4 minutes, or until fragrant. Add the jam, barbecue sauce, vinegar, your sweetener of choice and salt, giving the mixture a quick stir and scraping up any browned bits with a wooden spoon. Press START/STOP to turn off the SEAR/SAUTÉ function. 4. Place the browned roast in the pot. Close the lid and move the slider to PRESSURE. Ensure the pressure release valve is in the SEAL position. The temperature will default to HIGH, which is the correct setting. Set time to 35 minutes. Select START/STOP to begin cooking. 5. Once the timer beeps, press START/STOP. Allow the unit to release pressure naturally for 15 minutes. Then quick release pressure by turning the pressure release valve to the VENT position. Move slider to AIR FRY/ STOVETOP to unlock the lid, then carefully open it. 6. Carefully remove the roast, place on a large plate or cutting board and pull apart into shreds. Add the shredded pork back to the pot and stir to combine well, ensuring all the pork gets coated. 7. Close the lid and move the slider to PRESSURE. Ensure the pressure release valve is in the SEAL position. Set on high pressure for 5 minutes. 8. Once the timer beeps, press START/STOP and quick release the pressure, carefully open the lid. 9. Stir until everything is fully incorporated. Pour the shredded pork into a shallow dish. Allow the juices to set up and absorb into the meat for 15 minutes. 10. Serve immediately or refrigerate for later use.
Per Serving: Calories 279; Fat 13.7g; Sodium 369mg; Carbs 8.47g; Fibre 0.2g; Sugar 6.41g; Protein 28.57g

Savoury Cheese Steak Mushroom Sloppy Joes

Prep Time: 15 minutes | Cook Time: 20 minutes | Serves: 6

2 tsp (10 ml) olive oil
1 medium onion, sliced
1 green pepper, seeded and sliced
225 g mushrooms, sliced
455 g beef mince

1 (295-ml) can French onion soup
60 ml water
10 ml Worcestershire sauce
6 buns, split, buttered and toasted
6 slices provolone cheese

1. Move slider to AIR FRY/STOVETOP. Select SEAR/SAUTÉ and set to 3. Select START/STOP to begin preheating. Allow unit to preheat for 5 minutes. After 5 minutes, add the olive oil, then the onion, pepper and mushrooms. Cook, stirring occasionally, until the onion is soft and the mushrooms have released their liquid and it has evaporated, 5 to 7 minutes. 2. Add the beef and cook until almost no pink is left, about 5 minutes. Add the French onion soup and water, ensuring to scrape up any browned bits from the bottom. 3. Close the lid and move the slider to PRESSURE. Ensure the pressure release valve is in the SEAL position. The temperature will default to HIGH, which is the correct setting. Set time to 7 minutes. Select START/STOP to begin cooking. 4. When cooking is complete, turn the pressure release valve to the vent position for a quick pressure release. Move slider to the right to unlock the lid, then carefully open it. 5. Stir in Worcestershire sauce. Divide the meat mixture among the rolls and top each mixture with a slice of provolone
Per Serving: Calories 706; Fat 36.13g; Sodium 707mg; Carbs 64.54g; Fibre 5.5g; Sugar 18.34g; Protein 34.54g

Wholesome Pork and Chicken Noodles

Prep Time: 15 minutes | Cook Time: 1 hour and 50 minutes | Serves: 2

455 g pork spare ribs, cut into 6 cm pieces
225 g chicken wings
1 tablespoon oil
1 large onion, cut into thick slices

2 garlic cloves, smashed
1 (6 cm) piece peeled fresh ginger
Soy sauce, for seasoning
150 g Japanese ramen noodles, cooked according to package directions

1. Bring 720 ml of water to a boil in a big saucepan on the stove. While the water is boiling, place the ribs and wings inside the pot of the pressure cooker. Move slider to AIR FRY/STOVETOP. Select SEAR/SAUTÉ and set to 3. Select START/STOP to begin cooking. 2. Carefully pour the boiling water into the pot. Allow the meat to simmer for 10 minutes with the lid loosely covering the pot. 3. Press START/STOP to turn off the SEAR/SAUTÉ function. Carefully drain the water from the ribs and wings, transfer them to a large bowl of cold water, and remove any fat. Rinse the cooker pot, dry it thoroughly, and return to the cooker. 4. Select SEAR/SAUTÉ function and set the heat to 3 again. Press START/STOP to begin cooking. Add the oil when the pot is hot. Add the onion and brown for 8 to 10 minutes. Press START/STOP. Add the garlic and ginger, then add the ribs and wings. Fill the pot with water to the ¾ fill line or until everything is submerged. 5. Close the lid and move the slider to PRESSURE. Ensure the pressure release valve is in the SEAL position. The temperature will default to HIGH, which is the correct setting. Set time to 90 minutes. Select START/STOP to begin cooking. 6. When cooking is complete, naturally release the pressure for 20 minutes. Then quick release pressure by turning the pressure release valve to the VENT position. Move slider to AIR FRY/ STOVETOP to unlock the lid, then carefully open it. 7. Using a fine-mesh strainer, strain the stock into a large bowl; reserve the ribs and wings for another use and discard the other solids. Skim any surface oil off the stock, if desired. Season the stock with soy sauce. 8. Divide the ramen between two soup bowls. Pour the stock over the noodles, then serve with the toppings of your choice.
Per Serving: Calories 675; Fat 24.34g; Sodium 425mg; Carbs 32.28g; Fibre 1.4g; Sugar 3.74g; Protein 76.62g

Refreshing Carnitas Tacos with Avocado Crema

Prep Time: 15 minutes | Cook Time: 40 minutes | Serves: 2

For the Carnitas:
455 g boneless pork shoulder roast, cut into 6 cm chunks
Salt
Freshly ground black pepper
240 ml chicken stock
120 ml freshly squeezed orange juice
For the Avocado Crema:
1 medium avocado, halved and pitted, and cubed
15 g coarsely chopped fresh coriander
60 g sour cream

Juice of 1 lime
110 g sliced onion
2 garlic cloves, crushed
½ teaspoon ground cumin

Juice of 1 lime
½ teaspoon Salt

1. Place the pork shoulder meat in the pressure cooker pot. Season with salt and pepper. Add the stock, onion, orange juice, lime juice, garlic, and cumin. Mix well and let the pork marinate for 20 minutes. 2. Close the lid and move the slider to PRESSURE. Ensure the pressure release valve is in the SEAL position. The temperature will default to HIGH, which is the correct setting. Set time to 30 minutes. Select START/STOP to begin cooking. 3. When cooking is complete, naturally release the pressure for 10 minutes. Then quick release pressure by turning the pressure release valve to the VENT position. Press START/STOP. 4. Line a baking sheet with aluminum foil. 5. Transfer the pork to a plate. Carefully strain the juices from the pot through a fine-mesh sieve into a bowl, reserving the cooked onions. Use two forks to shred the meat, discarding any extra fat. Place the pork and onion in a single layer on the prepared baking sheet. 6. Place the Deluxe Reversible Rack in the lower position in the pot. Then place the baking sheet with food on the rack. 7. Move slider to AIR FRY/STOVETOP to BROIL. Set the time to 4-5 minutes. Press START/STOP to begin cooking. 8. Broil until the edges are crispy, then flip the meat, spoon on some of the reserved liquid if necessary, and broil for another 4 to 5 minutes. 9. Scoop the avocado from the skin into the bowl of a food processor fitted with the blade attachment (or into a blender) and add the coriander, sour cream, lime juice, and salt. Process until smooth, stopping to scrape down the side of the bowl with a rubber spatula as needed. 10. Transfer the crema to a small bowl. Cover with plastic wrap and store in the refrigerator for up to 2 hours if not using immediately.
Per Serving: Calories 776; Fat 43.49g; Sodium 1065mg; Carbs 41.26g; Fibre 15.1g; Sugar 11.72g; Protein 60.48g

Fresh Salsa Verde Pulled Pork

Prep Time: 15 minutes | Cook Time: 1 hour and 30 minutes | Serves: 8

220 g mild purchased salsa verde
60 ml liquid from a jar of pickled jalapeño rings
2 tablespoons pickled jalapeño rings
One bone-in pork shoulder or picnic ham, any skin and large bits of fat removed
10 g packed fresh coriander leaves, chopped

1. Mix the salsa verde, liquid from the jalapeño rings, and jalapeños in the pressure cooker pot. Add the pork and toss to coat on all sides. Lock the lid onto the pot. 2. Close the lid and move the slider to PRESSURE. Ensure the pressure release valve is in the SEAL position. The temperature will default to HIGH, which is the correct setting. Set time to 1 hour and 30 minutes. Select START/STOP to begin cooking. 3. When cooking is complete, naturally release the pressure for 30 minutes. Then quick release pressure by turning the pressure release valve to the VENT position. Move slider to AIR FRY/ STOVETOP to unlock the lid, then carefully open it. 4. Use a meat fork and a slotted spoon to transfer the pork pieces to a nearby cutting board. Remove and discard the bone. 5. Use a flatware tablespoon to skim any excess surface fat from the sauce in the pot. Shred the meat with two forks. Add these shreds to the pot along with the coriander. Stir well before serving warm.
Per Serving: Calories 283; Fat 8.64g; Sodium 462mg; Carbs 4.3g; Fibre 1.2g; Sugar 2.14g; Protein 43.82g

Homemade Chipotle Pulled Pork

Prep Time: 20 minutes | Cook Time: 1 hour 40 minutes | Serves: 8

360 ml beef or chicken stock
80 g cherry jam (not jelly or preserves)
Up to 2 canned chipotle chilis in adobo sauce, stemmed, seeded (if desired), and chopped
3 tablespoons mild paprika
2 tablespoons Worcestershire sauce
1 teaspoon ground cumin
½ teaspoon ground cloves
½ teaspoon ground dried mustard
1 (1.5 kg) bone-in pork shoulder or picnic ham, any skin and large chunks of fat removed

1. Whisk the stock, jam, chipotles, paprika, Worcestershire sauce, cumin, cloves, and dried mustard in the pot; add the pork and turn the piece in the sauce to coat all sides. 2. Close the lid, turn the pressure release valve to SEAL position, and then move the slider to PRESSURE. Select HI and set the cooking time to 90 minutes. Press START/STOP to begin cooking. When finished, release the pressure naturally. 3. Transfer the pork (or maybe pieces of it) to a nearby cutting board. Cut out and discard the bone. Then use a flatware tablespoon to skim the excess surface fat from the sauce in the pot. 4. Bring the sauce in the pot to a simmer at Lo2 on SEAR/SAUTÉ mode; cook then sauce for 5 to 10 minutes until thickened like barbecue sauce, stirring more and more frequently to prevent scorching. 5. Shred the meat with two forks. Once the sauce has reduced to the right consistency, stir the meat back into it. 6. Stop the process and serve.
Per Serving: Calories 370; Fat: 24.6g; Sodium: 2182mg; Carbs: 5.32g; Fibre: 0.9g; Sugar: 2.72g; Protein: 32.67g

Juicy Smoked Brisket Skewers

Prep Time: 15 minutes | Cook Time: 53 minutes | Serves: 6

900 g flat- or first-cut lean brisket, cut into 4 cm cubes
1 tablespoon mild smoked paprika
1 teaspoon onion powder
½ teaspoon garlic powder
½ teaspoon table salt
Twelve to sixteen 10 cm bamboo or metal skewers
240 ml water
One bottle liquid smoke

1. Toss the brisket cubes, smoked paprika, garlic powder, onion powder, and salt in a big bowl until the meat is well coated. Thread two cubes onto each of the skewers. 2. Pour the water and liquid smoke into the pot. Then place the bottom layer of the Deluxe Reversible Rack in the lower position in the pot. Pile the skewers onto the rack. 3. Close the lid and move the slider to PRESSURE. Ensure the pressure release valve is in the SEAL position. The temperature will default to HIGH, which is the correct setting. Set time to 50 minutes. Select START/STOP to begin cooking. 4. When cooking is complete, press START/STOP. Naturally release the pressure for 20 minutes. Then quick release pressure by turning the pressure release valve to the VENT position. 5. Move slider to AIR FRY/STOVETOP to BROIL. Set the time to 2-3minutes. Press START/STOP to begin cooking. 6. Broil the skewers (in batches in the grill pan) until crisp and browned, turning occasionally.
Per Serving: Calories 244; Fat 10.28g; Sodium 447mg; Carbs 1.28g; Fibre 0.5g; Sugar 0.31g; Protein 34.66g

Smoky Corned Beef with Original Potatoes

Prep Time: 15 minutes | Cook Time: 1 hour and 40 minutes | Serves: 8

1 teaspoon ground dried mustard
1 teaspoon ground coriander
1 teaspoon ground black pepper
One 1.3 – 1.4 kg corned beef, any spice packets removed and discarded, the meat well rinsed
480 ml water
Two bottles liquid smoke
900 g very small, red- or yellow-skinned potatoes, each about the size of a ping-pong balls, scrubbed of any surface dirt

1. In a small bowl, mix together the dried mustard, coriander, and pepper. Dry the corned beef with paper towels, then rub this mixture all over the meat. 2. Pour the water into the pressure cooker pot; stir in the liquid smoke. Then place the Cook & Crisp Basket in the lower position in the pot. 4. Place the coated corned beef on the basket. 3. Close the lid and move the slider to PRESSURE. Ensure the pressure release valve is in the SEAL position. The temperature will default to HIGH, which is the correct setting. Set time to 1 hour 30 minutes. Select START/STOP to begin cooking.4. When cooking is complete, naturally release the pressure for 40 minutes. Then quick release pressure by turning the pressure release valve to the VENT position, then carefully open it. 5. Transfer the corned beef to a nearby cutting board. Tent with foil to keep warm. 6. Remove the basket from the pot. Stir the potatoes into the liquid inside. Lock the lid. 7. Move slider to PRESSURE. Set to high temperature and set the time to 10 minutes. Select START/STOP to begin cooking. 8. When cooking is complete, naturally release the pressure for 5 minutes. Then quick release pressure by turning the pressure release valve to the VENT position. Move slider to AIR FRY/ STOVETOP to unlock the lid, then carefully open it. 9. Drain the potatoes from the pot into a colander set in the sink. Slice the corned beef against the grain into 1 cm-thick strips and serve with the potatoes.
Per Serving: Calories 269; Fat 18.15g; Sodium 1205mg; Carbs 9.41g; Fibre 0.6g; Sugar 7.6g; Protein 16.88g

Easy Egg Salad Sandwiches
Prep Time: 10 minutes | Cook Time: 5 minutes | Serves: 2

6 eggs
30 g chopped celery
2 tablespoons chopped spring onions
60 g mayonnaise
2 tablespoons Dijon mustard
½ teaspoon hot sauce
½ teaspoon Salt
¼ teaspoon freshly ground black pepper
¼ teaspoon paprika
4 slices sandwich bread

1. Add 240 ml to the pressure cooker pot and place the Deluxe Reversible Rack in the bottom. Put the eggs on the rack. 2. Close the lid and cook on high pressure for 5 minutes for hard-boiled eggs. When the timer beeps, naturally release the pressure for 2 to 3 minutes. Then quick release pressure by turning the pressure release valve to the VENT position. Move slider to AIR FRY/ STOVETOP to unlock the lid, then carefully open it. 3. Transfer the eggs to a large bowl and place under cold running water. Peel and chop the eggs as soon as they are cool enough to handle. Transfer to a medium bowl and add the celery and spring onions. 4. In a bowl, combine the mustard, mayonnaise, and hot sauce and mix well. Gently stir the mayo dressing into the egg mixture. Season with the salt, pepper, and paprika. 5. Serve some of the egg salad on the sandwich bread. Store the remaining egg salad in an airtight container in the refrigerator for up to 3 days.
Per Serving: Calories 607; Fat 40.39g; Sodium 1531mg; Carbs 25.83g; Fibre 2.6g; Sugar 4.98g; Protein 33.08g

Cheesy Beef Sandwiches
Prep Time: 20 minutes | Cook Time: 10 minutes | Serves: 6

2 tsp olive oil
1 (905-g) chuck roast
Coarse salt
Freshly ground black pepper
2 medium onions, sliced
475 ml beef stock
2 sprigs thyme
6 crusty rolls split, buttered and toasted
6 slices Swiss cheese
Dijon mustard

1. Season the chuck roast well with salt and pepper. 2. Select SEAR/SAUTÉ. Select Lo3, and then press START/STOP to begin cooking. 3. When hot, pour in the oil to the pot and brown the roast well on all sides. Transfer the roast to a plate and set aside. 4. Add the onions to the drippings in the pot, scraping up any browned bits on the bottom of the pot; sauté the onions for 10 minutes until they are soft and starting to caramelize. 5. Add the beef stock to the pot, taking care to scrape up any browned bits from the bottom of the pot. Place the roast and thyme sprigs directly into the liquid. Stop the process. 6. Close the lid, turn the pressure release valve to SEAL position, and then move the slider to PRESSURE. Select HI and set the cooking time to 40 minutes. Press START/STOP to begin cooking. When finished, release the pressure naturally. 7. Divide the meat among the roll bottoms and top each with a slice of Swiss cheese. Spread Dijon on the underside of the roll tops and place over the cheese.
Per Serving: Calories 451; Fat: 19.76g; Sodium: 1725mg; Carbs: 25.66g; Fibre: 1.5g; Sugar: 4.43g; Protein: 40.86g

Italian-Flavoured Pork Loin
Prep Time: 20 minutes | Cook Time: 15 minutes | Serves: 4

2 tsp olive oil
3 cloves garlic, minced
2 tsp Italian seasoning
1 tsp. coarse salt
½ tsp. freshly ground black pepper
680 g pork tenderloin
240 ml water or chicken stock

1. Mix the olive oil, garlic, Italian seasoning, salt and pepper in a small bowl. Rub the mixture all over the outside of the pork loin. 2. Pour the water or stock into the pot and insert the rack. Place the pork loin on the rack. 3. Close the lid, turn the pressure release valve to SEAL position, and then move the slider to PRESSURE. Select HI and set the cooking time to 25 minutes. Press START/STOP to begin cooking. When finished, release the pressure naturally. 4. Remove the pork and allow it to rest on a carving board for 5 minutes, then slice and serve.
Per Serving: Calories 289; Fat: 8.63g; Sodium: 893mg; Carbs: 4.51g; Fibre: 0.4g; Sugar: 0.3g; Protein: 45.28g

Authentic Pepperoncini Pot Roast
Prep Time: 35 minutes | Cook Time: 1 hour 35 minutes | Serves: 8

2 tsp. olive oil
1 (2.3-kg) chuck roast
1 large onion, sliced
1 (310-ml) can French onion soup
60 ml water
1 (30-g) packet dried ranch seasoning mix
1 (30-g) packet dried beef gravy mix
½ (455-g) jar pepperoncini peppers (half of both peppers and juice)
60 ml heavy cream

1. Select SEAR/SAUTÉ. Select Lo3, and then press START/STOP to begin cooking. 2. When the pot is hot, heat the olive oil. When the oil is shimmering, add the chuck roast and brown for 10 minutes on all sides. Transfer the roast to a plate and set aside. 3. Add the sliced onion and cook for 5 minutes until the onion is starting to soften. 4. Stop the process, and add the French onion soup and water to the pot, stirring well to scrape up any browned bits from the bottom. 5. Return the roast to the pot. Add the ranch and gravy mixes, then the pepperoncini and their juice. 6. Close the lid, turn the pressure release valve to SEAL position, and then move the slider to PRESSURE. Select HI and set the cooking time to 80 minutes. Press START/STOP to begin cooking. When finished, release the pressure naturally. 7. Place the dish on a serving platter. 8. Using a gravy or fat separator, or just a spoon skimming from the top, remove the fat from the liquid in the pot. Stir in the cream. 9. Pour the gravy over the roast, serving the extra on the side.
Per Serving: Calories 406; Fat: 14.05g; Sodium: 2905mg; Carbs: 13.56g; Fibre: 2g; Sugar: 5.32g; Protein: 54.73g

Tender Pork Chops with Onion Gravy

Prep Time: 20 minutes | Cook Time: 25 minutes | Serves: 4

4 (2.5-cm thick) bone-in pork chops
Coarse salt
Freshly ground pepper
2 tsp olive oil
1 large onion, sliced
240 ml beef stock
60 ml heavy cream
1 tbsp cornflour

---

1. Season the chops with salt and pepper. 2. Select SEAR/SAUTÉ. Select Lo3, and then press START/STOP to begin cooking. 3. When hot, pour in the olive oil and brown the chops for 5 minutes on both sides. Transfer the chops to a plate and set them aside. 4. Add the onion to the pot and cook for 5 minutes until the onion is starting to soften; add the beef stock, stirring to scrape up any browned bits from the bottom of the pot. Return the pork chops to the pot. 5. Close the lid, turn the pressure release valve to SEAL position, and then move the slider to PRESSURE. Select HI and set the cooking time to 10 minutes. Press START/STOP to begin cooking. When finished, release the pressure naturally. 6. Remove the chops and cover with foil to keep warm. 7. In a small bowl, mix together the cream and cornflour, then pour into the pot. Stir until the sauce is thickened, 2 to 3 minutes. Pour the sauce on top of the pork chops and serve.
Per Serving: Calories 426; Fat: 24.9g; Sodium: 245mg; Carbs: 6.78g; Fibre: 1g; Sugar: 2.42g; Protein: 41.49g

Perfect Mexican Beef Casserole

Prep Time: 20 minutes | Cook Time: 15 minutes | Serves: 4

2 tsp olive oil
1 medium onion, chopped
3 cloves garlic, minced
455 g beef mince
1 tbsp chipotle chili powder
1 tbsp ancho chili powder
1 tbsp ground cumin
120 ml water
195 g uncooked long-grain white rice
1 red pepper, seeded and chopped
1 poblano pepper, chopped
1 jalapeño pepper, minced
1 (455-g) jar red salsa
1 (410-g) can fire-roasted diced tomatoes
220 g Mexican-blend shredded cheese
2 green onions, chopped
10 g chopped fresh coriander

---

1. Select SEAR/SAUTÉ. Select Lo3, and then press START/STOP to begin cooking. 2. When hot, add olive oil and onion, and then cook them for 5 minutes until the onion is soft; add garlic, beef mince, chili powders and cumin, and cook the beef until no pink remains. 3. Add the water, taking care to scrape up any browned bits from the bottom of the pot. 4. Stop the process, and add the rice, the bell, poblano and jalapeño peppers, and the salsa and tomatoes in order without stirring. 5. Close the lid, turn the pressure release valve to SEAL position, and then move the slider to PRESSURE. Select HI and set the cooking time to 9 minutes. Press START/STOP to begin cooking. When finished, release the pressure naturally. 6. Stir in the cheese, and then top with green onions and coriander.
Per Serving: Calories 704; Fat: 32.59g; Sodium: 514mg; Carbs: 52.89g; Fibre: 5.9g; Sugar: 8.17g; Protein: 49.8g

Hearty Lamb Ragù

Prep Time: 20 minutes | Cook Time: 15 minutes | Serves: 2

3 tablespoons olive oil
1 large yellow onion, chopped
2 medium carrots, chopped
4 medium garlic cloves, peeled and minced
675 g boneless leg of lamb, cut into 5 cm pieces
240 ml chicken stock
2 tablespoons fresh rosemary leaves, chopped
2 tablespoons fresh sage leaves, chopped
½ teaspoon table salt
½ teaspoon ground black pepper
1 (150 g) can tomato paste

---

1. Select SEAR/SAUTÉ. Select Lo3, and then press START/STOP to begin cooking. 2. When hot, heat the oil for 1 to 2 minutes; add onion and carrot, and cook them for 5 minutes until the onion begins to soften. Stir in the garlic and cook for a few seconds; add the lamb pieces and stir them for 1 minute just until the lamb is thoroughly mixed into the vegetables. 3. Stop the process, and stir in the stock, rosemary, sage, salt, and pepper. 4. Close the lid, turn the pressure release valve to SEAL position, and then move the slider to PRESSURE. Select HI and set the cooking time to 30 minutes. Press START/STOP to begin cooking. When finished, release the pressure naturally. 5. Break up the meat into smaller pieces. Stir in the tomato paste until uniform. 6. Bring the sauce to a simmer at Lo2 on SEAR/SAUTÉ mode for 5 minutes until thickened. 7. Set the lid askew over the pot for 5 minutes to blend the flavors. 8. Serve and enjoy.
Per Serving: Calories 1012; Fat: 53.39g; Sodium: 1448mg; Carbs: 30.88g; Fibre: 7.3g; Sugar: 15.83g; Protein: 101.14g

Spicy Baby Back Ribs

Prep Time: 10 minutes | Cook Time: 35 minutes | Serves: 4

675g baby back ribs
2 tablespoons olive oil
1 teaspoon smoked paprika
1 teaspoon garlic powder
1 teaspoon onion powder
½ teaspoon cumin
1 teaspoon mustard powder
1 teaspoon dried thyme
Coarse sea salt and freshly cracked black pepper, to season

---

1. Toss all the recipe ingredients in a greased Cook & Crisp Basket. 2. Place the Cook & Crisp Basket in your Pressure Cooker Steam Fryer. 3. Put on the Smart Lid on top of the Ninja Foodi Steam Fryer. 4. Move the Lid Slider to the "Air Fry/Stovetop". Select the "Air Fry" mode for cooking. 5. Cook the pork ribs at 175°C for around 35 minutes, turning them over halfway through the cooking time. 6. Serve.
Per Serving: Calories: 440; Fat:33.3g; Carbs: 1.8g; Fibre: 0.4g; Sugars: 0.1g; Proteins: 33.7g

Tangy Pork Ragù

Prep Time: 5 minutes | Cook Time: 15 minutes | Serves: 4

900 g boneless pork shoulder, cut into 5 cm pieces and any large chunks of fat removed
900 g plum or Roma tomatoes, chopped
240 ml chicken stock
1 small yellow onion, chopped
2 medium celery stalks, thinly sliced
2 tablespoons fresh oregano leaves, finely chopped
2 tablespoons fresh rosemary leaves, finely chopped
½ teaspoon table salt
½ teaspoon ground black pepper
60 g heavy cream
10 g loosely packed parsley leaves, chopped

1. Mix the pork, tomatoes, stock, onion, celery, oregano, rosemary, salt, and pepper in the pot. 2. Close the lid, turn the pressure release valve to SEAL position, and then move the slider to PRESSURE. Select HI and set the cooking time to 45 minutes. Press START/STOP to begin cooking. When finished, release the pressure naturally. 3. Use a flatware tablespoon to skim any excess surface fat from the top of the sauce. Break up the pork pieces into smaller bits and shreds, stirring these into the sauce. 4. Bring the sauce to a simmer at Lo2 on SEAR/SAUTÉ mode, stir in the cream and cook them for 4 minutes until somewhat thickened. 5. Transfer the food to the serving plate and stir in the parsley. Enjoy.
Per Serving: Calories 625; Fat: 15.01g; Sodium: 716mg; Carbs: 56.56g; Fibre: 3g; Sugar: 52g; Protein: 65.61g

BBQ Pulled Pork Sandwiches

Prep Time: 15 minutes | Cook Time: 45 minutes | Serves: 2

½ tablespoon packed light brown sugar
½ teaspoon paprika
½ teaspoon salt
½ teaspoon ground mustard
¼ teaspoon ground cumin
¼ teaspoon freshly ground black pepper
455 g boneless pork shoulder roast
1 teaspoon oil
120 ml chicken stock
480 g classic barbecue sauce, divided

1. Combine the brown sugar, paprika, salt, mustard, cumin, and pepper in a small bowl. Rub the mixture all over the pork roast. 2. Select SEAR/SAUTÉ. Select Lo3, and then press START/STOP to begin cooking. 3. When hot, add oil and brown the pork for 2 to 3 minutes per side. 4. Stop the process, and then add stock and 240 g of barbecue sauce to the pot and stir them well. 5. Close the lid, turn the pressure release valve to SEAL position, and then move the slider to PRESSURE. Select HI and set the cooking time to 45 minutes. Press START/STOP to begin cooking. When finished, release the pressure naturally. 6. Transfer the pork to a large bowl. Stir and allow simmering for 10 to 12 minutes, or until thickened and reduced. 7. During cooking, use a spoon to remove any fat that rises to the top. Taste and adjust the seasonings as necessary. 8. Shred the pork with two forks. Return the meat to the pot, stir, and warm through. 9. Serve on hamburger buns or Portobello mushroom caps with additional barbecue sauce and coleslaw.
Per Serving: Calories 838; Fat: 14.29g; Sodium: 3716mg; Carbs: 119.3g; Fibre: 2.9g; Sugar: 96.12g; Protein: 54.9g

Tasty Beef Enchiladas

Prep Time: 30 minutes | Cook Time: 60 minutes | Serves: 2

1 tablespoon oil, plus more for greasing
455 g beef roast
Salt
Freshly ground black pepper
1 small onion, chopped
240 ml beef stock
110 g tomato salsa
1 tablespoon red wine vinegar
½ tablespoon ground cumin
1 (250 g) can enchilada sauce, divided
6 (15 cm) corn or flour tortillas
100 g shredded sharp Cheddar cheese

1. Season the beef with pepper and salt. 2. Select SEAR/SAUTÉ. Select Lo3, and then press START/STOP to begin cooking. 3. When hot, add 1 tablespoon of oil and sear the beef for 8 to 10 minutes on all sides. 4. Stop the process, and add onion, stock, salsa, vinegar, and cumin to the pot. 5. Close the lid, turn the pressure release valve to SEAL position, and then move the slider to PRESSURE. Select HI and set the cooking time to 60 minutes. Press START/STOP to begin cooking. When finished, release the pressure naturally. 6. Transfer the roast from the pot to a large bowl, discarding the liquid. Shred the roast. 7. Add 60 g of the enchilada sauce to the meat and toss to combine. Taste and adjust the seasonings if desired. 8. Coat a suitable baking pan with oil. Spread half of the remaining enchilada sauce (about 120 g on the bottom of the prepared baking pan. 9. Lay the tortillas out on a cutting board. Stuff each tortilla with the shredded beef mixture and 1 tablespoon of cheese. Roll up and place seam-side down in the baking dish. Pour the remaining enchilada sauce over the enchiladas and sprinkle with the remaining cheese. 10. Add the baking pan to the pot. Close the lid and move slider to AIR FRY/STOVETOP, then use the dial to select BAKE/ROAST. Adjust the cooking temperature to 175°C and set the cooking time to 20 minutes. Press START/STOP to begin cooking. 11. Transfer the dish to a cooling rack and let rest for 5 to 10 minutes before serving with sour cream, guacamole, salsa, and chopped coriander.
Per Serving: Calories 1289; Fat: 62.26g; Sodium: 3062mg; Carbs: 91.8g; Fibre: 8.3g; Sugar: 15g; Protein: 92.39g

Pork and Vegetables Skewers

Prep Time: 10 minutes | Cook Time: 15 minutes | Serves: 4

455g pork tenderloin, cubed
455g peppers, diced
455g aubergine, diced
1 tablespoon olive oil
1 tablespoon parsley, chopped
1 tablespoon coriander, chopped
Sea salt and black pepper, to taste

1. Place the Cook & Crisp Basket in your Pressure Cooker Steam Fryer. 2. Toss all the recipe ingredients in a suitable mixing bowl until well coated on all sides. 3. Thread the ingredients onto skewers and place them in the Cook & Crisp Basket. 4. Put on the Smart Lid on top of the Ninja Foodi Steam Fryer. 5. Move the Lid Slider to the "Air Fry/Stovetop". Select the "Air Fry" mode for cooking. 6. Then, cook the skewers at 200°C for around 15 minutes, turning them over halfway through the cooking time. 7. Serve.
Per Serving: Calories: 344; Fat:16.3g; Carbs: 18g; Fibre: 5.3g; Sugars: 10.1g; Proteins: 32.6g

Homemade Mongolian Beef

Prep Time: 5 minutes | Cook Time: 15 minutes | Serves: 4

455 g skirt steak
80 ml soy sauce (or tamari, to make it gluten-free)
3 tablespoons pure maple syrup
1 tablespoon raw apple cider vinegar
1 tablespoon minced fresh ginger (2.5 cm knob)
2 cloves garlic, minced
125 g sliced shiitake mushrooms
190 g bulgur (or white rice, to make it gluten-free)
300 ml plus 2 tablespoons water
2 heads baby bok choy
120 g sugar snap peas
120 g shredded carrots
1 tablespoon cornflour
60 g chopped green onions, tender white and green parts only
Chopped fresh coriander, for garnish
Sesame seeds, for garnish

1. Thinly cut the steak across the grain into 1 cm-thick slices. 2. Place the steak in the pot and add the soy sauce, maple syrup, vinegar, ginger, garlic, and mushrooms. Stir to coat the beef. 3. In an oven-safe bowl, combine the bulgur and 300 ml of the water. Arrange the rack over the meat and place the bowl on top. 4. Close the lid, turn the pressure release valve to SEAL position, and then move the slider to PRESSURE. Select HI and set the cooking time to 4 minutes. Press START/STOP to begin cooking. When finished, release the pressure naturally. 5. To prepare the bok choy, trim the ends, rinse well to remove any dirt, then slice crosswise into 2.5 cm pieces. 6. Lift the rack and the bowl out of the pot, then add the bok choy, snap peas, and carrots to the pot, and cook them at Lo3 on SEAR/SAUTÉ mode for 5 minutes until the vegetables are crisp-tender. 7. In a separate bowl, mix up the cornflour and the 2 tablespoons water to make slurry. Pour the slurry into the pot and stir for 1 to 2 minutes until the sauce thickens. 8. Serve the beef and vegetables over the cooked bulgur with a generous topping of green onions, coriander, and sesame seeds. 9. Store the leftovers in an airtight container in the fridge for 3 or 4 days.
Per Serving: Calories 513; Fat: 12.1g; Sodium: 1820mg; Carbs: 62.55g; Fibre: 4.4g; Sugar: 12.54g; Protein: 39.24g

Italian Pot Roast Ragù

Prep Time: 15 minutes | Cook Time: 60 minutes | Serves: 4

2 tablespoons olive oil
900 g boneless beef chuck, trimmed of any large chunks of fat and cut in half
1 can whole tomatoes
60 g frozen pearl onions (do not thaw)
180 ml light dry red wine, such as Pinot Noir
1 tablespoon drained and rinsed capers, chopped
1 medium garlic clove, peeled and minced (1 teaspoon)
1 tablespoon dried rosemary
2 teaspoons dried oregano
1 bay leaf
½ teaspoon table salt
½ teaspoon ground black pepper

1. Select SEAR/SAUTÉ. Select Lo3, and then press START/STOP to begin cooking. 2. When hot, heat the oil for 1 to 2 minutes, and then brown the beef pieces. Transfer the beef to a bowl. 3. Squeeze the whole tomatoes over the pot, and then add any remaining juice from the can. Add the pearl onions and stir well to scrape up all the browned bits on the bottom of the pot, and cook them for 2 minutes just until the onions begin to brown lightly. 4. Stop the process, and stir in wine, capers, rosemary, garlic, oregano, bay leaf, salt, and pepper, and then return the beef pieces and any juice in the bowl to the pot. 5. Close the lid, turn the pressure release valve to SEAL position, and then move the slider to PRESSURE. Select HI and set the cooking time to 55 minutes. Press START/STOP to begin cooking. When finished, release the pressure naturally. 6. Skim off any excess surface fat with a flatware tablespoon. Find and discard the bay leaf, then use two forks to shred the meat. 7. Bring the sauce to a full simmer at Lo2 on SEAR/ SAUTÉ mode for 5 minutes until reduced to a fairly wet ragù. 8. Stop the process and set the lid askew over the pot for 5 minutes to blend the flavors.
Per Serving: Calories 399; Fat: 19.9g; Sodium: 582mg; Carbs: 9.18g; Fibre: 1.4g; Sugar: 6.19g; Protein: 47.45g

Limey Steak Salad

Prep Time: 10 minutes | Cook Time: 12 minutes | Serves: 5

900g T-bone steak
1 teaspoon garlic powder
Sea salt and black pepper, to taste
2 tablespoons lime juice
60ml extra-virgin olive oil
1 pepper, seeded and sliced
1 red onion, sliced
1 tomato, diced

1. Place the Cook & Crisp Basket in your Pressure Cooker Steam Fryer. 2. Toss the steak with the garlic powder, salt, and black pepper; place the steak in the Cook & Crisp Basket. Put on the Smart Lid on top of the Ninja Foodi Steam Fryer. 3. Move the Lid Slider to the "Air Fry/Stovetop". Select the "Air Fry" mode for cooking. 4. Cook the steak at 200°C for around 12 minutes, turning it over halfway through the cooking time. 5. Cut the steak into slices and add in the remaining ingredients. Serve at room temperature or well-chilled. 6. Serve.
Per Serving: Calories: 316; Fat:16g; Carbs: 3.7g; Fibre: 0.7g; Sugars: 1.7g; Proteins: 38.2g

Simple Beef Dinner Rolls

Prep Time: 10 minutes | Cook Time: 15 minutes | Serves: 4

455g beef
½ teaspoon garlic powder
½ teaspoon onion powder
1 teaspoon paprika
Sea salt and black pepper, to taste
8 dinner rolls

1. Place the Cook & Crisp Basket in your Pressure Cooker Steam Fryer. 2. Mix all the recipe ingredients, except for the dinner rolls. Shape the mixture into four patties. 3. Put on the Smart Lid on top of the Ninja Foodi Steam Fryer. 4. Move the Lid Slider to the "Air Fry/Stovetop". Select the "Air Fry" mode for cooking. 5. Cook the burgers at 195°C for about 15 minutes or until cooked through; make sure to turn them over halfway through the cooking time. 6. Serve your burgers on the prepared dinner rolls and enjoy!
Per Serving: Calories: 406; Fat:16.2g; Carbs: 27g; Fibre: 2.6g; Sugars: 1.5g; Proteins: 35.2g

Tender and Juicy Filet Mignon

Prep Time: 10 minutes | Cook Time: 14 minutes | Serves: 4

675g filet mignon
2 tablespoons soy sauce
2 tablespoons butter, melted
1 teaspoon mustard powder
1 teaspoon garlic powder
Sea salt and black pepper, to taste

1. Place the Cook & Crisp Basket in your Pressure Cooker Steam Fryer. 2. Toss the filet mignon with the remaining ingredients; place the filet mignon in the Cook & Crisp Basket. 3. Put on the Smart Lid on top of the Ninja Foodi Steam Fryer. 4. Move the Lid Slider to the "Air Fry/Stovetop". Select the "Air Fry" mode for cooking. 5. Cook the filet mignon at 200°C for around 14 minutes, turning it over halfway through the cooking time. 6. Enjoy!
Per Serving: Calories: 393; Fat:26.2g; Carbs: 2.7g; Fibre: 0.2g; Sugars: 1.5g; Proteins: 36.2g

Garlic Beef Shoulder

Prep Time: 10 minutes | Cook Time: 55 minutes | Serves: 4

675g beef shoulder
Sea salt and black pepper, to taste
1 teaspoon cayenne pepper
½ teaspoon cumin
2 tablespoons olive oil
2 cloves garlic, minced
1 teaspoon Dijon mustard
1 onion, cut into slices

1. Place the Cook & Crisp Basket in your Pressure Cooker Steam Fryer. 2. Toss the beef with the spices, garlic, mustard, and olive oil; brush the Cook & Crisp Basket with oil and place the beef in it. 3. Put on the Smart Lid on top of the Ninja Foodi Steam Fryer. 4. Move the Lid Slider to the "Air Fry/Stovetop". Select the "Air Fry" mode for cooking. 5. Cook the beef at 200°C for around 45 minutes, turning it over halfway through the cooking time. 6. Pour in the onion and continue to cook an additional 10 minutes. 7. Serve.
Per Serving: Calories: 309; Fat:16.2g; Carbs: 2.2g; Fibre: 0.4g; Sugars: 0.7g; Proteins: 36.2g

Italian Herbed Pork Cut

Prep Time: 10 minutes | Cook Time: 55 minutes | Serves: 5

900g pork centre cut
2 tablespoons olive oil
1 tablespoon Italian herb mix
1 teaspoon red pepper flakes, crushed
Sea salt and black pepper, to taste

1. Toss all the recipe ingredients in a greased Cook & Crisp Basket. 2. Place the Cook & Crisp Basket in your Pressure Cooker Steam Fryer. 3. Put on the Smart Lid on top of the Ninja Foodi Steam Fryer. 4. Move the Lid Slider to the "Air Fry/Stovetop". Select the "Air Fry" mode for cooking. 5. Cook the pork at 180°C for around 55 minutes, turning it over halfway through the cooking time. 6. Serve warm and enjoy!
Per Serving: Calories: 356; Fat:21.7g; Carbs: 0.1g; Fibre: 0.1g; Sugars: 0.1g Proteins: 37.5g

Mustard Sausage with Fennel

Prep Time: 10 minutes | Cook Time: 15 minutes | Serves: 4

455g pork sausage
455g fennel, quartered
1 teaspoon garlic powder
½ teaspoon onion powder
2 teaspoons mustard

1. Place all the recipe ingredients in a greased Cook & Crisp Basket. 2. Place the Cook & Crisp Basket in your Pressure Cooker Steam Fryer. 3. Put on the Smart Lid on top of the Ninja Foodi Steam Fryer. 4. Move the Lid Slider to the "Air Fry/Stovetop". Select the "Air Fry" mode for cooking. 5. Air fry the sausage and fennel at 185°C for approximately 15 minutes, tossing the basket halfway through the cooking time. 6. Serve.
Per Serving: Calories: 433; Fat:35.7g; Carbs: 9.9g; Fibre: 3.7g; Sugars: 1g; Proteins: 17.8g

Spiced Pork Patties

Prep Time: 10 minutes | Cook Time: 15 minutes | Serves: 4

455g pork
1 small onion, chopped
1 garlic clove, minced
4 tablespoons tortilla chips, crushed
1 teaspoon fresh sage, minced
1 teaspoon fresh coriander, minced
1 tablespoon fresh parsley, minced
1 egg, beaten
½ teaspoon smoked paprika
Sea salt and black pepper, to taste

1. Place the Cook & Crisp Basket in your Pressure Cooker Steam Fryer. 2. In a suitable mixing bowl, mix all the recipe ingredients. Form the mixture into four patties. 3. Put on the Smart Lid on top of the Ninja Foodi Steam Fryer. 4. Move the Lid Slider to the "Air Fry/Stovetop". Select the "Air Fry" mode for cooking. 5. Cook the burgers at 195°C for about 15 minutes or until cooked through; make sure to turn them over halfway through the cooking time. 6. Serve.
Per Serving: Calories: 386; Fat:28.7g; Carbs: 9.2g; Fibre: 1.1g; Sugars: 1g; Proteins: 22.3g

Comforting Lamb and Vegetables Casserole
Prep Time: 15 minutes | Cook Time: 45 minutes | Serves: 4

455 g lamb stew meat, cubed
1 tbsp olive oil
3 cloves garlic, minced
2 tomatoes, chopped
455 g baby potatoes
2 carrots, chopped
1 onion, chopped
1 celery stalk, chopped

2 tbsp ketchup
2 tbsp red wine
480 ml chicken stock
1 tsp sweet paprika
1 tsp cumin, ground
¼ tsp oregano, dried
¼ tsp rosemary, dried
Salt and ground black pepper to taste

1. Move slider to AIR FRY/STOVETOP. Select SEAR/SAUTÉ and set to 3. Select START/STOP to begin preheating. Allow unit to preheat for 2 minutes. After 2 minutes, heat the oil. 2. Place in the lamb and cook until the meat has turned light brown. 3. Place in the garlic and sauté for 1 minute more. 4. Add all of the remaining ingredients and spices. Press START/STOP to turn off the SEAR/SAUTÉ function. 5. Close the lid and move slider to PRESSURE. Ensure the pressure release valve is in the SEAL position. The temperature will default to HIGH, which is the correct setting. Set time to 35 minutes. Select START/STOP to begin cooking. 6. When cooking is complete, naturally release the pressure for 10 minutes. Then turn the pressure relief valve to the VENT position for quick pressure relief. Move slider to AIR FRY/ STOVETOP to unlock the lid, then carefully open it. Serve.
Per Serving: Calories 368; Fat 11.37g; Sodium 361mg; Carbs 36.88g; Fibre 5.2g; Sugar 9.62g; Protein 30.07g

Palatable Pork Chops with Apples
Prep Time: 15 minutes | Cook Time: 15 minutes | Serves: 4

1 tsp nutmeg
1 tsp cinnamon
4 tbsp brown sugar
2 apples, sliced

4 tbsp butter
4 pork chops, 2 – 2.5 cm thick
Salt and ground black pepper to taste

1. Mix the nutmeg, cinnamon and brown sugar in a bowl. 2. Season the sliced apples with this mix and stir to coat well. 3. Move slider to AIR FRY/STOVETOP. Select SEAR/SAUTÉ and set to 3. Select START/STOP to begin preheating. Allow unit to preheat for 2 minutes. After 2 minutes, add the butter and melt it. 4. Add the apples to the pot and sauté, stirring occasionally, for 2 minutes. 5. Rub both sides of the pork chops with salt and pepper. 6. Put the pork on the apples. Press START/STOP to turn off the SEAR/SAUTÉ function. 7. Close the lid and move slider to PRESSURE. Ensure the pressure release valve is in the SEAL position. The temperature will default to HIGH, which is the correct setting. Set time to 10 minutes. Select START/STOP to begin cooking. 8. Once the timer beeps, turn the pressure relief valve to the VENT position for quick pressure relief. Move slider to the right to unlock the lid, then carefully open it. Serve.
Per Serving: Calories 517; Fat 29.27g; Sodium 180mg; Carbs 22.42g; Fibre 2.8g; Sugar 17.89g; Protein 40.85g

Spicy Pork Chops with Creamy Mushroom Gravy
Prep Time: 15 minutes | Cook Time: 40 minutes | Serves: 4

4 boneless pork loin chops
1 tsp onion powder
1 tsp salt
1 tsp black pepper
1 tsp garlic powder
1 tbsp paprika
¼ tsp cayenne pepper

2 tbsp coconut oil
½ medium onion, sliced
150 g baby bella mushrooms, sliced
1 tbsp butter
120 g heavy whipping cream
¼ – ½ tsp cornflour
1 tbsp chopped fresh parsley

1. Rinse the pork chops and dry with paper towel. 2. In a bowl, mix up the black pepper, onion powder, garlic powder, salt, paprika, and cayenne powder. 3. Season the pork chops with 1 tablespoon of the spice mix and rub all sides of the pork chops with the spice mix. 4. Move slider to AIR FRY/STOVETOP. Select SEAR/SAUTÉ and set to 3. Select START/STOP to begin preheating. Allow unit to preheat for 2 minutes. After 2 minutes, add and heat the oil. 5. Put the pork in the pot and cook for about 3 minutes on each side, until browned. 6. Transfer the meat to a plate and press START/STOP to turn off the SEAR/SAUTÉ function. 7. Place the onions and mushrooms into the pot. Place the pork chops on the top. 8. Close the lid and move slider to PRESSURE. Ensure the pressure release valve is in the SEAL position. The temperature will default to HIGH, which is the correct setting. Set time to 25 minutes. Select START/STOP to begin cooking. 9. When cooking is complete, naturally release the pressure for 10 minutes. Then turn the pressure relief valve to the VENT position for quick pressure relief. Move slider to AIR FRY/ STOVETOP to unlock the lid, then carefully open it. 10. Transfer the pork to a serving plate. 11. Move slider to AIR FRY/STOVETOP. Select SEAR/SAUTÉ and set to 3. Select START/STOP to begin cooking. add the heavy cream, butter, and remaining spice mix to the pot. Stir well. 12. Add the cornflour and mix well. Let the sauce simmer for 5 minutes until start to thicken. Press START/STOP. 13. Pour the gravy over the pork chops. Season with parsley and serve.
Per Serving: Calories 510; Fat 22.26g; Sodium 709mg; Carbs 35.29g; Fibre 5.9g; Sugar 1.67g; Protein 46.43g

Healthy Spiced Pork Strips with Lettuce

Prep Time: 15 minutes | Cook Time: 40 minutes | Serves: 4

900 g. pork tenderloin, cut into 5 cm strips
3 tbsp garlic, chopped
2 tbsp dried oregano
½ tbsp ground cumin
3 tbsp sweet paprika

½ tsp salt
½ tsp ground black pepper
2 tbsp olive oil
480 ml vegetable stock
90 g lettuce, chopped

1. Mix the garlic, paprika, oregano, cumin, salt and pepper in a large bowl. 2. Rub the pork strips all over until well coated. Let marinate for at least 30 minutes. 3. Move slider to AIR FRY/STOVETOP. Select SEAR/SAUTÉ and set to 3. Select START/STOP to begin preheating. Allow unit to preheat for 2 minutes. After 2 minutes, add and heat the oil. 4. Add the meat and cook for 10 minutes until browned. 5. Pour in the vegetable stock and stir well. Press START/STOP to turn off the SEAR/SAUTÉ function. 6. Close the lid and move slider to PRESSURE. Ensure the pressure release valve is in the SEAL position. The temperature will default to HIGH, which is the correct setting. Set time to 30 minutes. Select START/STOP to begin cooking. 7. When cooking is complete, naturally release the pressure for 15 minutes. Then turn the pressure relief valve to the VENT position for quick pressure relief. Move slider to AIR FRY/ STOVETOP to unlock the lid, then carefully open it. 8. Serve the cooked pork with the chopped lettuce.
Per Serving: Calories 472; Fat 16.83g; Sodium 713mg; Carbs 16.11g; Fibre 5.2g; Sugar 3.27g; Protein 63.84g

Delicious Pork and Cabbage Stew

Prep Time: 10 minutes | Cook Time: 50 minutes | Serves: 8

1.8 kg. pork roast, cut into chunks
3 tbsp coconut oil
4 cloves garlic, minced
2 large onions, chopped

1 tsp salt
1 tsp ground black pepper
240 ml water
1 head cabbage, chopped

1. Move slider to AIR FRY/STOVETOP. Select SEAR/SAUTÉ and set to 3. Select START/STOP to begin preheating. Allow unit to preheat for 2 minutes. After 2 minutes, add and heat the oil. 2. Add the garlic and onions and sauté for 5-6 minutes until the onion is translucent. 3. Put the pork chunks in the pot and cook for 5 minutes on all sides. 4. Season with pepper and salt; pour the water and stir well. 5. Press START/STOP to turn off the SEAR/SAUTÉ function. 6. Close the lid and move slider to PRESSURE. Ensure the pressure release valve is in the SEAL position. The temperature will default to HIGH, which is the correct setting. Set time to 35 minutes. Select START/STOP to begin cooking. 7. When cooking is complete, turn the pressure relief valve to the VENT position for quick pressure relief. Move slider to the right to unlock the lid, then carefully open it. 8. Cook on SEAR/SAUTÉ function and set the heat to 3. Add the cabbage, stir and bring to a simmer. 9. Simmer the dish for 5 minutes. Serve.
Per Serving: Calories 520; Fat 25.27g; Sodium 417mg; Carbs 9.45g; Fibre 2.2g; Sugar 4.32g; Protein 61.55g

Chapter 8 Seafood Mains

Thai Coconut Salmon Curry 83

Soy-Ginger Salmon and Broccoli 83

Cheesy Tuna Noodle Casserole 83

Lemony Cocktail Prawns 83

Quick Prawns Boil with Sausage 84

Garlicky Chili Fish Tacos 84

Honey-Soy Salmon 84

Homemade Pesto Tilapia with Sun-Dried Tomatoes 84

Lemony-Buttered Lobster Tails 85

Fantastic Brown Butter Pasta with Scallops & Tomatoes 85

Delicious Scallop Risotto with Spinach 85

Refreshing Salmon with Zesty Dill Sauce ... 85

Lemony Cajun Salmon 86

Fried Cheese Prawns 86

Traditional Prawns Scampi 86

Tasty Miso Salmon Fillets 86

Easy Crab Legs with Lemon Wedges 86

Creamy Scallops with Spinach 87

Marinated Salmon Fillets with Vegetable ... 87

Limey Garlic Salmon Fillets 87

Fresh Prawns and Broccoli 87

Coconut Salmon Cakes with Greens 88

Zesty Salmon Salad 88

Yummy Parmesan Cod 88

Quick Bacon Wrapped Scallops 88

Air Fried Cod with Spring Onions 89

Creamy Dill Salmon 89

Thai Coconut Salmon Curry

Prep Time: 10 minutes | Cook Time: 15 minutes | Serves: 4

1 tablespoon extra-virgin olive oil
½ red onion, chopped
1 tablespoon minced fresh ginger (about 2.5 cm knob)
1 tablespoon curry powder
1 red pepper, seeded and chopped
One can full-fat coconut milk
2 tablespoons pure maple syrup
1 tablespoon freshly squeezed lime juice
1 tablespoon soy sauce (or tamari, to make it gluten-free)
455 g wild-caught Alaskan salmon
½ teaspoon fine sea salt
Freshly ground black pepper
10 g chopped fresh basil
140 g cauliflower "rice"
Chopped fresh coriander or basil, for garnish

1. Add the oil to the pot. Select SEAR/SAUTÉ. Select Lo3, and then press START/STOP to begin cooking. 2. When the oil is hot, place in the red onion and sauté for 3 minutes until softened; add ginger and curry powder and stir them for 1 minute more. 3. Stop the process. 4. Pour a splash of water to the pan, scraping the bottom with the wooden spoon or a spatula to ensure nothing is stuck. 5. Add the pepper, coconut milk, maple syrup, lime juice, and soy sauce. Place a fish rack on top of the curry, then place the salmon on the rack, skin side down, in one layer. Sprinkle the fish with salt and a few grinds of pepper. 6. Close the lid, turn the pressure release valve to SEAL position, and then move the slider to PRESSURE. Select HI and set the cooking time to 2 minutes. Press START/STOP to begin cooking. When finished, release the pressure quickly. 7. Place the cooked fish directly into the sauce below. The skin will most likely stick to the rack, making it easy to flake the part you want to eat. Remove any small bones you see. Lift the rack out of the pot. 8. Simmer the sauce at Lo2 on SEAR/SAUTÉ mode for 3 minutes until the sauce reduces slightly. 9. Stir in the basil and riced cauliflower, and then stop the process. 10. Serve the curry warm with coriander sprinkled over the top. You can store the leftovers in an airtight container in the fridge for 3 days.
Per Serving: Calories 745; Fat: 29.41g; Sodium: 441mg; Carbs: 107.64g; Fibre: 12.9g; Sugar: 16.56g; Protein: 22.19g

Soy-Ginger Salmon and Broccoli

Prep Time: 5 minutes | Cook Time: 5 minutes | Serves: 4

455 g wild-caught Alaskan salmon, cut into four 100 g fillets
Fine sea salt and freshly ground black pepper
455 g broccoli, cut into florets
Sesame seeds, for garnish
Chopped green onions, tender white and green parts only, for garnish
Soy-Ginger Dressing:
6 tablespoons extra-virgin olive oil
2 tablespoons soy sauce or tamari
2 tablespoons raw apple cider vinegar
1 tablespoon minced fresh ginger (about 2.5 cm knob)
1 clove garlic
3 tablespoons pure maple syrup
1 teaspoon toasted sesame oil

1. 240 ml water into the pot and arrange the rack on the bottom. Place the salmon fillets on the rack in a single layer with skin side down. Sprinkle them generously with salt and pepper. 2. Close the lid, turn the pressure release valve to SEAL position, and then move the slider to PRESSURE. Select HI and set the cooking time to 1 minute. Press START/STOP to begin cooking. When finished, release the pressure naturally. 3. Remove the lid and place the broccoli directly on top of the cooked fish, and then cook them at HI on PRESSURE COOK for 5 minute. 4. Release the steam pressure quickly. 5. Transfer the steamed broccoli and salmon to serving plates. 6. Combine the olive oil, vinegar, ginger, maple syrup, soy sauce, garlic, and sesame oil in a blender and blend them for 1 minute until smooth. 7. Drizzle the dressing over the top and garnish with the green onions and sesame seeds. 8. You can store the leftovers in an airtight container in the fridge for 4 days.
Per Serving: Calories 207; Fat: 12.22g; Sodium: 341mg; Carbs: 21.17g; Fibre: 3.7g; Sugar: 11.28g; Protein: 5.37g

Cheesy Tuna Noodle Casserole

Prep Time: 5 minutes | Cook Time: 5 minutes | Serves: 6

480 ml chicken stock
240 ml regular or low-fat evaporated milk
100 g white button mushrooms, thinly sliced
2 medium celery stalks, thinly sliced
2 tablespoons butter
1 teaspoon onion powder
1 teaspoon ground dried mustard
¼ teaspoon table salt
300 g wide egg or no-yolk noodles
240 g heavy cream
Two 150 g cans tuna, preferably yellow fin tuna packed in oil, drained
200 g grated Swiss cheese

1. Mix the stock, evaporated milk, mushrooms, celery, butter, onion powder, dried mustard, and salt in the pot. Stir in the noodles until well coated. 2. Close the lid, turn the pressure release valve to SEAL position, and then move the slider to PRESSURE. Select HI and set the cooking time to 4 minutes. Press START/STOP to begin cooking. When finished, release the pressure quickly. 3. Stir in the cream, and then cook them at Lo3 on SEAR/SAUTÉ mode for 1 minute until the sauce is bubbling fairly well. 4. Stop the process, and gently stir in the tuna and cheese. Set the lid askew over the unit for a couple of minutes to melt the cheese. 5. Serve and enjoy.
Per Serving: Calories 537; Fat: 36.95g; Sodium: 798mg; Carbs: 7.99g; Fibre: 0.7g; Sugar: 3.26g; Protein: 42.44g

Lemony Cocktail Prawns

Prep Time: 20 minutes | Cook Time: 1 minute | Serves: 1

240 ml water
½ teaspoon salt
220 g frozen peeled and deveined jumbo prawns
2 tablespoons cocktail sauce
½ medium lemon

1. Add water, salt, and prawns to the pot. 2. Close the lid, turn the pressure release valve to SEAL position, and then move the slider to PRESSURE. 3. Cook the prawns at HI for 0 minute. When finished, release the pressure quickly. 4. Drain prawns. Place prawns in an ice bath 5 minutes to halt the cooking process. 5. Remove to a serving bowl and serve with cocktail sauce and lemon.
Per Serving: Calories 209; Fat: 1.28g; Sodium: 1691mg; Carbs: 4.08g; Fibre: 0.7g; Sugar: 2.02g; Protein: 46.23g

Quick Prawns Boil with Sausage

Prep Time: 5 minutes | Cook Time: 15 minutes | Serves: 4

240 ml chicken stock
1 teaspoon minced garlic
2 medium red potatoes, quartered
1 medium ear corn, husked
1 (75 g) link andouille sausage, cut into 4 pieces on the bias
½ tablespoon Old Bay seasoning
110 g peeled and deveined extra-large prawns
3 tablespoons butter, melted
½ medium lemon, for serving
1 tablespoon chopped fresh parsley

1. Add stock and garlic to the pot and then place in the rack. 2. Add potatoes, corn, and sausage, and then sprinkle Old Bay seasoning over everything. 3. Close the lid, turn the pressure release valve to SEAL position, and then move the slider to PRESSURE. Select HI and set the cooking time to 3 minutes. Press START/STOP to begin cooking. When finished, release the pressure quickly. 4. Add prawns, stir, then immediately replace the lid and wait for 5 to 8 minutes until the prawns is pink and cooked through. 5. Remove everything to a large bowl and serve with a side of butter, lemon, and sprinkle of parsley.
Per Serving: Calories 398; Fat: 18.34g; Sodium: 688mg; Carbs: 40.89g; Fibre: 5.3g; Sugar: 3.7g; Protein: 20.13g

Garlicky Chili Fish Tacos

Prep Time: 15 minutes | Cook Time: 5 minutes | Serves: 4

½ tablespoon olive oil
½ teaspoon minced garlic
⅛ teaspoon smoked paprika
⅛ teaspoon chili powder
⅛ teaspoon ground cumin
Spicy Lime Crema:
2 tablespoons sour cream
1 tablespoon mayonnaise
1 teaspoon lime juice
For Serving:
3 small tortillas, warmed
30 g shredded cabbage
1½ tablespoons pico de gallo
¼ teaspoon salt
⅛ teaspoon Cajun seasoning
2 (110 g) frozen tilapia fillets
240 ml water

⅛ teaspoon garlic salt
⅛ teaspoon salt
½ teaspoon sriracha sauce

1 tablespoon chopped coriander
½ medium lime

1. Mix together oil and all the spices in a small bowl, and then spread evenly over both sides of fillets. 2. Pour water into the pot and place in the rack. Place fish on rack. 3. Close the lid, turn the pressure release valve to SEAL position, and then move the slider to PRESSURE. Select HI and set the cooking time to 2 minutes. Press START/STOP to begin cooking. When finished, release the pressure quickly. 4. Carefully transfer fish to a small bowl. 5. In a separate small bowl, combine all Spicy Lime Crema ingredients and refrigerate until ready to use. 6. To serve, transfer tortillas to a serving plate. Evenly break up the fish between tortillas. Top the dish with cabbage, pico de gallo, Spicy Lime Crema, coriander, and a squeeze of lime.
Per Serving: Calories 209; Fat: 7.42g; Sodium: 584mg; Carbs: 31.21g; Fibre: 1.2g; Sugar: 11.8g; Protein: 4.92g

Honey-Soy Salmon

Prep Time: 5 minutes | Cook Time: 15 minutes | Serves: 2

60 ml soy sauce
2 tablespoons honey
½ tablespoon apple cider vinegar
½ tablespoon olive oil
1½ tablespoons brown sugar
½ teaspoon minced garlic
1 (125 g) frozen salmon fillet

1. Stir all of the ingredients together in the pot. 2. Close the lid, turn the pressure release valve to SEAL position, and then move the slider to PRESSURE. Select HI and set the cooking time to 3 minutes. Press START/STOP to begin cooking. When finished, release the pressure naturally. 3. Transfer the fish to a plate or bowl. 4. Cook the sauce at Hi5 on SEAR/SAUTÉ mode for 8 minutes until reduced and thickened. 5. Spoon 1 tablespoon sauce over fish and serve.
Per Serving: Calories 311; Fat: 14.26g; Sodium: 791mg; Carbs: 29.29g; Fibre: 0.7g; Sugar: 27.12g; Protein: 17.01g

Homemade Pesto Tilapia with Sun-Dried Tomatoes

Prep Time: 5 minutes | Cook Time: 5 minutes | Serves: 2

1 tablespoon butter
3 tablespoons chopped sun-dried tomatoes
55 g artichoke heart quarters
1 teaspoon lemon juice
⅛ teaspoon salt
⅛ teaspoon ground black pepper
120 ml chicken stock
1 tablespoon basil pesto
2 (110g) frozen tilapia fillets
2 tablespoons heavy cream
3 tablespoons shredded Parmesan cheese

1. Add butter, tomatoes, artichokes, lemon juice, salt, pepper, and stock to the pot. 2. Spread pesto all over the tops of fillets and place on the rack. Lower the rack into the pot. 3. Close the lid, turn the pressure release valve to SEAL position, and then move the slider to PRESSURE. Select HI and set the cooking time to 2 minutes. Press START/STOP to begin cooking. When finished, release the pressure quickly. 4. Carefully transfer fish to a serving plate. 5. Stir cream and Parmesan into the sauce. Ladle sauce over fish and serve.
Per Serving: Calories 387; Fat: 21.3g; Sodium: 701mg; Carbs: 30.64g; Fibre: 2.9g; Sugar: 22.45g; Protein: 20.55g

Lemony-Buttered Lobster Tails

Prep Time: 10 minutes | Cook Time: 0 minute | Serves: 2

2 (150 g) lobster tails
⅛ teaspoon Old Bay seasoning
240 ml water
½ teaspoon minced garlic

½ teaspoon salt
½ teaspoon chopped parsley
2 tablespoons clarified butter
2 lemon wedges

1. Cut down the centre of each lobster tail all the way to the bottom of the tail. 2. Carefully crack open the lobster to expose the meat underneath, and then slide the bottom of the meat with your fingers to loosen it from the bottom of the shell. 3. Pop the meat up and above the shell so it lies gently on the outer shell but is still connected to the tail. Sprinkle Old Bay seasoning over the lobster tails, then set aside. 4. Add water, garlic, and salt to the pot, then place in the rack and place the lobsters on it. 5. Close the lid, turn the pressure release valve to SEAL position, and then move the slider to PRESSURE. Select LO and set the cooking time to 0 minute. Press START/STOP to begin cooking. When finished, release the pressure naturally. 6. Take the internal temperature of lobster. It should be 60°C. If it is a little under, replace the lid and wait 2 minutes and check again. Lobster is extremely delicate and can be easy to overcook. 7. Remove lobster tails to a plate and top with parsley. Serve the dish with butter and lemon.
Per Serving: Calories 229; Fat: 12.77g; Sodium: 1310mg; Carbs: 3.61g; Fibre: 0.2g; Sugar: 1.23g; Protein: 25.13g

Fantastic Brown Butter Pasta with Scallops & Tomatoes

Prep Time: 5 minutes | Cook Time: 6 minutes | Serves: 4

240 ml chicken stock
1 teaspoon minced garlic
⅛ teaspoon crushed red pepper flakes
80 g uncooked angel hair pasta, broken in half
75 g frozen bay scallops

2 tablespoons brown butter
50 g halved cherry tomatoes
2 tablespoons heavy cream
1 tablespoon minced fresh parsley

1. Add stock, garlic, and red pepper flakes. Layer pasta in a crisscross pattern over the liquid to reduce clumping. 2. Close the lid, turn the pressure release valve to SEAL position, and then move the slider to PRESSURE. Select HI and set the cooking time to 1 minute. Press START/STOP to begin cooking. When finished, release the pressure quickly. 3. Immediately stir in scallops, brown butter, tomatoes, and cream, and stir them for 5 minutes until scallops are completely cooked through. 4. Transfer the dish to a serving dish and top with parsley. Serve.
Per Serving: Calories 225; Fat: 13.02g; Sodium: 407mg; Carbs: 9.04g; Fibre: 1.3g; Sugar: 0.39g; Protein: 17.36g

Delicious Scallop Risotto with Spinach

Prep Time: 5 minutes | Cook Time: 35 minutes | Serves: 2

75 g frozen bay scallops
⅛ teaspoon salt
⅛ teaspoon ground black pepper
2 tablespoons butter, divided
½ tablespoon dried onion flakes
½ teaspoon minced garlic

100 g uncooked Arborio rice
240 ml chicken stock
1 tablespoon white wine
1½ tablespoons lemon juice
15 g packed spinach

1. Season the scallops with salt and pepper. 2. Select SEAR/SAUTÉ. Select Hi5, and then press START/STOP to begin cooking. 3. Add 1 tablespoon butter to the pot and swirl for about 3 minutes until browned. Add scallops and stir them for about 3 to 5 minutes until fully cooked. Remove them to a serving plate. 4. Add remaining 1 tablespoon butter, onion flakes, garlic, and rice, and stir them for 2 to 3 minutes to toast the rice. 5. Add stock, wine, and lemon juice and deglaze the pot, scraping all the browned bits off the bottom of the pot. Stop the process. 6. Close the lid, turn the pressure release valve to SEAL position, and then move the slider to PRESSURE. Select HI and set the cooking time to 10 minutes. Press START/STOP to begin cooking. When finished, release the pressure naturally. 7. Stir spinach into risotto about 3 minutes until wilted. Stir in scallops and brown butter right before serving. 8. Transfer them to a serving plate and serve immediately.
Per Serving: Calories 435; Fat: 26.32g; Sodium: 971mg; Carbs: 20.09g; Fibre: 6.6g; Sugar: 1.3g; Protein: 37.34g

Refreshing Salmon with Zesty Dill Sauce

Prep Time: 5 minutes | Cook Time: 5 minutes | Serves: 4

60 ml water
60 ml lemon juice
2 sprigs fresh dill
1 (200 g) skinless salmon fillet
Zesty Dill Sauce:
1½ tablespoons sour cream
1½ tablespoons mayonnaise
½ teaspoon minced fresh dill
¼ teaspoon Dijon mustard

¼ teaspoon salt
¼ teaspoon ground black pepper
3 slices lemon

¼ teaspoon lemon zest
½ tablespoon lemon juice
⅛ teaspoon garlic salt

1. Add water, lemon juice, and fresh dill to the pot, and place in the rack. 2. Sprinkle salmon with salt and pepper on all sides, then place lemon slices on top of salmon. Place salmon on the rack. 3. Close the lid, turn the pressure release valve to SEAL position, and then move the slider to PRESSURE. Select HI and set the cooking time to 5 minutes. Press START/STOP to begin cooking. When finished, release the pressure naturally. 4. While the fish cooks, prepare the Zesty Dill Sauce. In a small bowl, mix up all sauce ingredients and refrigerate until ready to use. 5. Transfer salmon to a plate and serve immediately with dill sauce.
Per Serving: Calories 125; Fat: 6.52g; Sodium: 443mg; Carbs: 4.66g; Fibre: 0.3g; Sugar: 1.55g; Protein: 12.5g

Lemony Cajun Salmon

Prep Time: 10 minutes | Cook Time: 7 minutes | Serves: 1

1 salmon fillet
Cajun seasoning

Juice of half a lemon, to serve

---

1. Place the Cook & Crisp Basket in your Pressure Cooker Steam Fryer. 2. Sprinkle Cajun seasoning all over fish. Put on the Smart Lid on top of the Ninja Foodi Steam Fryer. 3. Move the Lid Slider to the "Air Fry/Stovetop". Select the "Air Fry" mode for cooking. 4. Adjust the cooking temperature to 180°C. Cook fish for around 7 minutes, skin side up on air fry pan. 5. Squeeze lemon juice over fish and serve.
Per Serving: Calories 414; Fat: 20.8g; Sodium 156mg; Carbs: 4.5g; Fibre: 0.4g; Sugars 1.6g; Protein 49.8g

Fried Cheese Prawns

Prep Time: 7 minutes | Cook Time: 10 minutes | Serves: 4

½ teaspoon oregano
65g shaved parmesan cheese
1 teaspoon basil
1 teaspoon pepper
1 teaspoon powdered onion

2 tablespoons sesame oil
900g peeled and deveined jumbo cooked prawns
4 minced garlic cloves
quartered lime
Cooking spray oil

---

1. Place the Cook & Crisp Basket in your Pressure Cooker Steam Fryer. 2. Using a suitable mixing bowl, add in the oil, powdered onion, basil, oregano, pepper, parmesan cheese, garlic and mix everything together. 3. Add the cooked prawns into the mixture and toss until well coated. 4. Grease the Cook & Crisp Basket with cooking spray oil then add in the coated prawns. Put on the Smart Lid on top of the Ninja Foodi Steam Fryer. 5. Move the Lid Slider to the "Air Fry/Stovetop". Select the "Air Fry" mode for cooking. 6. Air fry for around 10 minutes at 175°C. 7. Serve with a garnish of the lime juice and enjoy as desired.
Per Serving: Calories 506; Fat: 23.9g; Sodium 197mg; Carbs: 3.6g; Fibre: 0.7g; Sugars 1.2g; Protein 66.1g

Traditional Prawns Scampi

Prep Time: 5 minutes | Cook Time: 8 minutes | Serves: 4

455g raw prawns
1 tablespoon juiced lime
1 tablespoon minced garlic
1 tablespoon chopped chives

1 tablespoon fresh chopped basil
2 tablespoons chicken stock
2 teaspoons red pepper flakes
4 tablespoons melted butter

---

1. Place the Cook & Crisp Basket in your Pressure Cooker Steam Fryer. 2. Add the pepper flakes, garlic and melted butter into the Cook & Crisp Basket. Put on the Smart Lid on top of the Ninja Foodi Steam Fryer. 3. Move the Lid Slider to the "Air Fry/Stovetop". Select the "Air Fry" mode for cooking. 4. Air fry at 200°C for a minute, until the butter, garlic and pepper are all incorporated. Add in the remaining recipe ingredients into the Cook & Crisp Basket then mix together. 5. Air fry the prawns for around 7 minutes at 200°C. 6. Serve, garnished with extra herbs if desired and enjoy.
Per Serving: Calories 340; Fat: 27.7g; Sodium 109mg; Carbs: 12.6g; Fibre: 0.3g; Sugars 3g; Protein 15.7g

Tasty Miso Salmon Fillets

Prep Time: 10 minutes | Cook Time: 10 minutes | Serves: 2

120ml boiling water
½ teaspoon cracked black pepper
1 teaspoon diced ginger
1 teaspoon sesame seeds
1 teaspoons minced garlic cloves
2 tablespoons soy sauce

2 tablespoons white miso
2 chopped green spring onions
2 tablespoons brown sugar
2 (125g) salmon fillets
Non-stick cooking spray

---

1. Place the Cook & Crisp Basket in your Pressure Cooker Steam Fryer. 2. Using a suitable mixing bowl, add in the pepper, ginger, garlic, miso, brown sugar, soy sauce and boiling water then mix together. 3. Using a flat work station, place the salmon fillets then cover with the sauce mixture, ensuring even amount of coating all over. 4. Grease the Cook & Crisp Basket with cooking spray then add in the coated fillets. Put on the Smart Lid on top of the Ninja Foodi Steam Fryer. Move the Lid Slider to the "Air Fry/Stovetop". Select the "Air Fry" mode for cooking. Air Fry for around 12 minutes at 200°C. 5. Serve with a garnish of spring onions, sesame seeds and enjoy as desired.
Per Serving: Calories 305; Fat: 16.7g; Sodium 148mg; Carbs: 2.5g; Fibre: 1.1g ; Sugars 0.1g ; Protein 36.5g

Easy Crab Legs with Lemon Wedges

Prep Time: 5 minutes | Cook Time: 1 minute | Serves: 2

240 ml water
455 g crab legs
⅛ teaspoon Old Bay seasoning

2 tablespoons clarified butter
½ medium lemon cut into wedges

---

1. Pour water into pot and place in the rack. 2. Add crab legs and sprinkle with Old Bay seasoning. 3. Close the lid, turn the pressure release valve to SEAL position, and then move the slider to PRESSURE. Select LO and set the cooking time to 1 minute. Press START/STOP to begin cooking. When finished, release the pressure quickly. 4. Remove crab to a plate and serve with butter and lemon.
Per Serving: Calories 302; Fat: 14g; Sodium: 758mg; Carbs: 0.96g; Fibre: 0g; Sugar: 0.31g; Protein: 41.13g

Creamy Scallops with Spinach

Prep Time: 5 minutes | Cook Time: 10 minutes | Serves: 2

½ teaspoon salt
½ teaspoon black pepper
180g heavy whipping cream
1 teaspoon coconut oil
1 teaspoon minced garlic
1 tablespoon tomato paste

1 tablespoon chopped fresh basil
8 jumbo sea scallops
300g pack frozen spinach, drained and thawed
Nonstick cooking oil spray
Black pepper and salt, to taste

1. Place the Cook & Crisp Basket in your Pressure Cooker Steam Fryer. 2. Grease the Cook & Crisp Basket then add in the drained and thawed spinach and keep to the side. 3. Generously season the scallops all over with oil, a sprinkle of salt and black pepper and then place inside the pan on the spinach. 4. Using a suitable mixing bowl, add in the extra pepper, salt, basil, tomato paste, garlic, heavy cream and mix together. 5. Then pour the cream mixture over the scallops and place in the Ninja Foodi Pressure Steam Fryer. 6. Air fry the scallops for around 10 minutes at 175°C then serve and enjoy as desired.
Per Serving: Calories 315; Fat: 15g; Sodium 91mg; Carbs: 0g; Fibre: 0g; Sugars 0g; Protein 42.3g

Marinated Salmon Fillets with Vegetable

Prep Time: 20 minutes | Cook Time: 12 minutes | Serves: 2

60ml soy sauce
½ teaspoon salt
120ml fresh juiced orange
1 tablespoon avocado oil
1 tablespoon chopped ginger
For the Veggies:
½ teaspoon toasted sesame seeds
1 tablespoon sesame oil
50g stemmed dry shiitake mushrooms

2 minced garlic cloves
2 (125g) salmon fillets
2 teaspoons grated orange zest
3 tablespoons rice vinegar

2 halved heads baby bok choy
Salt, to taste

1. Place the Cook & Crisp Basket in your Pressure Cooker Steam Fryer. 2. Using a suitable mixing bowl, add in the avocado oil, soy sauce, salt, vinegar, orange juice, zest, ginger, garlic and mix until mixed. 3. Divide the marinade into 2 and reserve one then add the salmon fillets into a Ziploc bag and pour the remaining soy sauce mix in to marinate for an hour. 4. Transfer the marinated salmon into the Cook & Crisp Basket then put on the Smart Lid on top of the Ninja Foodi Steam Fryer. 5. Move the Lid Slider to the "Air Fry/Stovetop". Select the "Air Fry" mode for cooking. air fry for around 6 minutes at 200°C. 6. In the meantime, coat the mushroom and bok choy with the oil, season with the salt then set aside. 7. Add the vegetables into the Cook & Crisp Basket along with the salmon fillets and cook for an extra 6 minutes. 8. Serve, drizzled with the reserved marinade, a garnish of the sesame seeds and enjoy.
Per Serving: Calories 404; Fat: 19.4g; Sodium 187mg; Carbs: 5g; Fibre: 1.1g; Sugars 0.8g; Protein 52g

Limey Garlic Salmon Fillets

Prep Time: 5 minutes | Cook Time: 12 minutes | Serves: 4

½ lime juice
½ lime wedges
1 tablespoon coconut oil
1 teaspoon powdered garlic

455g diced salmon fillets
2 teaspoons seafood seasoning
2 teaspoons lime pepper seasoning
Salt, to taste

1. Place the Cook & Crisp Basket in your Pressure Cooker Steam Fryer. 2. Ensure the salmon fillets are completely dry then mix the lime juice and coconut oil together. 3. Coat the dry salmon with the oil mixture then sprinkle with the salt and remaining seasonings. 4. Prepare the Cook & Crisp Basket with parchment paper then place in the salmon fillets. Put on the Smart Lid on top of the Ninja Foodi Steam Fryer. Move the Lid Slider to the "Air Fry/Stovetop". Select the "Air Fry" mode for cooking. Air Fry at 180°C for around 12 minutes. 5. Allow the fillets to cool off for a bit then serve, garnished with the lime wedges and enjoy.
Per Serving: Calories 786; Fat: 24.2g; Sodium 252mg; Carbs: 31.6g; Fibre: 3.9g; Sugars 22.8g; Protein 106.9g

Fresh Prawns and Broccoli

Prep Time: 15 minutes | Cook Time: 6 minutes | Serves: 4

2 tablespoons avocado oil
2 medium shallots, peeled and diced
1 tablespoon minced garlic
180 ml chicken stock
1½ tablespoons lemon juice

½ teaspoon salt
½ teaspoon black pepper
675 g peeled, deveined jumbo prawns
225 g small broccoli florets

1. Move slider to AIR FRY/STOVETOP. Select SEAR/SAUTÉ and set to Lo1. Select START/STOP to begin cooking. Heat the oil for 1 minute or 2, then add the shallots. Cook the shallots for 3 minutes and then add the garlic and continue to cook for an additional 1 minute. 2. Add the stock and use a spoon to remove any brown bits that are stuck to the pot. Press START/STOP to turn off the SEAR/SAUTÉ function. 3. Add the lemon juice, salt, pepper, and prawns. Then add the broccoli to the top layer and do not stir. 4. Close the lid and move slider to PRESSURE. Ensure the pressure release valve is in the SEAL position. The temperature will default to HIGH, which is the correct setting. Set time to 1 minute. Select START/STOP to begin cooking. 5. When cooking is complete, turn the pressure relief valve to the VENT position for quick pressure relief. Move slider to the right to unlock the lid, then carefully open it. Serve.
Per Serving: Calories 118; Fat 7.89g; Sodium 368mg; Carbs 10.65g; Fibre 1.8g; Sugar 4.21g; Protein 3.35g

Coconut Salmon Cakes with Greens

Prep Time: 35 minutes | Cook Time: 15 minutes | Serves: 5

75g mashed avocado
10g chopped coriander, with extra
10g tapioca starch, with 4 extra teaspoons
½ teaspoon salt
40g coconut flakes
For the Greens
½ teaspoon salt
2 teaspoons olive oil

455g salmon
1½ teaspoon yellow curry powder
2 large eggs
Avocado oil

120g arugula and spinach mix

---

1. Place the Cook & Crisp Basket in your Pressure Cooker Steam Fryer. 2. Skin the salmon then chop into pieces and transfer into a suitable mixing bowl. 3. Add in the coriander, salt, curry powder, avocado and incorporate together. 4. Pour in the teaspoons of tapioca then mix until mixed then mold the patties into 10 even sizes. 5. Transfer the molded patties into a parchment paper prepared baking sheet then freeze for about 30 minutes. 6. In the meantime, mix the eggs in a suitable mixing bowl and pour the coconut flakes and tapioca into different bowls. 7. Coat the Cook & Crisp Basket with oil. 8. Run the chilled patties through the tapioca until coated, then dredge in the egg mix and finally coat with the coconut flakes. 9. Transfer the covered patties into the basket then Put on the Smart Lid on top of the Ninja Foodi Steam Fryer. 10. Move the Lid Slider to the "Air Fry/Stovetop". Select the "Air Fry" mode for cooking. Cook at 200°C for around 15 minutes until the crispy and tenderized. 11. Using a suitable pan, heat the olive oil up over medium heat then add in the spinach, arugula, salt and stir cook for a minute until wilted. 12. Serve the salmon cakes and greens together, enjoying with a garnish of coriander.
Per Serving: Calories 367; Fat: 22.9g; Sodium 101mg; Carbs: 8g; Fibre: 1.9g; Sugars 3g; Protein 31.8g

Zesty Salmon Salad

Prep Time: 15 minutes | Cook Time: 3 minutes | Serves: 4

455 g salmon
1 teaspoon salt, divided
½ teaspoon black pepper, divided
1 tablespoon lemon juice
1½ tablespoons extra-virgin olive oil
1 tablespoon fresh lemon juice
½ tablespoon apple cider vinegar
1 tablespoon chopped fresh parsley

2 teaspoons minced garlic
½ teaspoon dried oregano
120 g chopped romaine lettuce
1 large cucumber, diced
2 Roma tomatoes, cored and diced
1 medium red onion, peeled and sliced
1 medium avocado, peeled, pitted, and sliced
30 g pitted Kalamata olives, sliced

---

1. Season the salmon with ½ teaspoon salt, ¼ teaspoon pepper, and the lemon juice. 2. Place 240 ml water in the pot and place the Deluxe Reversible Rack in the lower position in the pot. Place the salmon on top of the rack. 3. Close the lid and move slider to PRESSURE. Ensure the pressure release valve is in the SEAL position. The temperature will default to HIGH, which is the correct setting. Set time to 3 minutes. Select START/STOP to begin cooking. 4. In the meantime, prepare the dressing and salad ingredients. In a small container with a tight lid, place the oil, lemon juice, vinegar, oregano, parsley, garlic, ½ teaspoon salt, and ¼ teaspoon pepper. Shake well until combined and set aside. 5. Place the lettuce, cucumber, tomatoes, avocado, red onion, and olives in a big bowl. Set aside. 6. When the timer beeps, turn the pressure relief valve to the VENT position for quick pressure relief. Move slider to the right to unlock the lid, then carefully open it. 7. Remove the salmon from the pot and allow it to cool completely. Once it is cool, cut it into bite-sized pieces. 8. Add the salmon pieces to the salad bowl. Drizzle with the dressing and gently toss to combine.
Per Serving: Calories 322; Fat 19.36g; Sodium 1212mg; Carbs 12.24g; Fibre 6.2g; Sugar 3.98g; Protein 26.27g

Yummy Parmesan Cod

Prep Time: 5 minutes | Cook Time: 15 minutes | Serves: 4

4 cod fillets, boneless
Salt and black pepper to the taste
100g parmesan

4 tablespoons balsamic vinegar
A drizzle of olive oil
3 spring onions, chopped

---

1. Place the Cook & Crisp Basket in your Pressure Cooker Steam Fryer. 2. Season fish with salt, pepper, grease with the oil, and coat it in parmesan. Put the fillets in the Cook & Crisp Basket. 3. Put on the Smart Lid on top of the Ninja Foodi Steam Fryer. Move the Lid Slider to the "Air Fry/Stovetop". Select the "Air Fry" mode for cooking. Air Fry at 185°C for around 14 minutes. 4. Meanwhile, in a suitable bowl, mix the spring onions with salt, pepper and the vinegar and whisk. 5. Divide the cod between plates, drizzle the spring onions mix all over and serve with a side salad.
Per Serving: Calories 636; Fat: 25g; Sodium 259mg; Carbs: 0.9g; Fibre: 0.5g; Sugars 0g; Protein 95.6g

Quick Bacon Wrapped Scallops

Prep Time: 15 minutes | Cook Time: 7 minutes | Serves: 4

1 teaspoon coriander
½ teaspoon paprika
¼ teaspoon salt
400g scallops

100g bacon, sliced
1 teaspoon sesame oil

---

1. Place the Cook & Crisp Basket in your Pressure Cooker Steam Fryer. 2. Sprinkle the scallops with coriander, paprika, and salt. Then wrap the scallops in the bacon slices and secure with toothpicks. Sprinkle the scallops with sesame oil. Put the scallops in the Cook & Crisp Basket. 3. Put on the Smart Lid on top of the Ninja Foodi Steam Fryer. Move the Lid Slider to the "Air Fry/Stovetop". Select the "Air Fry" mode for cooking. 3. Adjust the cooking temperature to 200°C. 4. Cook for them for around 7 minutes.
Per Serving: Calories 278; Fat: 15.4g; Sodium 321mg; Carbs: 1.3g; Fibre: 0.5g; Sugars 0.1g; Protein 32.1g

Air Fried Cod with Spring Onions

Prep Time: 5 minutes | Cook Time: 15 minutes | Serves: 2

2 cod fillets, boneless
Salt and black pepper to the taste

1 bunch spring onions, chopped
3 tablespoons ghee, melted

1. In the Cook & Crisp Basket, mix all the recipe ingredients, toss gently. 2. Place the Cook & Crisp Basket in your Pressure Cooker Steam Fryer. Put on the Smart Lid on top of the Ninja Foodi Steam Fryer. 3. Move the Lid Slider to the "Air Fry/Stovetop". Select the "Air Fry" mode for cooking. Air Fry at 180°C for around 15 minutes. 4. Divide the fish between plates and serve.
Per Serving: Calories 443; Fat: 16.3g; Sodium 305mg; Carbs: 37.4g; Fibre: 7.8g; Sugars 11.4g; Protein 38.5g

Creamy Dill Salmon

Prep Time: 5 minutes | Cook Time: 20 minutes | Serves: 4

4 salmon fillets, boneless
A pinch of salt and black pepper
120g heavy cream
1 tablespoon chives, chopped

1 teaspoon lemon juice
1 teaspoon dill, chopped
2 garlic cloves, minced
50g ghee, melted

1. In a suitable bowl, mix all the recipe ingredients except the salmon and mix well. Arrange the salmon in the Cook & Crisp Basket, drizzle the sauce all over. 2. Place the Cook & Crisp Basket in your Pressure Cooker Steam Fryer. 3. Put on the Smart Lid on top of the Ninja Foodi Steam Fryer. Move the Lid Slider to the "Air Fry/Stovetop". Select the "Air Fry" mode for cooking. Air Fry at 180°C for around 20 minutes. 4. Divide everything between plates and serve.
Per Serving: Calories 423; Fat: 18.4g; Sodium 137mg; Carbs: 4.6g; Fibre: 1.9g; Sugars 0.8g; Protein 56.2g

Chapter 9 Desserts

Sweet Stewed Pears in Red Wine 91	Mouthwatering Chocolate Rice Pudding ... 95
Simple Chocolate Molten Lava Cake 91	Banana Pudding Cake with Pecans............ 95
Easy Egg Custard 91	Traditional Lava Cake........................ 95
Basic Butter Vanilla Cake 91	Sweet Cranberry Stuffed Apples............... 96
Super-Simple Cheesecake 91	Arroz con Leche 96
Tangy Dark Chocolate Fondue 92	Classic Bread Pudding 96
Creamy Chocolate Cake 92	Red Wine Braised Bartlett Pears............... 96
Chocolate Peanut Butter Popcorn 92	Perfect Lemony Tapioca Pudding 96
Almond Bundt Cake with Berries 92	Delicious White Chocolate Pots De Crème 97
Healthy Cinnamon Apples with Dates 92	Fluffy Carrot Coconut Cake with Pecans ... 97
Creamy Cinnamon Raisin Brown Rice Pudding 93	Red Wine-Braised Apples with Raisins 97
Yummy Creamy Rice Pudding 93	Cranberry Stuffed Apples 97
Soft Vanilla Banana Bread 93	Chocolate Chip-Berry Mug Cake 98
Blueberry Crisp 93	Stuffed Peaches 98
Cinnamon Walnuts-Oats Stuffed Apples...... 94	Wine Poached Apricots 98
Authentic Peach Cobbler 94	Homemade Vanilla Almond Milk 98
Homemade Sweet Cranberry Applesauce ... 94	Cinnamon Apples 99
Quick Lemon Blueberry Compote 94	Simple Cinnamon Pineapple 99
Flavourful Cinnamon Dried Fruit Compote 95	Easy Applesauce 99
	Tasty Strawberry Compote 99

Sweet Stewed Pears in Red Wine

Prep Time: 30 minutes | Cook Time: 10 minutes | Serves: 4-6

720 ml red wine
1 tsp. ginger powder
4 cloves
1 tsp. ground cinnamon

1 bay leaf
400 g brown sugar
6 pears, peeled, leave the stems

1. Combine the red wine, ginger, cloves, cinnamon, bay leaf and sugar in the pot until the sugar has dissolved. Put the pears into the pot. 2. Close the lid, turn the pressure release valve to SEAL position, and then move the slider to PRESSURE. Select HI and set the cooking time to 4 minutes. Press START/STOP to begin cooking. When finished, release the pressure naturally. 3. Transfer the pears to a serving plate. Remove the bay leaf. 4. Select SEAR/SAUTÉ and cook the sauce in the pot at Lo3 for 4 to 5 minutes to reduce the liquid. 5. Serve the pears with this sauce.
Per Serving: Calories 404; Fat: 0.26g; Sodium: 11mg; Carbs: 104.22g; Fibre: 5.8g; Sugar: 92.59g; Protein: 1.24g

Simple Chocolate Molten Lava Cake

Prep Time: 25 minutes | Cook Time: 10 minutes | Serves: 1-2

480 ml water
1 egg, beaten
1 tsp. vanilla extract
55 g semi-sweet chocolate chips

4 tbsp. butter, soft
2 tbsp. flour
30 g powdered sugar

1. Grease the ramekin with butter. 2. Whisk the egg and vanilla in a small bowl. 3. Melt the chocolate with butter in a saucepan over medium heat, and then let the mixture cool for about 30 seconds. 4. Add the egg mix, flour and sugar to the chocolate mixture, stir them to combine. 5. Fill the ramekin halfway-full. 6. Pour the water into the pot and place in the rack. Place the ramekin on the rack. 7. Close the lid, turn the pressure release valve to SEAL position, and then move the slider to PRESSURE. Select HI and set the cooking time to 7minutes. Press START/STOP to begin cooking. When finished, release the pressure naturally. 8. Serve and enjoy.
Per Serving: Calories 423; Fat: 32.79g; Sodium: 241mg; Carbs: 27.79g; Fibre: 1g; Sugar: 20.17g; Protein: 6.09g

Easy Egg Custard

Prep Time: 25 minutes | Cook Time: 10 minutes | Serves: 6

6 big eggs, beaten
150 g sugar
A pinch of salt
1 tsp. vanilla extract

960 ml milk
360 ml water
¼ tsp. cinnamon

1. Whisk the eggs, sugar, salt, vanilla, and milk in a bowl until combined. 2. Pour the mixture into six ramekins and cover with foil. 3. Poke some holes in the foil. 4. Pour the water into the pot and place in the rack. Place the ramekins on the rack. 5. Close the lid, turn the pressure release valve to SEAL position, and then move the slider to PRESSURE. Select HI and set the cooking time to 7 minutes. Press START/STOP to begin cooking. When finished, release the pressure naturally. 6. Remove the ramekins from the pot and let them cool for 3 minutes. 7. Sprinkle the dish with cinnamon and serve.
Per Serving: Calories 213; Fat: 9.51g; Sodium: 160mg; Carbs: 20.75g; Fibre: 0.1g; Sugar: 20.69g; Protein: 10.66g

Basic Butter Vanilla Cake

Prep Time: 20 minutes | Cook Time: 40 minutes | Serves: 6-8

240 ml water
110 g unsalted butter, melted
15 g stevia sweetener
4 large eggs, beaten
185 g plain flour

180 g heavy cream
2 tsp. baking powder
½ tbsp. vanilla extract
¼ tsp. salt

1. Whisk the butter, stevia sweetener, and eggs in a bowl until combined. Stir in the flour, heavy cream, baking powder, vanilla extract, and salt. Stir the mixture until just smooth. 2. Grease a baking pan with butter. Arrange the batter onto the pan and cover with foil. 3. Pour the water into the pot and place in the rack. Place the pan on the rack. 4. Close the lid, turn the pressure release valve to SEAL position, and then move the slider to PRESSURE. Select HI and set the cooking time to 40 minutes. Press START/STOP to begin cooking. When finished, release the pressure naturally. 5. Let the cake cool for a few minutes and serve.
Per Serving: Calories 233; Fat: 14.49g; Sodium: 120mg; Carbs: 19.07g; Fibre: 0.7g; Sugar: 0.57g; Protein: 6.26g

Super-Simple Cheesecake

Prep Time: 25 minutes | Cook Time: 30 minutes | Serves: 6

3 large eggs, beaten
200 g white sugar

720 g cream cheese, room temperature
½ tbsp. vanilla extract

1. Combine the eggs, sugar, cream cheese, and vanilla in a medium bowl. 2. Place the mixture to a baking dish that can fit into the pot. Cover the pan tightly with aluminum foil. 3. Pour the water into the pot and place in the rack. Place the pan on the rack. 4. Close the lid, turn the pressure release valve to SEAL position, and then move the slider to PRESSURE. Select HI and set the cooking time to 30 minutes. Press START/STOP to begin cooking. When finished, release the pressure naturally. 5. Let the cheesecake cool for a few minutes and serve.
Per Serving: Calories 449; Fat: 36.58g; Sodium: 528mg; Carbs: 21.27g; Fibre: 0g; Sugar: 20.69g; Protein: 9.87g

Tangy Dark Chocolate Fondue

Prep Time: 20 minutes | Cook Time: 5 minutes | Serves: 3-6

1 (100 g) bar dark chocolate 70-85%, cut into large chunks
1 tbsp. sugar
1 tsp. amaretto liqueur
120 g heavy cream
480 ml water

1. Divide the chocolate, sugar, amaretto liqueur, and heavy cream between 3 ramekins. 2. Pour the water into the pot and place in the rack. Place the ramekins on the rack. 3. Close the lid, turn the pressure release valve to SEAL position, and then move the slider to PRESSURE. Select HI and set the cooking time to 3 minutes. Press START/STOP to begin cooking. When finished, release the pressure naturally. 4. Remove the ramekins from the pot. 5. Quickly stir the contents of the ramekins vigorously for about 1 minute until the texture is smooth and thick. 6. Serve the dish with fresh fruit or bread pieces.
Per Serving: Calories 144; Fat: 10.88g; Sodium: 9mg; Carbs: 9.79g; Fibre: 1.8g; Sugar: 5.99g; Protein: 1.52g

Creamy Chocolate Cake

Prep Time: 25 minutes | Cook Time: 30 minutes | Serves: 6-8

185 g plain flour
¼ tsp. baking powder
65 g cocoa powder, unsweetened
15 g stevia sweetener
35 g protein powder, chocolate or vanilla flavour
¼ tsp. salt
4 large eggs, beaten
110 g unsalted butter, melted
180 g heavy cream
1 tsp. vanilla extract

1. Combine the flour, cocoa powder, baking powder, stevia sweetener, protein powder, and salt in a large bowl. 2. Add the eggs, butter, cream, and vanilla. Stir to combine. 3. Pour the mixture into a baking pan. 4. Pour the water into the pot and place in the rack. Place the pan on the rack. 5. Close the lid, turn the pressure release valve to SEAL position, and then move the slider to PRESSURE. Select HI and set the cooking time to 30 minutes. Press START/STOP to begin cooking. When finished, release the pressure naturally. 6. Let the cake cool for a few minutes and serve.
Per Serving: Calories 261; Fat: 16.25g; Sodium: 106mg; Carbs: 23.86g; Fibre: 3.2g; Sugar: 0.93g; Protein: 8.28g

Chocolate Peanut Butter Popcorn

Prep Time: 5 minutes | Cook Time: 5 minutes | Serves: 4

1 tablespoon coconut oil
60 g popcorn kernels
1 tablespoon creamy peanut butter
2 tablespoons dairy-free dark chocolate chips

1. Select SEAR/SAUTÉ. Select Lo3, and then press START/STOP to begin cooking. 2. When the pot is hot, heat the coconut oil; add the popcorn kernels and cook until they begin to sizzle; place the lid on the pot but do not lock it, and then cook them for 5 to 6 minutes or until the kernels stop popping on a regular basis. 3. Stop the process and remove the lid; stir in the chocolate chips. 4. Serve the dish warm or let the chocolate set at room temperature before eating.
Per Serving: Calories 136; Fat: 7.2g; Sodium: 151mg; Carbs: 15.97g; Fibre: 2.2g; Sugar: 3.15g; Protein: 2.43g

Almond Bundt Cake with Berries

Prep Time: 10 minutes | Cook Time: 45 minutes | Serves: 6

Nonstick cooking spray
185 g almond flour, plus 1 tablespoon
1 teaspoon baking soda
¼ teaspoon salt
2 eggs, beaten
120 ml buttermilk
70 g pure maple syrup
½ teaspoon pure almond extract
130 g fresh berries

1. Grease a Bundt pan with nonstick cooking spray. 2. Combine almond flour, the baking soda, and salt in a medium bowl. 3. In a separate bowl, whisk together the buttermilk, eggs, maple syrup, and almond extract. 4. Add the egg mixture into the flour mixture and combine to form a batter. 5. In a small bowl, mix the berries with 1 tablespoon of almond flour until thoroughly coated. Fold the berry mixture into the batter. 6. Pour the batter into the prepared Bundt pan and cover the top with aluminum foil. 7. Pour 240 ml of water into the pot and place in the rack. Place the pan on the rack. 8. Close the lid, turn the pressure release valve to SEAL position, and then move the slider to PRESSURE. Select HI and set the cooking time to 45 minutes. Press START/STOP to begin cooking. When finished, release the pressure naturally. 9. Carefully remove the lid and lift out the Bundt pan. Remove the foil and allow the cake to cool on the rack for 1 hour. 10. Cut the cake into six slices and serve.
Per Serving: Calories 171; Fat: 5.74g; Sodium: 454mg; Carbs: 25.78g; Fibre: 0.7g; Sugar: 17.72g; Protein: 4.76g

Healthy Cinnamon Apples with Dates

Prep Time: 15 minutes | Cook Time: 3 minutes | Serves: 6

4 large Granny Smith or Pink Lady apples, peeled, cored, and sliced
120 ml water
30 g chopped pitted dates
1 teaspoon ground cinnamon
¼ teaspoon vanilla extract
1 teaspoon unsalted butter

1. Place the apples, dates, water, and cinnamon in the pot. Close the lid and move the slider to PRESSURE. Ensure the pressure release valve is in the SEAL position. The temperature will default to HIGH, which is the correct setting. Set time to 3 minutes. Select START/STOP to begin cooking. 2. When the timer beeps, quick-release the pressure. Open the lid. Stir in vanilla and butter. Serve hot or chilled.
Per Serving: Calories 114; Fat 1.05g; Sodium 5mg; Carbs 27.88g; Fibre 3.4g; Sugar 24.1g; Protein 0.44g

Creamy Cinnamon Raisin Brown Rice Pudding

Prep Time: 10 minutes | Cook Time: 25 minutes | Serves: 4

185 g short-grain brown rice
320 ml water
1 tablespoon vanilla extract
1 cinnamon stick

1 tablespoon butter
120 ml raisins
3 tablespoons honey
120 g heavy cream

1. Add rice, water, vanilla, cinnamon stick, and butter to the pot. 2. Close the lid and move the slider to PRESSURE. Ensure the pressure release valve is in the SEAL position. The temperature will default to HIGH, which is the correct setting. Set time to 20 minutes. Select START/STOP to begin cooking. 3. When cooking is complete, naturally release the pressure for 10 minutes. Then quick release pressure by turning the pressure release valve to the VENT position. Move slider to AIR FRY/ STOVETOP to unlock the lid, then carefully open it. 4. Discard the cinnamon stick. Stir in the raisins, honey, and cream. 5. Move slider to AIR FRY/STOVETOP. Select SEAR/SAUTÉ and set to Lo1. Select START/STOP to begin cooking. Simmer unlidded for 5 minutes. Serve warm.
Per Serving: Calories 319; Fat 8.72g; Sodium 32mg; Carbs 55.06g; Fibre 2.5g; Sugar 13.88g; Protein 3.72g

Yummy Creamy Rice Pudding

Prep Time: 15 minutes | Cook Time: 20 minutes | Serves: 6

185 g basmati rice
300 ml water
480 ml milk
60 g maple syrup

A pinch of salt
1 tsp vanilla extract
180 g heavy cream

1. Rinse the rice well. 2. Add the rice, water, milk, maple syrup, and salt to the pot. Stir well. 3. Close the lid and move the slider to PRESSURE. Ensure the pressure release valve is in the SEAL position. The temperature will default to HIGH, which is the correct setting. Set time to 20 minutes. Select START/STOP to begin cooking. 4. When cooking is complete, naturally release the pressure for 10 minutes. Then quick release pressure by turning the pressure release valve to the VENT position. Move slider to AIR FRY/ STOVETOP to unlock the lid, then carefully open it. 5. Add the vanilla and cream. Mix well. 6. Serve warm with any toppings as you like.
Per Serving: Calories 200; Fat 12.32g; Sodium 161mg; Carbs 22.97g; Fibre 4.1g; Sugar 12.73g; Protein 5.5g

Soft Vanilla Banana Bread

Prep Time: 15 minutes | Cook Time: 45 minutes | Serves: 8

2 large eggs, beaten
100 g sugar
100 g. butter, room temperature
4 medium bananas, mashed

1 tsp vanilla extract
240 g plain flour
1 tsp baking powder
240 ml water

1. In a large bowl, whisk together the eggs, sugar and butter until well combined. Stir in the bananas and vanilla. 2. In a separate bowl, mix up the flour and baking powder. 3. Pour the egg mixture into the flour mixture. Stir until the batter is smooth. 4. Grease a baking pan that fits the pot with butter. Pour the batter in the pan. 5. Pour water to the pot and arrange the Deluxe Reversible Rack in the lower position in the pot. 6. Put the pan on the rack. 7. Close the lid and move the slider to PRESSURE. Ensure the pressure release valve is in the SEAL position. The temperature will default to HIGH, which is the correct setting. Set time to 45 minutes. Select START/STOP to begin cooking. 8. When cooking is complete, naturally release the pressure for 10 minutes. Then quick release pressure by turning the pressure release valve to the VENT position. Move slider to AIR FRY/ STOVETOP to unlock the lid, then carefully open it. 9. Let the bread cool for a few minutes and serve.
Per Serving: Calories 311; Fat 13.13g; Sodium 96mg; Carbs 44.22g; Fibre 2.4g; Sugar 13.65g; Protein 4.67g

Blueberry Crisp

Prep Time: 15 minutes | Cook Time: 17 minutes | Serves: 4

For the Filling:
1 (250 g) bag frozen blueberries
2 tablespoons fresh orange juice
15 g erythritol
For the Topping:
100 g almond flour
15 g erythritol
80 g old fashioned rolled oats
60 g sliced almonds

1 teaspoon pure vanilla extract
2 tablespoons almond flour
1 teaspoon orange zest

1½ teaspoons pure vanilla extract
60 ml coconut oil
2 tablespoons fresh orange juice

1. To make the Filling: In a medium bowl, mix together the filling ingredients and transfer to a cake pan that fits the pot, set aside. 2. To make the Topping: In another bowl, mix together the topping ingredients. Use your hands to incorporate the oil into the rest of the ingredients evenly. 3. Pour the topping over the blueberry filling. 4. Pour 480 ml water into the pot and place the Deluxe Reversible Rack in the lower position in the pot. Place the cake pan on the rack. 5. Close the lid and move slider to PRESSURE. Make sure the pressure release valve is in the SEAL position. The temperature will default to HIGH, which is the correct setting. Set time to 17 minutes. Select START/STOP to begin cooking. 6. When cooking is complete, turn the pressure relief valve to the VENT position for quick pressure relief. Move slider to the right to unlock the lid, then carefully open it. 7. Spoon into four bowls and serve.
Per Serving: Calories 976; Fat 24.9g; Sodium 16mg; Carbs 205.04g; Fibre 42.1g; Sugar 136.08g; Protein 10.36g

Cinnamon Walnuts-Oats Stuffed Apples
Prep Time: 10 minutes | Cook Time: 6 minutes | Serves: 4

30 g chopped walnuts
20 g gluten-free rolled oats
3 teaspoons coconut oil
1 teaspoon maple syrup

1 teaspoon ground cinnamon
⅛ teaspoon salt
4 apples, cored

---

1. In a small bowl, mix together the walnuts, oats, maple syrup, coconut oil, cinnamon, and salt. Spoon the mixture into the cored apples. 2. Pour 240 ml into the pot and place the bottom layer of the Deluxe Reversible Rack in the lower position in the pot. Place the apples on the rack. 3. S Close the lid and move the slider to PRESSURE. Ensure the pressure release valve is in the SEAL position. The temperature will default to HIGH, which is the correct setting. Set time to 6 minutes. Select START/STOP to begin cooking. 4. When cooking is complete, turn the pressure release valve to the vent position for a quick pressure release. Move slider to the right to unlock the lid, then carefully open it. 5. Serve the apples warm.
Per Serving: Calories 177; Fat 7.37g; Sodium 80mg; Carbs 31.34g; Fibre 6g; Sugar 20.14g; Protein 2.28g

Authentic Peach Cobbler
Prep Time: 15 minutes | Cook Time: 10 minutes | Serves: 6

125 g spelt flour
1 tablespoon baking powder
2 teaspoons coconut sugar
⅛ teaspoon Salt
240 ml buttermilk

900 g frozen sliced peaches
60 ml water
½ teaspoon ground cinnamon
¼ teaspoon ground coriander

---

1. In a medium bowl, mi together the flour, baking powder, coconut sugar, and salt. Stir in the buttermilk to form a thick dough. 2. Combine the peaches, water, cinnamon, and coriander in the pot. Drop the dough, one tablespoon at a time, on top of the peaches, being careful to not let the dough touch the bottom or sides of the pot. 3. Close the lid and move the slider to PRESSURE. Ensure the pressure release valve is in the SEAL position. The temperature will default to HIGH, which is the correct setting. Set time to 10 minutes. Select START/STOP to begin cooking. 4. When cooking is complete, turn the pressure release valve to the vent position for a quick pressure release. Move slider to the right to unlock the lid, then carefully open it. 5. Let the cobbler cool for 5 to 10 minutes before serving.
Per Serving: Calories 263; Fat 1.27g; Sodium 143mg; Carbs 60.75g; Fibre 6g; Sugar 38.29g; Protein 6.54g

Homemade Sweet Cranberry Applesauce
Prep Time: 15 minutes | Cook Time: 5 minutes | Serves: 8

130 g whole cranberries
4 medium tart apples, peeled, cored, and grated
4 medium sweet apples, peeled, cored, and grated
1½ tablespoons grated orange zest
60 ml orange juice
60 g dark brown sugar
50 g granulated sugar

1 tablespoon unsalted butter
2 teaspoons ground cinnamon
½ teaspoon ground cloves
¼ teaspoon ground black pepper
⅛ teaspoon salt
1 tablespoon lemon juice

---

1. Place all ingredients in the pot and stir well. 2. Close the lid and move the slider to PRESSURE. Ensure the pressure release valve is in the SEAL position. The temperature will default to HIGH, which is the correct setting. Set time to 5 minutes. Select START/STOP to begin cooking. 3. When cooking is complete, naturally release the pressure for 25 minutes. Then quick release pressure by turning the pressure release valve to the VENT position. Move slider to AIR FRY/ STOVETOP to unlock the lid, then carefully open it. 4. Lightly mash fruit with a fork. Stir well. Serve warm or cold.
Per Serving: Calories 153; Fat 1.35g; Sodium 43mg; Carbs 37.76g; Fibre 4.8g; Sugar 29.8g; Protein 0.67g

Quick Lemon Blueberry Compote
Prep Time: 10 minutes | Cook Time: 5 minutes | Serves: 8

1 (400 g) bag frozen blueberries, thawed
50 g sugar
1 tablespoon lemon juice
2 tablespoons cornflour

2 tablespoons water
¼ teaspoon vanilla extract
¼ teaspoon grated lemon zest

---

1. Add the blueberries, lemon juice and sugar to the pot. Close the lid and move the slider to PRESSURE. Ensure the pressure release valve is in the SEAL position. The temperature will default to HIGH, which is the correct setting. Set time to 1 minute. Select START/STOP to begin cooking. 2. When cooking is complete, press START/STOP and quick release pressure by turning the pressure release valve to the VENT position. Move slider to the right to unlock the lid, then carefully open it. 3. Move slider to AIR FRY/STOVETOP. Select SEAR/SAUTÉ and set to Lo1. Select START/STOP to begin cooking. In a bowl, combine cornflour and water. Stir into blueberry mixture and cook until mixture comes to a boil and thickens, about 3 to 4 minutes. Press the START/STOP button and stir in vanilla and lemon zest. Serve right away or refrigerate until ready to serve.
Per Serving: Calories 599; Fat 7.26g; Sodium 12mg; Carbs 143.11g; Fibre 30.6g; Sugar 38.95g; Protein 4.78g

Flavourful Cinnamon Dried Fruit Compote

Prep Time: 15 minutes | Cook Time: 9 minutes | Serves: 6

200 g dried apricots, quartered
200 g dried peaches, quartered
120 g golden raisins

360 ml orange juice
1 cinnamon stick
4 whole cloves

1. Place all ingredients in the pot. Stir to combine. Close the lid and move the slider to PRESSURE. Ensure the pressure release valve is in the SEAL position. The temperature will default to HIGH, which is the correct setting. Set time to 3 minutes. Select START/STOP to begin cooking. 2. When the timer beeps, let pressure release naturally, about 20 minutes. Press the START/STOP button and open lid. 3. Discard the cinnamon stick and cloves. Press the SEAR/SAUTÉ button and set to Lo1, simmer for 5–6 minutes. Serve warm or allow to cool, and then cover and refrigerate for up to a week.

Per Serving: Calories 178; Fat 0.46g; Sodium 12mg; Carbs 45.97g; Fibre 3.1g; Sugar 36.05g; Protein 1.83g

Mouthwatering Chocolate Rice Pudding

Prep Time: 15 minutes | Cook Time: 20 minutes | Serves: 6

480 ml almond milk
185 g long-grain brown rice
2 tablespoons Dutch-processed cocoa powder

60 g maple syrup
1 teaspoon vanilla extract
55 g chopped dark chocolate

1. Combine the almond milk, rice, maple syrup, cocoa, and vanilla in the pot. Stir well. 2. Close the lid and move the slider to PRESSURE. Ensure the pressure release valve is in the SEAL position. The temperature will default to HIGH, which is the correct setting. Set time to 20 minutes. Select START/STOP to begin cooking. 3. When the timer beeps, let pressure release naturally for 15 minutes, then quick release the remaining pressure. Press the START/STOP button and open lid. Serve warm, sprinkled with chocolate.

Per Serving: Calories 317; Fat 11.86g; Sodium 43mg; Carbs 46.32g; Fibre 3.7g; Sugar 16.96g; Protein 6.81g

Banana Pudding Cake with Pecans

Prep Time: 15 minutes | Cook Time: 20 minutes | Serves: 6

3 tablespoons ground golden flaxseed meal
10 tablespoons water, divided
3 mashed bananas
60 ml avocado oil
1 teaspoon pure vanilla extract
250 g almond flour

50 g erythritol
1 teaspoon baking powder
¼ teaspoon salt
65 g chopped pecans
½ teaspoon ground cinnamon

1. Combine the flaxseed and 9 tablespoons water in a small bowl and give it time to gel. 2. In a big bowl, whisk together the flaxseed and water mixture, oil, banana, and vanilla. 3. Stir in the flour, baking powder, erythritol, and salt. 4. Spray a cake pan that fits the pot with nonstick cooking spray. Pour the batter into the pan. 5. In a bowl, mix the chopped pecans, cinnamon, and 1 tablespoon water. Sprinkle on top of the cake batter. 6. Pour 240 ml water into the inner pot and place the Deluxe Reversible Rack in the lower position in the pot. Place the pan on top of the rack. 7. Close the lid and move the slider to PRESSURE. Ensure the pressure release valve is in the SEAL position. The temperature will default to HIGH, which is the correct setting. Set time to 20 minutes. Select START/STOP to begin cooking. 8. When cooking is complete, turn the pressure release valve to the vent position for a quick pressure release. Move slider to the right to unlock the lid, then carefully open it. 9. Spoon into six bowls and serve.

Per Serving: Calories 304; Fat 17.93g; Sodium 101mg; Carbs 37.43g; Fibre 5.3g; Sugar 22.46g; Protein 2.93g

Traditional Lava Cake

Prep Time: 15 minutes | Cook Time: 20 minutes | Serves: 8

125 g plain flour
205 g packed brown sugar, divided
5 tbsp. baking cocoa, divided
2 tsp. baking powder
¼ tsp. salt
120 ml fat-free milk

2 tbsp. rapeseed oil
½ tsp. vanilla extract
⅛ tsp. ground cinnamon
300 ml hot water
Optional toppings: Fresh raspberries and ice cream

1. In a large bowl, mix up the flour, 105 g brown sugar, 3 tbsp. baking powder, cocoa, and salt. In another bowl, whisk the oil, milk, and vanilla until blended. Add to flour mixture and stir just until moistened. 2. Spread the mixture into a baking dish coated with cooking spray. 3. In a small bowl, mix up the cinnamon and remaining brown sugar and 2 tbsp. cocoa; stir in hot water. Pour over batter but do not stir. 4. Add 240 ml water to the pot and place the rack in the pot. Cover the baking dish with foil. 5. Fold a piece of foil lengthwise into thirds, making a sling. Using the sling, lower the dish onto the rack. 6. Close the lid, turn the pressure release valve to SEAL position, and then move the slider to PRESSURE. Select HI and set the cooking time to 20 minutes. Press START/STOP to begin cooking. When finished, release the pressure naturally. 7. Carefully remove the baking dish. Allow to stand 15 minutes. A toothpick inserted in cake portion should come out clean.

Per Serving: Calories 150; Fat: 4.12g; Sodium: 83mg; Carbs: 27.17g; Fibre: 1.4g; Sugar: 13.11g; Protein: 2.75g

Sweet Cranberry Stuffed Apples

Prep Time: 10 minutes | Cook Time: 5 minutes | Serves: 5

5 medium apples
85 g fresh or frozen cranberries, thawed and chopped
55 g packed brown sugar
2 tbsp. chopped walnuts
¼ tsp. ground cinnamon
⅛ tsp. ground nutmeg
Optional toppings: Whipped cream or vanilla ice cream

1. Core apples, leaving bottoms intact. Peel top third of each apple. 2. Add 240 ml water to the pot and place in the rack. 3. Combine the cranberries, brown sugar, walnuts, cinnamon and nutmeg; spoon into apples. Place apples on rack. 4. Close the lid, turn the pressure release valve to SEAL position, and then move the slider to PRESSURE. Select HI and set the cooking time to 3 minutes. Press START/STOP to begin cooking. When finished, release the pressure naturally. 5. Serve the dish with whipped cream or ice cream if desired.
Per Serving: Calories 195; Fat: 2.18g; Sodium: 6mg; Carbs: 46.2g; Fibre: 4.7g; Sugar: 37.75g; Protein: 1.26g

Arroz con Leche

Prep Time: 10 minutes | Cook Time: 20 minutes | Serves: 6

200 g long-grain white rice, rinsed until the water runs clear
480 ml milk
300 ml water
2 tablespoons granulated sugar
⅛ teaspoon fine sea salt
1 (250 g) can sweetened condensed milk
1 teaspoon vanilla extract

1. Combine the rice, milk, water, sugar, and salt in the pot. 2. Close the lid, turn the pressure release valve to SEAL position, and then move the slider to PRESSURE. Select HI and set the cooking time to 20 minutes. Press START/STOP to begin cooking. When finished, release the pressure naturally. 3. Stir in the vanilla and sweetened condensed milk. 4. Serve the dish warm or let cool to room temperature.
Per Serving: Calories 206; Fat: 4.53g; Sodium: 111mg; Carbs: 33.72g; Fibre: 0.4g; Sugar: 9.41g; Protein: 6.36g

Classic Bread Pudding

Prep Time: 5 minutes | Cook Time: 25 minutes | Serves: 8

480 ml milk
5 large eggs
75 g granulated sugar
1 teaspoon vanilla extract
½ loaf cubed bread (5 cm cubes)
Nonstick cooking spray
2 tablespoons unsalted butter, cut into small pieces

1. In a medium bowl, mix up the milk, sugar, eggs, and vanilla and stir until the sugar dissolves. Place in the bread cubes and stir to coat well. Refrigerate them for 1 hour. 2. Grease the pot with nonstick cooking spray. Pour in the bread mixture. Scatter the butter pieces on top. 3. Close the lid, turn the pressure release valve to SEAL position, and then move the slider to PRESSURE. Select HI and set the cooking time to 25 minutes. Press START/STOP to begin cooking. When finished, release the pressure naturally. 4. Allow the pudding to cool for a few minutes before serving.
Per Serving: Calories 165; Fat: 7.5g; Sodium: 140mg; Carbs: 18.3g; Fibre: 0.6g; Sugar: 8.48g; Protein: 5.66g

Red Wine Braised Bartlett Pears

Prep Time: 15 minutes | Cook Time: 3 minutes | Serves: 4

480 ml water
480 ml red wine
60 g honey
4 whole cloves
2 cinnamon sticks
1 star anise
1 teaspoon vanilla bean paste
4 Bartlett pears, peeled

1. Place all ingredients in the pot. Stir to combine. Close the lid and move the slider to PRESSURE. Ensure the pressure release valve is in the SEAL position. The temperature will default to HIGH, which is the correct setting. Set time to 3 minutes. Select START/STOP to begin cooking. 2. When cooking is complete, turn the pressure release valve to the vent position for a quick pressure release. Move slider to the right to unlock the lid, then carefully open it. With a slotted spoon, remove pears to a plate and let cool for 5 minutes. Serve warm.
Per Serving: Calories 206; Fat 0.89g; Sodium 19mg; Carbs 50.49g; Fibre 8g; Sugar 36.54g; Protein 2.06g

Perfect Lemony Tapioca Pudding

Prep Time: 10 minutes | Cook time: 10 minutes | Serves: 2-4

360 g milk
95 g tapioca
50 g sugar
Zest of 1 lemon

1. Pour the water into the pot and place the bottom layer of the Deluxe Reversible Rack in the lower position in the pot. 2. In a baking dish that can fit into the pot, combine the milk, tapioca, sugar and lemon zest. 3. Place the baking dish on the rack. Close the lid and move slider to PRESSURE. Ensuring the pressure release valve is in the SEAL position. The temperature will default to HIGH, which is the correct setting. Set time to 10 minutes. Select START/STOP to begin cooking. 4. When cooking is complete, release the pressure quickly by turning the pressure release valve to the VENT position. Move slider to the right to unlock the lid, then carefully open it. Serve.
Per Serving: Calories 201; Fat 4.03g; Sodium mg; Carbs 37.72g; Fibre 0.3g; Sugar 15.56g; Protein 3.95g

Delicious White Chocolate Pots De Crème

Prep Time: 15 minutes | Cook time: 20 minutes | Serves: 4

4 large egg yolks
2 tablespoons sugar
Pinch of salt
¼ teaspoon vanilla extract

360 ml milk
80 g white chocolate chips
480 ml water

1. First, mix egg yolks, sugar, salt, and vanilla in a small bowl and keep it aside. Then, heat milk in a saucepan over medium-low heat until it reaches a low simmer. 2. Next, take a spoonful of the hot mixture and whisk it into the egg mixture to temper the eggs. Slowly pour this egg mixture into the saucepan with the remaining milk. 3. Add white chocolate chips and stir continuously over a simmer until the chocolate melts, which takes around 10 minutes. 4. Once the chocolate is melted, remove the mixture from heat and distribute it evenly among four custard ramekins. 5. Pour water into the pot. Then place the bottom layer of the Deluxe Reversible Rack in the lower position in the pot. 6. Place the ramekins on the rack. Close the lid and move slider to PRESSURE. Ensuring the pressure release valve is in the SEAL position. The temperature will default to HIGH, which is the correct setting. Set time to 6 minutes. Select START/STOP to begin cooking. 7. When cooking is complete, naturally release the pressure for 10 minutes. Then release the pressure quickly by turning the pressure release valve to the VENT position. Move slider to AIR FRY/ STOVETOP to unlock the lid, then carefully open it. 8. Transfer custards to a plate and refrigerate covered for 2 hours. Serve.
Per Serving: Calories 294; Fat 15.96g; Sodium 204mg; Carbs 31.35g; Fibre 0.1g; Sugar 27.2g; Protein 6.83g

Fluffy Carrot Coconut Cake with Pecans

Prep Time: 10 minutes | Cook time: 20 minutes | Serves: 4

60 g coconut oil, melted
100 g sugar
1 large egg
½ teaspoon ground cinnamon
Pinch of ground nutmeg
½ teaspoon vanilla extract

30 g peeled, grated carrot
30 g unsweetened coconut flakes
60 g plain flour
½ teaspoon baking powder
30 g chopped pecans
240 ml water

1. Combine oil, sugar, egg, carrot, coconut flakes, cinnamon, vanilla, nutmeg, flour, and baking powder in a medium-sized bowl using a whisk. Be careful not to mix too much. 2. Add pecans by folding them in. Place the batter into a 15 cm cake pan that has been greased. 3. Pour water into the pot. Then place the bottom layer of the Deluxe Reversible Rack in the lower position in the pot. 4. Place the cake pan on the rack. Close the lid and move slider to PRESSURE. Ensuring the pressure release valve is in the SEAL position. The temperature will default to HIGH, which is the correct setting. Set time to 20 minutes. Select START/STOP to begin cooking. 5. When cooking is complete, naturally release the pressure for 5 minutes. Then release the pressure quickly by turning the pressure release valve to the VENT position. Move slider to AIR FRY/ STOVETOP to unlock the lid, then carefully open it. 6. Remove cake pan from the pot and transfer to a rack until cool. Flip cake onto a serving platter.
Per Serving: Calories 310; Fat 20.89g; Sodium 24mg; Carbs 29.46g; Fibre 1.9g; Sugar 14.9g; Protein 3.1g

Red Wine-Braised Apples with Raisins

Prep Time: 10 minutes | Cook time: 10 minutes | Serves: 6

6 medium apples, cored
1 tsp cinnamon powder
100 g white sugar

25 g raisins
240 ml red wine

1. Add the apples to the pot. Add the cinnamon, raisins, sugar, and red wine, toss to coat. 2. Close the lid and move slider to PRESSURE. Ensuring the pressure release valve is in the SEAL position. The temperature will default to HIGH, which is the correct setting. Set time to 10 minutes. Select START/STOP to begin cooking. 3. When cooking is complete, naturally release the pressure for 10 minutes. Then release the pressure quickly by turning the pressure release valve to the VENT position. Move slider to AIR FRY/ STOVETOP to unlock the lid, then carefully open it. 4. Transfer the apples to a serving plate. 5. Pour the remaining liquid over the apples and serve.
Per Serving: Calories 149; Fat 3.55g; Sodium 6mg; Carbs 31.75g; Fibre 5.2g; Sugar 23.8g; Protein 1.31g

Cranberry Stuffed Apples

Prep Time: 10 minutes | Cook time: 5 minutes | Serves: 6

120 ml water
2 tbsp walnuts, chopped
⅛ tsp ground nutmeg
40 g fresh cranberries, chopped

55 g brown sugar
¼ tsp cinnamon powder
5 medium apples, cored

1. Mix together the walnuts, sugar, nutmeg, cranberries, and cinnamon in a bowl. 2. Stuff each apple with the mixture. 3. Pour the water in the pot and add the apples. 4. Add the leftover filling to the pot. Close the lid and move slider to PRESSURE. 5. Ensuring the pressure release valve is in the SEAL position. The temperature will default to HIGH, which is the correct setting. Set time to 5 minutes. Select START/STOP to begin cooking. 6. When cooking is complete, naturally release the pressure for 10 minutes. Then release the pressure quickly by turning the pressure release valve to the VENT position. Move slider to AIR FRY/ STOVETOP to unlock the lid, then carefully open it. 7. Serve.
Per Serving: Calories 138; Fat 1.83g; Sodium 5mg; Carbs 32.19g; Fibre 3.9g; Sugar 26.34g; Protein 1.04g

Chocolate Chip-Berry Mug Cake

Prep Time: 10 minutes | Cook time: 10 minutes | Serves: 2

35 g almond flour
1 egg, beaten
1 tbsp maple syrup
Salt to taste

1½ tbsp chocolate chips
60 g berries of choice (blueberries, strawberries, raspberries)
½ tsp vanilla

1. Add the flour, egg, maple syrup, berries, chocolate chips, vanilla, and salt to a small bowl. Mix well. 2. Pour the mixture in a mug that can fit into the pot. 3. Cover the mug tightly with aluminum foil. Add water to the pot and place the bottom layer of the Deluxe Reversible Rack in the lower position in the pot. 4. Place the mug on the rack. Close the lid and move slider to PRESSURE. Ensuring the pressure release valve is in the SEAL position. The temperature will default to HIGH, which is the correct setting. Set time to 10 minutes. Select START/STOP to begin cooking. 5. When cooking is complete, release the pressure quickly by turning the pressure release valve to the VENT position. Move slider to the right to unlock the lid, then carefully open it. 6. Let the cake cool for a few minutes and serve.
Per Serving: Calories 177; Fat 10.39g; Sodium 172mg; Carbs 13.28g; Fibre 2.6g; Sugar 8.37g; Protein 6.35g

Stuffed Peaches

Prep Time: 10 minutes | Cook time: 3 minutes | Serves: 6

2 tbsp butter
⅛ tsp sea salt
50 g sugar
30 g flour

50 g tsp pure almond extract
½ tsp ground cinnamon
5-6 medium peaches, cored
240 ml water

1. Mix together the flour, butter, salt, almond extract, sugar, and cinnamon in a bowl. Stuff each peach with the mixture. 2. Pour water into the pot and place bottom layer of the Deluxe Reversible Rack in the lower position in the pot. 3. Carefully put the peaches on the rack. 4. Add the leftover filling to the pot. Close the lid and move slider to PRESSURE. Ensuring the pressure release valve is in the SEAL position. The temperature will default to HIGH, which is the correct setting. Set time to 3 minutes. Select START/STOP to begin cooking. 5. When cooking is complete, release the pressure quickly by turning the pressure release valve to the VENT position. Move slider to the right to unlock the lid, then carefully open it. 6. Allow to cool for 10-12 minutes. Serve.
Per Serving: Calories 199; Fat 8.96g; Sodium 83mg; Carbs 28.74g; Fibre 3.5g; Sugar 21.21g; Protein 3.84g

Wine Poached Apricots

Prep Time: 5 minutes | Cook Time: 1 minute | Serves: 6

300 ml water
60 g marsala wine
50 g sugar

1 teaspoon vanilla bean paste
8 medium apricots, sliced in half and pitted

1. Place all ingredients in the pot. Stir to combine. Close the lid and move slider to PRESSURE. Make sure the pressure release valve is in the SEAL position. The temperature will default to HIGH, which is the correct setting. Set time to 1 minute. Select START/STOP to begin cooking. 2. When cooking is complete, turn the pressure relief valve to the VENT position for quick pressure relief. Move slider to the right to unlock the lid, then carefully open it. 3. Let stand for 10 minutes. Carefully remove apricots from poaching liquid with a slotted spoon. Serve warm or at room temperature.
Per Serving: Calories 31; Fat 0.03g; Sodium 4mg; Carbs 7.75g; Fibre 0.4g; Sugar 7.05g; Protein 0.28g

Homemade Vanilla Almond Milk

Prep Time: 10 minutes | Cook Time: 1 minute | Serves: 6

120 g raw almonds
1.1 L filtered water, divided

1 teaspoon vanilla bean paste
½ teaspoon pumpkin pie spice

1. Add almonds and 240 ml water to the pot. Close the lid and move slider to PRESSURE. Make sure the pressure release valve is in the SEAL position. The temperature will default to HIGH, which is the correct setting. Set time to 1 minute. Select START/STOP to begin cooking. 2. When the timer beeps, turn the pressure relief valve to the VENT position for quick pressure relief. Move slider to the right to unlock the lid, then carefully open it. Strain almonds and rinse under cool water. Transfer to a high-powered blender with remaining water. Purée for 2 minutes on high speed. 3. Pour mixture into a nut milk bag set over a big bowl. Squeeze bag to extract all liquid. Stir in vanilla and pumpkin pie spice. 4. Transfer to a Mason jar or sealed jug and refrigerate for 8 hours. Stir or shake gently before serving.
Per Serving: Calories 4; Fat 0.12g; Sodium 5mg; Carbs 0.71g; Fibre 0.1g; Sugar 0.4g; Protein 0.12g

Cinnamon Apples

Prep Time: 10 minutes | Cook Time: 4 minutes | Serves: 4

1 tablespoon coconut oil
5 medium apples, peeled, cored, and cut into large chunks
1½ teaspoons ground cinnamon
1 tablespoon water
1 tablespoon lemon juice

1. Move slider to AIR FRY/STOVETOP. Select SEAR/SAUTÉ and set to 3. Select START/STOP to begin preheating. Allow unit to preheat for 2 minutes. 2. After 2 minutes, heat the oil for 1 minute, add the apples, water, cinnamon, and lemon juice and stir to combine. Press START/STOP to turn off the SEAR/SAUTÉ function. 3. Close the lid and move slider to PRESSURE. Make sure the pressure release valve is in the SEAL position. The temperature will default to HIGH, which is the correct setting. Set time to 1 minute. Select START/STOP to begin cooking. 4. When cooking is complete, turn the pressure relief valve to the VENT position for quick pressure relief. Move slider to the right to unlock the lid, then carefully open it. Serve warm.
Per Serving: Calories 151; Fat 3.81g; Sodium 2mg; Carbs 32.47g; Fibre 6g; Sugar 23.75g; Protein 0.64g

Simple Cinnamon Pineapple

Prep Time: 10 minutes | Cook Time: 5 minutes | Serves: 6

2 tablespoons coconut oil
1 large pineapple, cored and cut into 6 cm pieces
1½ teaspoons ground cinnamon

1. Move slider to AIR FRY/STOVETOP. Select SEAR/SAUTÉ and set to 3. Select START/STOP to begin preheating. Allow unit to preheat for 2 minutes. 2. After 2 minutes, heat the oil for 1 minute, add the pineapple and cinnamon and stir to combine. Press START/STOP to turn off the SEAR/SAUTÉ function. 3. Close the lid and move slider to PRESSURE. Make sure the pressure release valve is in the SEAL position. The temperature will default to HIGH, which is the correct setting. Set time to 2 minutes. Select START/STOP to begin cooking. 4. When cooking is complete, turn the pressure relief valve to the VENT position for quick pressure relief. Move slider to the right to unlock the lid, then carefully open it.
Per Serving: Calories 116; Fat 4.76g; Sodium 2mg; Carbs 20.26g; Fibre 2.7g; Sugar 13.86g; Protein 0.94g

Easy Applesauce

Prep Time: 15 minutes | Cook Time: 4 minutes | Serves: 16

1.3 kg apples, cored, cut into large chunks
80 ml water
1 tablespoon freshly squeezed lemon juice

1. Combine the apples, water, and lemon juice in the pot. Close the lid and move slider to PRESSURE. Make sure the pressure release valve is in the SEAL position. The temperature will default to HIGH, which is the correct setting. Set time to 4 minutes. Select START/STOP to begin cooking. 2. When cooking is complete, naturally release the pressure for 10 minutes. Then turn the pressure relief valve to the VENT position for quick pressure relief. Move slider to AIR FRY/ STOVETOP to unlock the lid, then carefully open it. 3. Using a potato masher, mash the apples to your desired chunkiness. Using a pair of tongs or a fork, transfer the apple peels to a deep, narrow container and blend using an immersion blender. Return to the pot and stir to combine. 4. Store in the fridge for up to 4 weeks in a covered container.
Per Serving: Calories 44; Fat 0.15g; Sodium 1mg; Carbs 11.81g; Fibre 2g; Sugar 8.86g; Protein 0.22g

Tasty Strawberry Compote

Prep Time: 15 minutes | Cook Time: 4 minutes | Serves: 6

700 g frozen strawberries
50 g sugar
1 tablespoon freshly squeezed lemon juice

1. Combine the strawberries, sugar, and lemon juice in the pot. Stir to coat the berries. Close the lid and move slider to PRESSURE. Make sure the pressure release valve is in the SEAL position. The temperature will default to HIGH, which is the correct setting. Set time to 4 minutes. Select START/STOP to begin cooking. 2. When cooking is complete, naturally release the pressure for 10 minutes. Then turn the pressure relief valve to the VENT position for quick pressure relief. Move slider to AIR FRY/ STOVETOP to unlock the lid, then carefully open it. 3. Using a potato masher, mash the berries until they are broken down completely. Pour into a container and chill. The compote will thicken as it cools. 4. Store in the fridge for up to 4 weeks in a covered container.
Per Serving: Calories 68; Fat 0.17g; Sodium 3mg; Carbs 17.78g; Fibre 3.1g; Sugar 10.86g; Protein 0.64g

Conclusion

The Ninja Foodi Deluxe Tendercrisp Pressure Cooker comes in as a handy appliance when you wish be fast when cooking. With the multiple programmed functions it offers, you will enjoy the results. It can cook all the varieties of your favorite meals from main course, seafood, meat to side dishes. Through this guide, we've not only explored the functionality of this magnificent appliance but also delved deep into the heart of the UK's rich culinary experience.

With each recipe and tip, there is addition of a dash of British charm and a sprinkle of global flavor, creating a symphony of tastes right in our homes. But remember, this cookbook is just the beginning. The real magic begins when you go in the kitchen and get busy with the meal preparation. Cheers to the Ninja Foodi Deluxe Tendercrisp Pressure Cooker adventures awaiting you!

Appendix 1 Measurement Conversion Chart

VOLUME EQUIVALENTS (LIQUID)

US STANDARD	US STANDARD (OUNCES)	METRIC (APPROXIMATE)
2 tablespoons	1 fl.oz	30 mL
¼ cup	2 fl.oz	60 mL
½ cup	4 fl.oz	120 mL
1 cup	8 fl.oz	240 mL
1½ cup	12 fl.oz	355 mL
2 cups or 1 pint	16 fl.oz	475 mL
4 cups or 1 quart	32 fl.oz	1 L
1 gallon	128 fl.oz	4 L

VOLUME EQUIVALENTS (DRY)

US STANDARD	METRIC (APPROXIMATE)
⅛ teaspoon	0.5 mL
¼ teaspoon	1 mL
½ teaspoon	2 mL
¾ teaspoon	4 mL
1 teaspoon	5 mL
1 tablespoon	15 mL
¼ cup	59 mL
½ cup	118 mL
¾ cup	177 mL
1 cup	235 mL
2 cups	475 mL
3 cups	700 mL
4 cups	1 L

TEMPERATURES EQUIVALENTS

FAHRENHEIT (F)	CELSIUS (C) (APPROXIMATE)
225 °F	107 °C
250 °F	120 °C
275 °F	135 °C
300 °F	150 °C
325 °F	160 °C
350 °F	180 °C
375 °F	190 °C
400 °F	205 °C
425 °F	220 °C
450 °F	235 °C
475 °F	245 °C
500 °F	260 °C

WEIGHT EQUIVALENTS

US STANDARD	METRIC (APPROXINATE)
1 ounce	28 g
2 ounces	57 g
5 ounces	142 g
10 ounces	284 g
15 ounces	425 g
16 ounces (1 pound)	455 g
1.5 pounds	680 g
2 pounds	907 g

Appendix 2 Recipes Index

A

Air Fried Cod with Spring Onions 89
Almond Bundt Cake with Berries 92
Aromatic Chicken Vindaloo 69
Arroz con Leche 96
Artichoke and Spinach Stuffed Aubergine 29
Asian Chicken Coleslaw Noodles Wraps 58
Asian-Spiced Duck Breast 65
Authentic Bulgur Pilaf with Chickpeas 34
Authentic Caribbean Chipotle Pork Sliders 54
Authentic Peach Cobbler 94
Authentic Pepperoncini Pot Roast 75

B

Banana Pudding Cake with Pecans 95
Barbecued Apricot Pulled Pork 72
Basic Butter Vanilla Cake 91
Basil Green Beans with Tomatoes and Pine Nuts 36
BBQ Chicken Patties 65
BBQ Pulled Pork Sandwiches 77
Beef and Cabbage Rice Soup 43
Beef Lentil Sliders 57
Best Potatoes Au Gratin 24
Black-Eyed Peas and Smoked Ham Soup 48
Blueberry Crisp 93
Blueberry Muffins 14
Breakfast Kale Soufflé 13
Brie with Cherry Tomatoes 54
Broccoli, Potato, and Sausage Tots 50
Buffalo Chicken Lettuce Wraps 62
Butter-Maple Glazed Carrots 31

C

Cheese Chicken Nacho Scoops 57
Cheese Courgette Drop Biscuits 12
Cheese Sausage–Stuffed Peppers 68
Cheesy Baked Eggs 16
Cheesy Beef Sandwiches 75
Cheesy Black Bean and Corn Quesadillas 40
Cheesy Chicken Artichoke Casserole 62
Cheesy Egg in a Hole 19
Cheesy Ham Muffins 18
Cheesy Ham Polenta Muffins 18
Cheesy Ham Strata 16
Cheesy Tuna Noodle Casserole 83
Cheesy White Beans with Lemon 35
Chicken & Quinoa Bowls 66
Chicken and Italian Sausage Ragu 63
Chicken Wings with Honey-Orange Sauce 50
Chicken, Mushrooms and Rice Bowls 68
Chinese Vegetable Fried Rice 40
Chinese Vegetable Spring Rolls 51
Chocolate Chip-Berry Mug Cake 98
Chocolate Peanut Butter Popcorn 92
Chocolate-Strawberry Quinoa 13
Cinnamon Apples 99
Cinnamon Coconut Muesli Stuffed Apples 13
Cinnamon Walnuts-Oats Stuffed Apples 94
Classic Beef Burgundy 72
Classic Bread Pudding 96
Classic Enchilada Casserole 20
Classic Indian Spiced Kidney Bean Stew 27
Classic Lentils & Bulgur 28
Classic Reuben Potato Skins 51
Coconut Chicken and Mushroom Stroganoff 64
Coconut Chicken Bites 55
Coconut Prawn and Rice Soup 48
Coconut Rice and Red Beans 34
Coconut Salmon Cakes with Greens 88
Comforting Lamb and Vegetables Casserole 80
Cranberry Stuffed Apples 97
Creamy Artichoke Crab Dip 52
Creamy Blueberries Clafouti 21
Creamy Buffalo Cheese Chicken Dip 55
Creamy Cheddar Broccoli and Potato Soup 45
Creamy Cheddar Broccoli Soup 42
Creamy Cheese Polenta 59
Creamy Cheese Tomato Soup with Basil 48
Creamy Chocolate Cake 92
Creamy Cinnamon Raisin Brown Rice Pudding 93
Creamy Dill Salmon 89
Creamy Mushroom and Chicken 61
Creamy Mushroom Chicken Soup 44
Creamy Scallops with Spinach 87
Crispy Avocado Fries 53
Crispy Cheese Beef Meatballs 50
Crispy Cheese Broccoli Pizza 29
Crispy Crusted Chicken Tenders 64
Crispy Fried Parmesan Polenta 26
Crispy Ranch Potato Chips 53
Crispy Spicy Potato Chips 59
Crispy Toast Sticks 17
Crunchy Dill Pickles with Ranch Dip 54
Crustless Feta and Spinach Quiche 15
Crustless Gruyère and Bacon Quiche 17
Crustless Mini Quiche Bites with Olives 17

D

Delicious Chicken Puttanesca 67
Delicious Hoisin Meatballs with Sesame Seeds 52
Delicious Miso Pork Ramen 71
Delicious Pork and Cabbage Stew 81
Delicious Potato and Cauliflower Curry 23
Delicious Scallop Risotto with Spinach 85
Delicious White Chocolate Pots De Crème 97
Dill Pickle Dijon Deviled Eggs 52

E

Easy Applesauce 99
Easy Boiled Peanuts 51

Easy Cauliflower "Rice" 32
Easy Chili Mac 44
Easy Crab Legs with Lemon Wedges 86
Easy Crispy Parmesan Artichokes 29
Easy Egg Custard 91
Easy Egg Salad Sandwiches 75
Easy Peach Jam 57
Easy Traditional Shakshuka 16
Egg White Bites with Ham 20

F

Fantastic Braised Chickpeas with Swiss Chard 39
Fantastic Brown Butter Pasta with Scallops & Tomatoes 85
Farro with Cremini Mushrooms and Parmesan 34
Faux-Tisserie Chicken 67
Flavourful Aubergine, Courgette & Tomatoes 32
Flavourful Brown Basmati Rice Pilaf with Spiced Beef 35
Flavourful Cinnamon Dried Fruit Compote 95
Flavourful Creamy Chicken and Brown Rice 66
Flavourful Turkey Cabbage Dumplings 53
Fluffy Carrot Coconut Cake with Pecans 97
Fluffy Garlic Cheese Bread 12
Fluffy Raspberry Breakfast Cake 21
Freekeh Bowls with Chickpeas 23
Fresh Barley & Beans Taco Salad with Zesty Lime Vinaigrette 38
Fresh Prawns and Broccoli 87
Fresh Salsa Verde Pulled Pork 74
Fried Banana PB&J Sandwich 18
Fried Cheese Prawns 86

G

Garlic Beef Shoulder 79
Garlic Cannellini Beans with Tomatoes 26
Garlic Chickpea Curry 27
Garlicky Chili Fish Tacos 84
Garlicky Potatoes and Kale 31
Greek Fried Rice with Eggs and Cucumber 36

H

Healthy Cinnamon Apples with Dates 92
Healthy Collard Greens with Bacon 23
Healthy Eggs in a Boat 21
Healthy Pesto Chicken Quinoa 67
Healthy Spiced Pork Strips with Lettuce 81
Hearty Chicken Sausage Gumbo 63
Hearty Cranberry Beans with Spanish Chorizo & Red Cabbage 39
Hearty Lamb Ragù 76
Hearty Pork and Pinto Bean Stew with Tomatoes 44
Herbed Black-Eyed Peas and Swiss Chard 38
Herbed Carrots and Parsnips 24
Herbed Ham and Potatoes 14
Herbed Kidney Bean and Sausage Soup with Cabbage 47
Herbed Mashed Sweet Potatoes 30
Herbed Pomegranate Chicken Chunks 61
Herbed White Beans 35
Herbed Whole Chicken 62
Homemade Barbecue Sauce 59
Homemade Black Bean and Chorizo Soup 43
Homemade Chipotle Pulled Pork 74
Homemade Chocolate Banana Bread 20
Homemade Mongolian Beef 78
Homemade Parmesan-Lemon Chicken Risotto 37
Homemade Pesto Tilapia with Sun-Dried Tomatoes 84
Homemade Sour Cream Deviled Eggs with Olives 53
Homemade Sweet Cranberry Applesauce 94
Homemade Vanilla Almond Milk 98
Honey Corn Muffins with Carrot and Pepper 19
Honey-Soy Salmon 84

I

Italian Duck Breasts with Tomatoes 67
Italian Herbed Pork Cut 79
Italian Herbed Turkey Breast 65
Italian Pot Roast Ragù 78
Italian-Flavoured Pork Loin 75

J

Jalapeño-Cheddar Bagel and Egg Casserole 12
Juicy Orange Pulled Pork Sliders 52
Juicy Smoked Brisket Skewers 74
Juicy Vinegary Beef Steak 51

L

Lemony Brussels Sprout 28
Lemony Cajun Salmon 86
Lemony Cocktail Prawns 83
Lemony Garlic Broccoli 26
Lemony Garlic Chicken Breasts 62
Lemony Garlic Smashed Red Potatoes 24
Lemony Mashed Chickpeas with Spring Onions 34
Lemony Roasted Cauliflower 29
Lemony-Buttered Lobster Tails 85
Limey Garlic Salmon Fillets 87
Limey Steak Salad 78

M

Marinated Salmon Fillets with Vegetable 87
Mashed Potatoes and Cauliflower 30
Minty Red Lentil and Bulgur Soup 27
Mouthwatering Chocolate Rice Pudding 95
Mouthwatering Potpie Chicken Soup 42
Mouthwatering Spiced Chicken Wings 61
Mozzarella Sandwich with Puttanesca Sauce 56
Mustard Sausage with Fennel 79

N

Nutritious Lamb and Potato Soup 46
Nutty Carrot Muffins 19

O

Oat Muffins with Dry Fruit 19

P

Palatable Pork Chops with Apples 80
Peach Oatmeal with Pecans 12
Pepperoni Pizza Casserole 15
Perfect French Onion Soup 45
Perfect Lemony Tapioca Pudding 96
Perfect Mexican Beef Casserole 76

Persian Pearled Barley-Lentil Soup with Spinach 46
Pinto Bean & Squash Soup with Tomato Salsa 43
Pork and Vegetables Skewers 77
Pork Sausage-Stuffed Mushrooms 50

Q

Quick Avocado Fries with Salsa Fresca 55
Quick Bacon Wrapped Scallops 88
Quick Lemon Blueberry Compote 94
Quick Prawns Boil with Sausage 84
Quick Spicy Lentil & Walnut Tacos 39
Quick Stuffed Potato Soup 43
Quinoa Endive Boats 31

R

Red Pepper Hummus 58
Red Wine Braised Bartlett Pears 96
Red Wine Braised Mushroom with Carrot 25
Red Wine-Braised Apples with Raisins 97
Refreshing Carnitas Tacos with Avocado Crema 73
Refreshing Lemony Broccoli Salad 29
Refreshing Salmon with Zesty Dill Sauce 85
Rich Thai Orange Chicken 63
Rich Vegan Sweet Potato Soup 42

S

Savoury Cheese Mushroom Risotto 36
Savoury Cheese Steak Mushroom Sloppy Joes 73
Savoury Ketchup 58
Savoury Sweet Potatoes and Bacon 15
Sesame Carrots Sticks 28
Sesame Prawn Toasts 55
Simple Air-Fried Chicken Breasts 64
Simple Asian Quinoa and Carrot Salad 36
Simple Beef Dinner Rolls 78
Simple Chocolate Molten Lava Cake 91
Simple Cinnamon Pineapple 99
Simple Sour Cream Cabbage 24
Simple Spicy Black Bean Soup 45
Smoked Salmon, Leek, and Potato Soup 45

Smoky Corned Beef with Original Potatoes 74
Smooth Celery Root and Cauliflower Mash 25
Soft Blueberry French Bread 14
Soft Vanilla Banana Bread 93
Soy-Ginger Salmon and Broccoli 83
Spanish Rice with Salsa 40
Spiced Lime Hummus 56
Spiced Pork Patties 79
Spicy Air-Fried Chicken Legs 65
Spicy Baby Back Ribs 76
Spicy Broiled Chicken Breasts 69
Spicy Chicken Thighs 65
Spicy Pinto Beans 30
Spicy Pork Chops with Creamy Mushroom Gravy 80
Spicy Prawn Soup with White Beans 47
Spicy Red Kidney Beans & Sausage Stew with Rice 37
Spicy Sweet Potato Hash with Eggs 13
Spicy Turkey Sweet Potato Boats 66
Steamed Artichokes with Lemony Dijon Dipping Sauce 23
Stir-Fried Vegetables and Brown Rice 37
Stuffed Peaches 98
Super-Easy Cinnamon Applesauce 28
Super-Simple Cheesecake 91
Sweet & Spicy Red Cabbage 32
Sweet & Spicy Tomato Jam with Toast 16
Sweet Cranberry Stuffed Apples 96
Sweet Pecan Steel-Cut Oats 15
Sweet Potato and Wild Rice Chowder 44
Sweet Potato Fries with Sriracha Ranch Sauce 57
Sweet Stewed Pears in Red Wine 91
Sweet-and-Sour Beef Short Ribs 72
Szechuan Beans with Sesame Seeds 28

T

Tangy Dark Chocolate Fondue 92
Tangy Pork Ragù 77
Tangy Shredded Beef with Pineapple 71

Tasty Beef Enchiladas 77
Tasty Butternut Squash Mash 31
Tasty Herbed Veggie & Bread Casserole 25
Tasty Jerk-Spiced Chicken Wings 64
Tasty Miso Salmon Fillets 86
Tasty Strawberry Compote 99
Tender and Juicy Filet Mignon 79
Tender Pork Chops with Onion Gravy 76
Thai Coconut Red Lentil Soup 46
Thai Coconut Salmon Curry 83
Thai-Style Curried Butternut Bisque 47
Traditional Hummus 38
Traditional Lava Cake 95
Traditional Prawns Scampi 86
Turmeric Basmati Rice with Yellow Onion 35

V

Vegan Chickpeas Hummus 30
Vegetable and Sausage Soup 42
Veggie Bacon Frittatas 17

W

Wholesome Cheese Corned Beef & Cabbage Slaw 26
Wholesome Pork and Chicken Noodles 73
Wine Poached Apricots 98
Wonderful Pulled Beef Brisket 71

Y

Yogurt Egg Salad 14
Yummy Chicken & Sausage Jambalaya 68
Yummy Chipotle Black Beans with Bacon 40
Yummy Creamy Rice Pudding 93
Yummy Mushroom Boat Eggs 18
Yummy Parmesan Cod 88
Yummy Spicy Black Bean Dip 56

Z

Zesty Salmon Salad 88

Printed in Great Britain
by Amazon